Track-II Diplomacy

The BCSIA Studies in International Security book series is edited at the Belfer Center for Science and International Affairs at Harvard University's John F. Kennedy School of Government and published by The MIT Press. The series presents books on contemporary issues in international security policy, as well as their conceptual and historical foundations. Topics of particular interest to the series include the spread of weapons of mass destruction, internal conflict, the international effects of democracy and democratization, and U.S. defense policy.

A complete list of BCSIA Studies appears at the back of this volume.

Track-II Diplomacy

Lessons from the Middle East

Hussein Agha, Shai Feldman, Ahmad Khalidi, and Zeev Schiff
Shai Feldman, Project Director

BCSIA Studies in International Security

The MIT Press
Cambridge, Massachusetts
London, England

ISBN: 0-262-01209-X hc; 0-262-51180-0 pbk
Library of Congress Control Number: 2003114235

10 9 8 7 6 5 4 3 2 1

Printed in the United States of America

Contents

Preface

This book is an example of Arab-Israeli cooperation. It was originally conceived as a book to be written with Zeev Schiff, defense editor of *Ha'aretz*. In 1996, as I began the research for this book, I went to London to interview Hussein Agha and Ahmad Khalidi, who had taken part in many Middle East Track-II talks. They became equal partners to the project.

When we entered the first phase of our four-way cooperation, we assumed that there would be wide gaps between the perceptions of the two Arabs and two Israelis regarding the causes and consequences of the Track-II process. Specifically, we thought that our understanding of the record of Track-II discussions in the Middle East would be very different, requiring that we provide readers with two separate histories of the process. We also thought that our analysis of the factors accounting for the successes and failures of the different Track-II venues would be very different, necessitating separate Arab and Israeli analyses.

As the four of us convened for successive authors' meetings, we gradually discovered that our perceptions of the record of Track-II talks in the Middle East were not that different, allowing us to present a common history of these talks. Later, we also discovered that although our analyses of the factors affecting the course and the consequences of the region's Track-II process were not identical, there was sufficient congruence between our approaches to permit a common assessment of the process.

We also agreed that the enormous value of a joint Arab-Israeli evaluation of the Track-II process merited a special effort to bridge the remaining differences in our analysis. Bridging these differences, however, was not easy; the effort was often exhausting, sometimes bringing us to the point of despair. Happily, we were eventually able to produce an "agreed text," whose substance—we hope—was not compromised in the process of consensus-building.

The four of us also held conversations with other participants and sponsors of Track-II talks. We also interviewed individuals who were close to Arab and Israeli leaders when these talks had taken place to ascertain the leaders' attitudes regarding the Track-II efforts. Due to the sensitivity of the subject matter, almost all these inter- views were conducted on a "not for attribution" basis. We are grateful to these individuals for giving us some of their scarce time and their energy.

The project resulting in this book was initiated while I was a senior research fellow at the Belfer Center for Science and International Affairs at Harvard University's John F. Kennedy School of Government. I am indebted to Graham Allison, director of the Belfer Center, and to Steven Miller, director of the Center's International Security Program, for the opportunity they gave me to be part of an institution of enormous intellectual power. I am also grateful for the encouragement and support they provided throughout my years at Harvard and for the continuous enthusiasm they displayed about this project.

Jill Harris, the Rockefeller Foundation, and the Carnegie Corporation provided critical financial support without which this book project could not have been implemented. I am particularly indebted to David Speedie at Carnegie and to Thomas Graham, then at the Rockefeller Foundation, who have been very helpful in arranging the required funding. In this context I am also grateful for the support and advice I received from Jane Holl, former executive director of the Carnegie Commission for Preventing Deadly Conflict.

The completion of this project took longer than expected since in late 1997, I returned to Israel to become head of Tel Aviv University's Jaffee Center for Strategic Studies. The combined pace of substantive work at the Center, orchestrating its research agenda, editing its products, fundraising, and teaching, caused repeated delays in bringing this book to print.

Finally, I would like to thank those who were responsible for making sure that this book eventually got published. First, my three co-conspirators who—to varying degrees—tolerated the delays induced by my other preoccupations. And second, those at the Belfer Center and at the MIT Press who helped bring this volume to publication: Miriam Avins, who edited the manuscript; Sean Lynn-Jones, who presided over the quality control process; and, last but most, Karen Motley, who immediately recognized the significance of this book and managed every aspect of bringing it to print.

Shai Feldman
Project Director

Chapter 1

What Are Track-II Talks?

This book is a product of a three-year study, undertaken jointly by Arab and Israeli scholars. It is an evaluation of the Middle East Track-II process, primarily in the late 1980s and the first half of the 1990s. It assesses the contribution of these talks to conflict resolution in the region and attempts to ascertain under what conditions such talks may contribute to peacemaking in regions beyond the Middle East. More generally, the book aims to evaluate the circumstances under which Track-II talks can prove a useful tool in conflict resolution and to identify the factors that determine their successes and failures. We hope that this book may help to improve the use of Track-II talks in the Middle East and highlight the possible contribution of this tool for peacemaking in other regions.

Track-II Talks

Track-II talks are discussions held by non-officials of conflicting parties in an attempt to clarify outstanding disputes and to explore the options for resolving them in settings or circumstances that are less sensitive than those associated with official negotiations. The non-officials involved usually include scholars, senior journalists, former government officials, and former military officers. Government and other officials, acting in an informal capacity, sometimes also participate in such talks alongside the non-officials involved.

The four coauthors of this study have taken part in many Middle East Track-II talks. These have focused on various facets of the Arab-

Israeli conflict: bilateral talks centering on the disputes between Israel and its various neighbors, and multilateral talks devoted to the prospects for regional security and arms control in the Middle East.

A number of Track-II venues have been hosted by third-party governments. Most Track-II talks, however, have been hosted by non-official institutions such as universities, research institutes, and dedicated nongovernmental organizations (NGOs). On some occasions, research centers have convened Track-II talks on behalf of their national governments.

Track-II talks can also be defined by what they are not: neither academic conferences nor secret diplomacy conducted by government representatives. In this study, academic conferences in which Arab and Israeli scholars participated and communicated with one another do not constitute Track-II talks. Rather, Track-II talks are convened specifically to foster informal interaction among participants regarding the political issues dividing their nations and to find ways of reducing the tensions or resolving the conflict between them. The purpose of Track-II exercises is to provide participants with a setting that is conducive to achieving such objectives.

Track-II talks should also be distinguished from secret diplomacy, which involves covert interactions between government officials. Officials taking part in secret diplomacy normally operate as representatives of their respective governments and follow their superiors' instructions. By contrast, officials who take part in Track-II talks usually do so in an informal capacity and in a manner that does not commit their governments to any positions taken in these talks. At the same time, if Track-II talks prove exceptionally successful, they can lead to secret formal negotiations, as occurred in mid-1993, during the later stages of the Oslo talks between Israel and the Palestine Liberation Organization (PLO).

Do Track-II talks require the parallel conduct of formal and official (Track-I) negotiations? They do not. Track-II talks may be held separately and independently of any official negotiations taking place or not taking place at the time. Indeed, at times Track-II talks are often held precisely because the relevant parties cannot or will not engage one another in formal Track-I negotiations. A broad range of PLO-Israeli contacts prior to Oslo fall within this category. Similarly, talks initiated in the late 1980s to explore the prospects for regional security in the Middle East were held without prior or concurrent Track-I negotiations. At the time, it was not expected that within a few years Israel, the Palestinians, and thirteen Arab countries would be engaged in formal negotiations on Arms Control and Regional Security (ACRS).

A subcategory of discussions included both non-officials and officials participating in a non-official capacity. In the following pages, these discussions will be referred to as Track-I½ talks.

While Track-II talks need not necessarily be linked to concurrent Track-I negotiations, participants in the former must have some relations with officials in their countries' decision-making circles for such talks to be effective. The exercise would be pointless if leaders and officials who can affect the course of national policy were not made aware of the information and impressions gained in these talks.

"Hard" and "Soft" Track-II Talks

The purposes of Track-II talks vary, but they are all related to reducing tensions or facilitating the resolution of a conflict. At a minimum, Track-II talks are aimed at an exchange of views, perceptions, and information between the parties to improve each side's understanding of the other's positions and policies. These may be termed "soft" Track-II exercises. Such talks may also help participants familiarize themselves with one another, increasing their understanding of the human dimensions of the struggle in which they are engaged. By informing their respective publics, elites, and governments of the perceptions and insights they have gained, participants may indirectly contribute to the formation of new national political priorities and policies.

A less modest purpose for Track-II talks might be to help negotiate political agreements between governments. These may be termed "hard" Track-II talks. Here, use is made of the informal standing of Track-II participants to initiate talks on sensitive issues that cannot be dealt with in formal settings or between parties that have not yet recognized each other and hence cannot engage one another in official negotiations. The objective in these cases is to reach a political agreement or understanding that will be acceptable to the conflicting parties.

One desirable outcome of "soft" Track-II talks is that participants widely share the impressions they gain in these talks among their formal or informal constituencies. Indeed, these talks are often aimed at publishing the final results of their deliberations. For example, the American Academy of Arts and Sciences (AAAS) published a set of monographs contrasting Israeli and Palestinian views on such central issues as Jerusalem and the Palestinians' "Right of Return." Similarly, the Search for Common Ground's Initiative for Peace in the Middle East (IPCME), now known as Search for Common Ground in the Middle East, has published monographs presenting Israeli and Arab approaches to resolving the conflict over Lebanon and to addressing the security problems entailed in the redeployment of the Israeli Defense Forces (IDF) in the West Bank.

By contrast, "hard" Track-II talks—aimed at negotiating an agreement between the parties involved—often require absolute secrecy. Any leak from these discussions—even if only revealing that such talks have taken place—may endanger the entire enterprise. In this case, the greater the number of officials and other individuals who are made aware that the talks are being conducted and are briefed about their contents, the greater the likelihood that sensitive information will find its way to the media's front pages.

In describing and analyzing Track-II talks, we often refer to the "sponsors" and "mentors" of these talks, as well as to the parties' national "leaders." In this book, the term "sponsor" refers either to the institution issuing the invitation to participate in the talks, or it refers to the institution on whose behalf the talks are being held. For example, if a research institute provided a Track-II venue but served merely as a conduit for its national government, the government would be considered the real sponsor of the talks.

In this book, the term "leaders" refers to each party's highest political echelon—for example, the prime minister and the minister for foreign affairs (in Israel), the chairman (for the PLO), or the president (in Egypt). The term "mentor" refers to a high-level political leader who serves as a chaperon for the talks. Many of the Middle East Track-II talks have been held on the mentor's behalf: he was the one who initiated the talks and who would later convince the national leaders of their import. Mentors also brought the information and the impressions gained in the talks, as well as the understandings and agreements reached in their framework, to the leaders' attention. The Middle East Track-II talks have differed with regard to the extent to which mentors within each party orchestrated the talks and in the degree to which their existence was critical to the talks' success.

In "soft" talks that aimed at dialogue, familiarization, exchange of information, assessments, and security concerns, the role of the mentor was less central than in "hard" Track-II venues. On the whole, the data gathered in "soft" talks may be disseminated without the sponsorship of a high official. By contrast, for "hard" Track-II talks that are aimed at achieving a breakthrough in the efforts to resolve the conflict, the role of the mentor has proven critical. Indeed, it is difficult to see how the Oslo talks could have evolved without the guidance and backing provided by the Israeli and Palestinian mentors of these talks.

The Middle East experience suggests that effective mentors may need to meet three requirements beyond access to the top leaders: a belief that

Track-II talks may be a useful tool for conflict resolution; sufficient time and energy to initiate, navigate, and orchestrate such talks, or at least to monitor these talks on a regular basis; and a readiness to "enlarge the envelope" by encouraging Track-II talks without necessarily obtaining their leaders' prior approval for the talks—or at least not initially, when the results of the talks are far from certain.

Establishing criteria for judging the success or failure of Track-II talks may be very difficult. In one case—the Israeli-Palestinian Oslo talks—Track-II talks eventually led to a historical breakthrough: an agreement that began a process of reconciliation among the two peoples. But Oslo was an extreme case and it would not be fair to judge other venues by the unique yardstick that it created. Most Track-II efforts were launched with much more modest purposes in mind: to enhance communication among participants and to provide them with settings that are more conducive than official negotiations for exploring their disagreements, understanding their different perspectives, and helping to bridge the gap between their different perspectives. Indeed, even the Oslo talks were initially aimed at assisting the stalled Track-I negotiations in Washington—rather than replacing these official discussions. Thus it seems more appropriate to judge the success or failure of Track-II talks by the purposes defined by those who convened and those who participated in these talks. If the initiators of the talks intended them merely to help identify the problems dividing the conflicting parties and to assist in the process of addressing these problems, then the extent to which these objectives were achieved may serve as a reasonable criteria for judging their success.

The Scope of the Study

Talks involving Arabs and Israelis were launched as early as the late 1960s, almost immediately after the 1967 War. The pioneering contribution of these talks and the utility of the discussions held in the 1970s and the 1980s was considerable, and these venues are discussed in Chapter 2, a survey of Track-II talks in the Middle East. However, to avoid an excessively long manuscript, we decided to focus our examination on the past decade, beginning just before the Gulf War.

One of the main characteristics of Track-II talks is that they are relatively free of media coverage. Except in rare cases, even the fact that the talks took place—let alone their subsequent impact—is not made public. As a result, there is very little documented information about these talks. Hence, this study largely relies on interviews with Track-II organizers and participants and on the authors' personal recollections for generating and demonstrating hypotheses about the factors that affect such talks.

Chapter 2 describes the early efforts to foster Track-II discussions in the Middle East. In this chapter we describe the most important Arab-Israeli discussions that, in our judgment, formed the background for the more important Middle East Track-II talks of the 1990s.

In Chapters 3 through 8 we present six case studies of Track-II talks held in the 1990s: the Israeli-Palestinian talks held in 1992–1993 in Norway, leading to the Oslo accords; Palestinian-Israeli talks held in the early 1990s under the auspices of the American Academy of the Arts and Sciences (AAAS); the Stockholm talks—Palestinian-Israeli discussions convened in 1994–1995 by the government of Sweden in an attempt to bridge the gap between the parties' positions with respect to the main "final status" issues; the talks held in 1995–1996 between Israeli settlers in the West Bank and representatives of the Palestinian Authority; meetings held in 1992–1994 between Israelis and Syrians, under the auspices of Search for Common Ground; and arms control and regional security–related talks—Arab-Israeli discussions that were convened throughout the 1990s by numerous research centers and other nongovernmental organizations in an attempt to explore the issues related to arms control and regional security in the Middle East. In each case we attempt to provide some sense of the purpose, the course of the talks and their outcome, the participants taking part in the discussions, and the role of the mentors, leaders, sponsors, and other third parties in these talks.

In Chapter 9 we present an analysis of the Middle East experience with the use of Track-II talks and in Chapter 10 we suggest lessons that can be derived from this experience. These two chapters provide the conclusions all four of us have reached regarding the factors affecting the success of Track-II talks and their potential application to other areas of conflict. Chapter 10 is also aimed at providing Track-II sponsors and participants with an operational guide that may facilitate their current or future work. We hope that these lessons will help improve the use of this tool for conflict management and resolution in the Middle East as well as in other regions.

With the failure of final status talks and the outbreak of the second Palestinian *intifada* in late 2000, the Arab-Israeli peace process experienced its most severe crisis since the signing of the Oslo accords in 1993. The resulting violence gave rise to a deep sense of despair among Israelis and Palestinians alike, and contributed to a growing sense of the intractability of the conflict amongst regional and international parties alike.

Yet, the deep crisis in Palestinian-Israeli relations that emerged from developments at the end of 2000 should not obscure the enormous progress made in the previous decade toward a resolution of the conflict, and the contribution of Track-II talks to this progress. Nor should it be permitted to overshadow the considerable long-term impact of the efforts made during this period to solve other aspects of the Arab-Israeli conflict.

For one thing, the peace process brought about significant political and territorial changes that will serve future efforts to reach an Israeli-Palestinian permanent status agreement. The establishment of the Palestine Authority (PA) on Palestinian land in 1994 marked a historical shift in the terms of reference of the conflict, setting the necessary foundations for a settlement based on the two-state solution and partition of Mandatory Palestine. Indeed, and regardless of any intervening turbulence, the ultimate resolution of the conflict is unlikely to differ substantially from the understandings developed in the Stockholm talks in 1994–1995 described in Chapter 5. Other developments in the 1990s should also be seen in historical perspective: The transfer of land to the Palestinians negotiated by Prime Minister Benjamin Netanyahu in 1998 shattered the Israeli right's ideological commitment to the concept of the "Greater Land of Israel," and the effort to reach a permanent status agreement during the tenure of Prime Minister Ehud Barak in 1999–2001 resulted in the breaking of a series of taboos—most notably Israel's long-standing insistence on the unity of Jerusalem under Israel's sole sovereignty—a precondition for any future resolution of the Jerusalem issue.

From this long-term perspective, and against the backdrop of renewed Israeli-Palestinian violence, a number of points about the significance of Track-II talks are worth making.

First, the recent history of Palestinian-Israeli formal negotiations emphasizes the potential of Track-II discussions. For example, the prospects of success at the Camp David summit of July 2000 could have been significantly enhanced had it been preceded by sufficient Track-II preparation. Such talks were in fact proposed by the Palestinian side, but were not followed through as conceived. In March 2000 a senior Palestinian leader approached the Swedish Social Democratic government with the idea of initiating an informal and nonbinding Track-II exercise with a view to laying the basis for a final status agreement. The idea was that the political and psychological pressures inherent in formal talks would prevent any real progress toward a resolution of the conflict. The Swedish side conveyed this message to Israeli Premier Ehud Barak, who rejected the idea of Track-II in favor of formal but secret Track-I talks.

This latter idea was adopted by the Swedes and secret Track-I talks were initiated in Stockholm in May 2000. However, the Stockholm channel only served to alienate members of the Palestinian leadership who saw them as an attempt to bypass the existing political process. The secret talks were promptly exposed, and they collapsed with highly negative consequences. On the one hand, public exposure forced Palestinian negotiators into taking more hardline positions than would otherwise have been likely in an informal and nonbinding context. On the other hand, the tentative and incomplete nature of the secret Stockholm talks gave a misleading impression of what was possible at Camp David. The Israeli side, in particular, emerged from Stockholm with unwarrantedly high expectations regarding the contours of an acceptable final status deal. A pre–Camp David Track-II would have been less damaging all around: it would have protected the formal "deal-makers" on both sides from the dangers of premature exposure, and it would have allowed for a deeper and wide-ranging discussion of substantive issues but without any real costs in case of failure.

Israelis and Palestinians are unlikely to exit the cycle of violence without considerable further Track-II efforts. For if negotiations are to be renewed, a new understanding must be created about the purpose of such talks and their ultimate outcome, and it is difficult to imagine how such an understanding can be rebuilt except through Track-II channels given the prevailing circumstances. Finally, it appears that major new Track-II efforts may be needed to diminish the likelihood and impact of any future miscommunication and misunderstanding between the two sides. For while Track-II talks may not guarantee perfect understanding, the absence of such talks is almost sure to pave the way to further crises and breakdowns.

Chapter 2

Early Contacts

Track-II experiences in the Middle East have grown out of the overall changes in the political environment surrounding the Arab-Israeli conflict and the search for a comprehensive negotiated peace settlement since the 1967 war. (While the period prior to the establishment of Israel in 1948 saw numerous politico-diplomatic contacts between the conflicting parties, efforts at resolving the conflict through direct formal or informal diplomacy had petered out by the late 1950s.) The aftermath of the 1967 War—fought principally by Israel, Egypt, Syria, and Jordan—set a formal framework for a peaceful settlement with the adoption of United Nations Security Council Resolution (UNSCR) 242 based on the formula of "land for peace" and secure and recognized borders for all the states in the area. Although in November 1967 this resolution was accepted in principle by Israel, Egypt, and Jordan, no progress toward a settlement was achieved in spite of the efforts of the UN and other external mediators.

The outbreak of the 1973 October war gave renewed urgency to the search for peace. By the end of the war, the UN Security Council adopted Resolution 338 reaffirming UNSCR 242 and calling on the parties to begin peace negotiations. Postwar Egyptian moves toward peace with Israel indicated that the era of all-out Arab confrontation with the Jewish state was begining to end. Further important changes were taking place elsewhere within the Arab camp: In 1974, Syria formally committed itself to a negotiated settlement based on UNSCR 242 for the first time, and accepted a U.S.-brokered disengagement agreement including a partial Israeli withdrawal from the Golan Heights. Coupled with the 1975 Israeli-Egyptian disengagement agreement in Sinai, progress on the Syrian-Israeli track suggested that a comprehensive peace on all major Arab-Israeli fronts was now possible. Although postwar diplomacy did not fully meet such expectations, by late 1977 Egypt had embarked on its own separate course with Israel, culminating in the U.S.-sponsored 1978 Camp David Accords that brought about the first-ever peace treaty between Israel and an Arab state.

As a result of such developments, the Palestinian Liberation Organization (PLO) leadership began a process of strategic reappraisal of its own goals. The 1973 war had seen the acceptance by all the major regional protagonists of UNSCR 338 calling for a U.S.-Soviet-sponsored international conference to end the conflict. Soon afterwards, the PLO leadership came to the conclusion that such a conference was inevitable given the post-1973 regional and international balance of power. One of its most pressing priorities therefore was to ensure its place in this projected conference and in any subsequent negotiations as the "sole representative of the Palestinian people." It finally secured this representative status at the Rabbat Arab summit of October 1974 and continued to develop its political platform in a manner that would enhance its prospects for participation in the peace process.

Accordingly, the PLO's politico-diplomatic program turned increasingly away from "armed struggle" as the sole basis of its attempt to regain Palestine and closer toward acceptance of a negotiated settlement with Israel based on the "two-state solution." This stipulated coexistence between a Palestinian state in East Jerusalem, the West Bank, and the Gaza Strip (the territories occupied by Israel in the 1967 War) and the state of Israel within its pre-1967 borders. The shift in policy was cautious and often wrapped in conflicting signals but nonetheless reflected the emergent pragmatism of the Palestinian movement and in particular that of its dominant Fateh leadership.[1] As part of an overall attempt to engage the Israeli side on the basis of a negotiated two-state settlement, the PLO leadership became more interested in contacts with the Israeli side.

This new environment set the stage for a surge of Arab-Israeli exchanges. Often prompted by interested third parties, such contacts were also propelled by a genuine desire by various Israeli and Palestinian individuals and groups to establish a meaningful dialogue and promote the prospects of peace with the other side. A number of Israeli activists were interested in developing contacts with the Palestinians and did not always wait for a Palestinian initiative. However, in most instances Israeli

---

1. Fateh, the largest of the movements constituting the PLO, was founded in the late 1950s, and has been headed by Yasser Arafat since the late 1960s.

peace activists were isolated and their activities met with sharp criticism in the Israeli press, the Knesset (Israel's parliament), and among the public at large. Nonetheless, most persevered without giving up hope. Many of these early encounters did not resemble any structured attempt at a Track-II exercise, and were often closer in style and substance to "therapy" sessions. Other efforts took on the more serious aspect of secret diplomacy, depending on the contacts and political outlook of the parties involved.

Although there were a number of Israeli contacts with other Arab parties (particularly with Egypt after President Sadat's visit to Jerusalem in 1977 and the Camp David Accords in 1978), until the late 1980s the Palestinian-Israeli track was by far the most active venue of Arab-Israeli contacts. This was the result of four factors. First, the PLO leadership was relatively uninhibited about initiating and pursuing such contacts, and believed that this served the Palestinian national interest. Second, the Palestinian leadership was largely unencumbered by any formal or bureaucratic restraints and was highly responsive to personal initiatives that came from within or without the organization's establishment. Third, the vast political and existential chasm between the two sides highlighted the need for dialogue and the urgency and value of any useful contact. Fourth, and perhaps most importantly, was the PLO leadership's ceaseless quest to obtain recognition from the Israeli side as a valid and acceptable negotiating partner. This quest for legitimacy took on an additional aspect after U.S. Secretary of State Henry Kissinger's 1975 commitments to Israel not to open a dialogue with the PLO unless it overtly and unequivocally recognized UNSCR 242, accepted Israel's right to exist, and "renounced terrorism." Henceforth, both Israel and the United States were the targets of a concerted effort to overcome the obstacles to direct negotiations.

The First Contacts

During the mid-1970s a number of Palestinian-Israeli channels were developed. As early as November 1973, the PLO's London representative, Said Hammami, had come out publicly in favor of the two-state solution. Hammami's articles in the *Times* of London drew the attention of Uri Avneri, Knesset member and long-time peace activist, and the two men met in London for the first time in early 1975. The Hammami-Avneri contacts helped to encourage Hammami to continue with his public support for the two-state solution with a major speech at the National Liberal Club in London in mid-1975. Another overlapping channel that was particularly active was initiated partly through the good offices of Henri Curiel—a Paris-based Egyptian Jewish communist. Curiel arranged for meetings between Hammami and Israeli physicist Danny Amit.

After a number of meetings, the Paris channel succeeded in producing a joint document outlining the shape and structure of a two-state solution. This was announced publicly in February 1976 by Maj. Gen. (res.) Matityahu Peled (the head of logistics on the Israeli General Staff during the 1967 War who later became a member of Knesset and one of the leaders of the Israeli peace movement). These contacts paved the way for a larger Palestinian-Israeli meeting in Paris in April 1976. The Palestinian side included Issam Sartawi, a Palestinian surgeon and "reformed" guerrilla leader, acting as the personal representative of PLO Chairman Yasser Arafat, alongside Sabri Jiryis—an Israeli Arab lawyer who had been recently deported by the Israeli authorities. The Israeli side was largely made up of members of the newly founded Israel Council for Israel-Palestine Peace (ICIPP), which had been set up in Tel Aviv in 1975. Present at the Paris meeting with Avneri were council members Peled, former Secretary General of the Labor Party Lova Eliav, historian Meir Pail, former treasury official Yaacov Arnon, and Danny Amit.[2]

The meetings held between Hammami, Sartawi, and their Israeli counterparts were no secret in Israel. Israeli participants took some trouble to report on their talks and disseminate their results among the Israeli leadership and public. However, the February 1976 document on a two-state solution met with strong criticism on both sides, hobbling the prospects for further work in this direction. Nevertheless, the PLO leadership made a special effort to sustain and upgrade its dialogue with the Israeli peace camp.[3]

Palestinian-Israeli contacts in this and later periods elicited considerable international interest. The degree of international support can be judged by the participation of Pierre Mendes-France (former prime minister of France) in the Sartawi-Peled group and the active encouragement given to this endeavor by Austria's Chancellor Bruno Kreiski. Kreiski later recruited other senior European political figures to the cause of Mid-

---

2. For details of the Hammami-Sartawi-Curiel meetings and other early contacts, see Mordechai Bar-On, *In Pursuit of Peace: A History of the Israeli Peace Movement* (Washington, D.C.: United States Institute for Peace, 1996).

3. The Palestinian National Council (PNC), the PLO's parliament in exile and highest policy-making organ, officially endorsed the establishment of ties and relations with Jewish "democratic and progressive" forces at its thirteenth session in 1977. By its eighteenth session, in 1988, this formulation had changed subtly but meaningfully to "enhancing relations with Israeli democratic forces."

dle East peace, including former chancellor Willy Brandt of Germany in his capacity as head of the Socialist International after 1976. In most cases the third parties' primary role was to facilitate and provide an umbrella, but Kreiski played an increasingly valuable role as intermediary and facilitator between the PLO and Israel. Later, until his death in July 1990, he became an open advocate of PLO-Israeli negotiations and the two-state solution.

The Hammami-Avneri and Sartawi-Peled channels set an important precedent for Palestinian-Israeli (and to some extent Arab-Israeli) contacts for the following two decades. By breaking previous taboos and allowing engagement and public debate with the other side, these contacts crossed previous psychological and political red lines and helped to create the climate for subsequent talks, including Track-II engagements and ultimately formal negotiations. The PLO leadership's support for Hammami's and Sartawi's activities was often shy and equivocal due to very vocal opposition from Palestinian radical factions and strong resistance from Arab parties that feared a PLO "sell-out." On the other hand, without the tacit support and encouragement of the leadership such activities would have been impossible.

THE PLO'S ATTITUDE

In many ways Hammami's and Sartawi's discourse was closer to the "real" positions of the PLO than that officially articulated by the organization at the time. Hammami's and Sartawi's views represented those of the PLO's inner circle, especially Fateh's leadership, which consisted of Arafat, military commander Khalil Wazir (nom de guerre: Abu Jihad), security chiefs Salah Khalaf (Abu Iyyad) and Hayil Abdul-Hamid (Abu al-Houl) as well as political leader Mahmoud Abbas (Abu Mazin).[4] However, the leadership's political and moral support could not guarantee the safety of those concerned. In January 1978, Hammami was assassinated in his London office by suspected agents of the PLO renegade Abu Nidal, acting on behalf of the Iraqi regime, which was then in a serious political confrontation with the PLO. Issam Sartawi was assassinated five years later, in April 1983, while attending a meeting of the Socialist International in Portugal, also at the hands of Abu Nidal agents thought to be directed from Baghdad.

The loss of Hammami and Sartawi did not, however, deter the development of Palestinian-Israeli contacts. Various Eastern European coun-

---

4. Abu Jihad was assassinated by an Israeli commando unit in Tunis in March 1988, and both Abu Iyyad and Abu al-Houl were killed by an agent of the Palestinian dissident Abu Nidal in February 1991.

tries in particular encouraged a dialogue between the two sides. President Tito of Yugoslavia and President Ceausescu of Romania were both active facilitators of such meetings. Among the more interesting of these encounters were the first PLO meetings, in Prague in May 1977, with Arab members of the Communist (*Rakah*) Party in the Israeli Knesset. In 1983, Abu Iyyad, Arafat's senior security official, met in Budapest with members of the Israeli Council for Peace in the Middle East (ICPME), an Israeli peace research group founded in 1981 by figures close to the Labor movement. By the mid-1980s such contacts had become almost routine: Abu Mazin, the PLO executive committee member tasked with following up on these meetings, records his own participation in three major conferences with senior representatives of the Sephardic-Moroccan communities in Israel and abroad during the period 1986–1989.[5]

The PLO's diplomatic drive was not merely the product of post-1973 "new thinking" by the organization's leadership. The PLO's embroilment in the Lebanese civil war after 1975 dissipated much of the organization's energies and resources, but equally constrained the leadership's political freedom of action. Pursuit of a policy toward Israel "independent" of Syria became increasingly difficult given the delicate balance of relations between the PLO and Syria, and Syria's concerns that a Palestinian defection from the Arab ranks (along Egyptian lines) would decisively tilt the balance of power against Damascus. In this respect, the Israeli invasion of Lebanon and the eviction of the PLO from Lebanese territory helped to consolidate the PLO's political options and release it from Syria's tutelage. The PLO's military defeat in the 1982 war and its relocation to Tunis some 1,500 kilometers away from the shores of Palestine thus made it increasingly clear that the "armed struggle" had reached a dead-end and that other means had to be found to achieve Palestinian national goals.

The outbreak of the first *intifada* (popular uprising) in the occupied territories in late 1987 provided a new opportunity to develop the PLO's politico-diplomatic approach. By refocusing world and Arab attention on the fate of the Palestinian people under occupation since 1967, the *intifada* succeeded in raising pertinent questions in Israel and abroad about the political future of the Gaza Strip and the West Bank. By late 1988, the PLO took a conscious decision to "capitalize on the gains" of the *intifada* and translate this into an overt and apparently realistic program for peace. At the November 1988 meeting of the Palestinian National Council (PNC) in Algiers, the PLO voted for the first time to accept the partition of Pales-

---

5. See Abbas's (Abu Mazin's) account of the purpose and importance of these encounters in Mahmoud Abbas, *Through Secret Channels* (London: Garnet, 1995), pp. 16–18.

tine (the land between the Mediterranean and the Jordan river), the two-state solution, and UNSC Resolution 242. This was intended as a clear message to the Israelis that the Palestinians were formally ready for peace.

ISRAELI ATTITUDES

The PLO's drive to engage the Israelis can be contrasted with the attitude and objective of successive Israeli governments in the 1970s and the 1980s. The ascendancy of the right-wing Likud Party after 1977 clearly hardened Israeli official attitudes against any contact or dialogue with the PLO, but there was also a broad consensus within the Israeli politico-security establishment that steadfastly opposed any opening to the PLO. Paradoxically, the Israeli debate on the PLO seemed to stand on its head Israel's longstanding call for direct negotiations with the Arabs. After years of calling for direct face-to-face talks as tangible evidence of Arab recognition of the Jewish state, many on the Israeli side now argued that direct dialogue with the PLO was a slippery slope tantamount to recognition of the Palestinians' national rights at Israel's expense. With few exceptions, the Israeli leadership—both Labor and Likud—was thus unwilling to consider dialogue with the PLO for political, ideological, and psychological reasons. The PLO's image as a terrorist organization also had wide resonance among the Israeli public.

While the PLO leadership had concluded by the mid-1980s that only a sustained campaign of contacts and political mobilization with Israel would generate a change in Israeli politics, there is not much evidence that the Israeli side—apart from some dedicated peace activists—had really absorbed the importance of the internal Palestinian debate or the growing backing for a "peace offensive" within the PLO leadership. Far from actively pursuing the possibilities of dialogue with the PLO, the Israeli leadership—with few exceptions—was looking elsewhere.

On the one hand, the Israeli side pursued its attempts to weaken or destroy the PLO militarily with a relentless campaign of preemptive and punitive strikes aimed at the burgeoning Palestinian presence in Lebanon and culminating in the all-out assault on this presence in 1982. On the other hand, there were tireless Israeli efforts designed to encourage a "local substitute" for the PLO. These included the establishment of the Village Leagues in the West Bank in 1979, and even initial support of the then politically quiescent Islamic movement Hamas in the hope that it could act as a counterweight to the nationalist aspirations embodied by the PLO. These Israeli efforts extended into the early 1990s with hopes that "insider" members of the Palestinian delegation to the post-1991 Gulf War Madrid-Washington peace talks—delegates from Gaza and the

West Bank—would split from the PLO Tunis-based "outsiders." Although the "insiders" may have often chafed under the restrictions and constraints placed on them by the "outsiders," the former were fully aware that they had neither the moral nor the political legitimacy to take a fundamentally divergent line from that pursued by the PLO outside.

Those on the Israeli side who encouraged the Palestinian "insiders" failed to understand the subtleties of the relationship between the PLO national leadership then still in the Diaspora and the local West Bank and Gaza individuals who often dealt with the Israelis on a day-to-day basis. While dissension, competition, and a measure of mutual suspicion frequently marked the relationship between the outside leadership and the "insiders," the latter were essentially subservient to the former. This was fundamentally because the PLO outside the West Bank and Gaza (and the Palestinian groups that preceded it) had initiated, organized, and directed the military and political struggle against Israel since the late 1950s, and had borne its heaviest and most direct human and material costs. In the eyes of the vast majority of Palestinians, the PLO leadership's legitimacy was indisputable. The local leaders lacked the base to challenge the PLO leadership even if they believed this was possible. Indeed, the local leaders were well aware of the danger of splitting the Palestinian polity and were genuinely consistent in their call for Israel (and others) to recognize and deal with the PLO directly.

Besides the largely elusive hope of fostering a local alternative to the PLO, many Israelis—particularly in the Labor Party—still hoped that Jordan could be induced to act as an alternative interlocutor to the PLO on the future of the West Bank. Dialogue and contact with the Jordanians to this end continued for much of the 1970s and the 1980s. Israeli efforts and designs ranged from the evisceration of the PLO, as in the invasion of Lebanon in 1982, to the establishment of a Jordanian-Israeli condominium in the West Bank, as in the abortive Peres-Hussein London understanding of 1987.[6] By 1988, as a result of the *intifada*, King Hussein of Jordan had formally "disengaged" from the West Bank, reducing the possibility of a direct Jordanian political role in the territories. Yet even after 1991, the Likud continued to believe that a Jordanian "return" of some kind to the West Bank could be engineered through the Madrid process.

---

6. The understanding negotiated secretly by the two leaders called for the establishment of an Israeli-Jordanian-Palestinian federation in which the Palestinian entity was to be ruled by "local Palestinians."

Israel Contacts the PLO

Yet the official Israeli aversion to contacts with the PLO leadership was not absolute. The first recorded contact took place in September 1986. Maj. Gen. (res.) Avraham Tamir, then Director General of the Israeli Foreign Ministry under Shimon Peres in the Likud-Labor national unity government headed by Yitzhak Shamir, took the initiative to meet with PLO Chairman Yasser Arafat in the unlikely setting of Mozambique. With Peres's consent, contact was made with the PLO in Europe and the meeting was arranged with the help of an Israeli adviser well connected with the president of Mozambique. The Israeli ambassador to Botswana came to the meeting but did not participate. On the Palestinian side, Fateh military commander Abu Jihad was also present in Mozambique but did not attend the meeting.

Tamir asked for and received a private audience with Arafat. Meeting in a guest house on the coast outside the capital, Arafat and Tamir had a broad-ranging discussion. Of most interest to Arafat was how Israel (which he saw as a strong regional power) could be apprehensive about making peace with the PLO. Tamir responded that Israel feared that a Palestinian state would become a base for terrorism against Israel and would ultimately force the Israeli side to wage war and reoccupy it.[7]

Little of substance emerged from the Arafat-Tamir meeting. The Israeli side later informed the U.S. consulate in Jerusalem, but with no evident reaction. Peres's complicity in the meeting is noteworthy but it is unclear whether or what he reported back to his partner in government, Prime Minister Shamir. Nonetheless, the Arafat-Tamir meeting seems to have set a precedent for subsequent attempts by the Labor Party leadership to test the possibility of a dialogue with the PLO.

Indeed, both Foreign Minister Peres and Israeli Defense Minister Yitzhak Rabin appear to have become less and less certain of the viability of an outright veto on the PLO as potential interlocutor after the outbreak of the Palestinian *intifada* in the occupied territories in late 1987. Without prior consultation with Prime Minister Shamir, Rabin and Peres appear to have authorized new "unofficial" contacts with the PLO. Meeting in Europe in late summer 1988, these contacts aimed at seeking some trade-off between a reduction in the level of the *intifada* and an Israeli release of Palestinian prisoners, as well as the promise of potential further talks if the initial steps proved mutually satisfactory.

---

7. Zeev Schiff interview with Major General (ret.) Avraham Tamir, March 1999.

The talks took place in Paris and Brussels in August and September 1988. They involved Arafat associates Hani al-Hassan and Said Kamal on the Palestinian side, and former Head of Israeli Military Intelligence Shlomo Gazit on the Israeli side. Newly retired from the presidency of Beersheva University, Gazit had been approached by Peres—then Prime Minister under the rotation agreement upon which the national unity government was based—to carry out discreet contacts with the PLO with the ostensible purpose of soliciting PLO aid in locating Israeli soldiers still missing in action since the Lebanese war in 1982. Facilitated by the Canadian Jewish academic Steve Cohen, the talks had a wider political purpose, focusing on the future of Israeli-PLO relations. Yossi Ginossar, then deputy head of Israel's General Security Services, helped to organize the talks and participated in the debate. On the Palestinian side, the talks were supported by Arafat and security chief Abu Iyyad. On the Israeli side, Peres, Defense Minister Rabin, and Foreign Minister Yitzhak Shamir were all briefed on the talks. The effort was aborted after the failure of Peres in Israel's October 1988 elections.[8]

Although the 1988 contacts petered out without any obvious change in the Israeli government's attitude toward the PLO, this attitude was nonetheless subject to a slow but sure evolution. Long before 1992, Rabin had become convinced that the Palestinians could not be ignored when deciding the fate of the occupied territories. The *intifada* had also made it increasingly clear to him that Jordan would not ultimately speak for the Palestinians.

Shortly before his return to office as prime minister in the summer of 1992, Rabin was beginning to articulate this view. In a visit to Washington in March 1992, he informed his hosts that the post–Gulf War environment in the region had created a great opportunity to make peace with the Palestinians. In Rabin's view, the Jordanian option was dead and henceforth only the Palestinians could speak for themselves. Rabin further postulated that the Palestinians were the party that was most ready to make peace, and that they would be followed by the Jordanians, and only then by the Syrians. Accordingly, Rabin believed that talks should start with the Palestinians first. Interestingly, however, it appears that Rabin was noncommittal on the shape of a final settlement and argued for the need to first test the possibility of peaceful coexistence in an interim settlement.

---

8. Based on interviews with Major General (ret.) Shlomo Gazit by Shai Feldman in 1997 and by Zeev Schiff in 1999. See also detailed report on 1988 meetings by A. Shavit in *Ha'aretz*, February 12, 1999. Gazit was also involved in another set of meetings with senior PLO Official Khalid al-Hassan in Washington in 1990 but Rabin, who felt that they were politically inopportune at the time, aborted these talks.

As the prospects of a negotiated settlement grew after 1987–1988, Rabin's first choice was to see whether Palestinians from the territories would be willing to speak out on behalf of the Palestinians as a whole. Later he realized that the process would not move forward without the PLO, although it took a while longer before Rabin became completely disillusioned with the Palestinian "insiders." This attitude eventually served to facilitate the 1993 Oslo accord.

The Growth of the Israeli Peace Movement

The post-1973 period had also seen the growth of an active and vociferous Israeli peace movement. Uri Avneri, Matityahu Peled, and others represented a growing segment of Israeli society that had been galvanized by the near disaster of 1973 into action aimed at ending the conflict. "Peace Now," which was established in 1973 as a mass popular movement, eventually brought forth more organized parties such as *Ratz* and *Shinui,* which joined the Knesset in 1981. Starting in 1976, for almost a decade the ICIPP under Peled played a pivotal role in Israeli peace politics. The more mainstream ICPME also kept international figures, such as Brandt, Mendes-France, and World Jewish Congress leader Nahum Goldman, engaged in peace activities.

The 1982 Lebanon War and its aftermath played a significant role in transforming the attitude of the Israeli public toward the Palestinians. The trauma of the Sabra and Shatilla massacre,[9] and the failure of Defense Minister Sharon's grand design—to destroy the PLO in Lebanon and crush Palestinian national aspirations in the West Bank and Gaza—only highlighted the limitations of Israel's military activism as an instrument of political change. Among other things, the Lebanon war helped to demonstrate to Israelis that perpetuating the dispute would only lead to more bloodshed, and that other alternatives had to be found to resolve the longstanding conflict with the Palestinians.

By the mid-1980s, the Likud government felt it necessary to take direct legal measures to prevent any further erosion of the traditional official position on dealing with the PLO. In 1986, the Shamir government passed a law banning any contact between Israeli citizens and members of the PLO. This impediment played an important but not decisive role in raising the political and legal costs of dialogue with the PLO.

9. Sabra and Shatilla are two Palestinian refugee camps in West Beirut. During the Israeli invasion of Lebanon in September 1982, the IDF allowed Christian Phalangist forces into the camps to flush out PLO "armed elements." Thousands of Palestinian and Lebanese civilians were massacred as a result.

By 1991, the ban had been lifted and the Israeli peace camp felt considerably freer to appear in public with PLO officials. This led peace activists such as Dudi Tzuker and Yossi Sarid to meet with Arafat in Tunis. By 1992, the political party Meretz (representing a coalition of the smaller Israeli peace parties) was part of the ruling governmental coalition led by Rabin and the Labor Party and was in a position to affect Israeli decision-making directly.

In contrast to the Palestinian side, the Israeli participants in this phase of contacts had no real concerns about their personal safety, although there was some concern about how their contacts would affect their political and personal standing within their professional and broader communities. Israeli participants record their awareness that the Palestinian side most often represented the PLO leadership or was mandated on its behalf, whereas the Israelis invariably represented themselves or a more amorphous "peace camp" within their society. Nonetheless, Israeli participants often reported back to their national leadership. For example, Peled kept Rabin informed of his contacts, although these reports were mostly received with "cold indifference."[10]

"Academic" Conferences

Academic conferences began to come to the fore as a mechanism for Palestinian-Israeli contacts after the mid-1980s. The 1986 Israeli law banning contacts between citizens and members of the PLO left open the possibility of conducting meetings in the context of "legitimate academic conferences." That is, the presence of a third-party umbrella offered Israeli participants a legal fig leaf and helped to redirect the early more politicized efforts to a less visible domain.

One early such effort was launched in the early 1980s by the American Psychiatry Association (APA) to bring together Israeli and Egyptian participants and—at a later phase—Palestinian participants. The meetings were prompted by the speech given by Egypt's President Anwar Sadat to the Israeli Knesset during his path-breaking visit to Israel in November 1977. In his speech, Sadat stated his conviction that 90 percent of the Arab-Israeli conflict was psychological. Accordingly, the APA-initiated meetings were designed to explore the psychological dimensions of the conflict and to examine what steps adversaries can take to humanize one another.

---

10. Bar-On, *In Pursuit of Peace*, p. 207. Rabin's reported angry response to a briefing from Lova Eliav in 1976 was more expressive: "I will meet them on the battlefield." See Shmuel Segev, *Crossing the Jordan* (New York: St. Martin's, 1998), p. 290.

The Israelis taking part in these talks included a number of psychologists—most notably, Nechama De-Shalit—as well as a number of historians, such as Shimon Shamir and Gabriel Cohen from Tel Aviv University, and former Israeli intelligence officials such as Aluf Hareven, Aharon Yariv, and Shlomo Gazit. The Egyptian participants also included a number of psychologists as well as prominent former officials including Ambassador Tahseen Bashir, and political analysts such as Muhammad Ramadan from *Al-Ahram*. Palestinians who later joined the talks included former mayor of Gaza, Rashad as-Shawa, and Elias Freij, then mayor of Bethlehem.

A number of meetings were convened over a span of three years and some options for meeting the purpose of the initiative were discussed. One was to arrange meetings among Israeli, Egyptian, and Palestinian peers within professional groups such as physicians or psychologists. Another idea was to examine the parties' education systems and the textbooks used and to correct all manifestations of the dehumanizing of adversaries. However, none of the ideas discussed were implemented and the APA leadership soon lost interest in the project.

The Washington-based Brookings Institution launched a more concerted effort in 1988–1989, orchestrated by William Quandt, who had been director for Middle East affairs at the National Security Council under U.S. President Jimmy Carter. Under his sponsorship, a series of meetings in Europe brought together PLO representatives such as Nabil Shaath and Leila Shahid with a wide spectrum of Israeli participants including Ephraim Sneh from the Labor Party and Ezra Sadaan from the right-wing Israeli *Hatihyah* Party. The Brookings group discussed the shape of a political and security agreement for a Palestinian state as part of a more general move by Quandt to encourage serious thinking on both sides regarding a settlement.[11]

Although the APA and Brookings meetings did not produce any conclusive results, their effect can best be seen as part of a cumulative and continuing process. Throughout the mid- to late 1980s, the "academic" circuit continued to provide the framework for a broad and extensive dialogue between the two sides. The rest of this chapter surveys three particularly important encounters.

---

11.   Quandt had been especially active during this period in trying to open a direct channel between the U.S. administration and the PLO. Subsequently, Sneh and Shaath were to develop their own separate back channel, which was used by the PLO and the Israeli Labor Party leadership to exchange messages after the return of the Labor Party to power in 1992.

"Gaza First": The Ontell Project

In the wake of the Camp David Accords, the Institute for World Politics, a semi-independent affiliate of San Diego State University in California, attempted to foster Arab-Israeli contacts (with funds provided by a grant from the Hansen Foundation for World Peace). Initially, Bob Ontell, the Institute's Middle East coordinator, focused on sponsoring meetings between Israeli and Egyptian governmental and nongovernmental agricultural experts. Much of this work was kept confidential to accommodate Egyptian sensitivities. The Hansen Foundation then raised funds for wider projects to combat desertification throughout the Middle East. Much later—and at the behest of the Egyptian side—the emphasis shifted to the Palestinian-Israeli track.

A number of meetings were held in 1987–1988. Among the Israeli participants in the Ontell project were former head of Military Intelligence Yehoshafat Harkabi, Labor Party leader Binyamin (Fuad) Ben-Eliezer, former Minister of Justice Haim Zadok (also of the Labor Party), Secretary General of the Mapam party Elazar Granot, and Zeev Schiff, defense editor of *Ha'aretz*. The Palestinian participants included political activists and academics such as Sari Nusseibeh and Fayiz Abu-Rahme, Bethlehem Mayor Elias Freige, and Jerusalem publisher Hanna Seniora. Meetings took place in California and Maryland, and in Jerusalem and other locations in Israel. The project came to a halt with the outbreak of the first *intifada* in the occupied territories after 1988.

The Ontell project was primarily aimed at clarifying the positions of the two sides. While various issues were discussed (such as the conditions that could lead to a halt of the *intifada*), perhaps the most interesting aspect of the Ontell meetings was that they seem to have provided the occasion for the first serious Palestinian-Israeli discussion of the "Gaza first/plus" idea. The essence of this idea was that Israel would withdraw from the Gaza Strip as a first step toward a more comprehensive settlement. The notion of "Gaza first" was not entirely novel and had been revived most recently as a possible interim follow-up to the Camp David Accords. Seniora and Abu-Rahme suggested to their Israeli counterparts during the course of the meetings that "Gaza first" was possible but that it could only begin to make sense from the Palestinian point of view if matched with a territorial "plus" on the West Bank, such as a withdrawal from Jericho. From the Palestinian point of view, the danger was that an Israeli withdrawal from Gaza could turn into "Gaza first and last," and diminish the prospects for any further withdrawals from the West Bank. The Palestinian side further suggested that a Gaza-Jericho withdrawal could be implemented as the first "experimental" stage in a phased process lasting a number of years and, if successful, would be followed by further Israeli withdrawals to be negotiated sequentially and separately.

The Ontell project's deliberations were eventually overtaken by events on the ground. At first, the uprising in the occupied territories after 1987 helped to heighten Palestinian expectations that a more comprehensive settlement would be reached than that offered by the "Gaza first/plus" option. Hence, there was little interest or discussion of this option for a number of years until it was revived at the Oslo talks of 1993. But the Ontell project did take on aspects of a Track-II exercise because some of the same Palestinian participants had close connections with the PLO leadership, and they reported back to Abu Jihad and Abu Mazin. Both leaders had a longstanding interest in promoting and widening contacts with the Israeli side. As Abu Jihad's brother-in-law, Fayiz Abu-Rahme had a direct personal link to him. The leadership input, however, was asymmetrical and lacked the element of an engagement or interest on the part of the Israeli leadership or the willingness to develop the exercise into a full-fledged negotiating channel. The personal security of the Palestinian participants was nonetheless at stake: Abu Jihad informed both Seniora and Abu-Rahme that their lives could be at risk. This important consideration continued to mark the difference between Palestinian and Israeli participation in such events for some time. Indeed, until well after the Madrid Conference in 1991, the element of physical danger was rarely absent for the Palestinian side.

Feelers from the "Right": The Amirav-Nusseibeh Channel

In the summer of 1987, Likud Party Central Council member Moshe Amirav and prominent Palestinian academic Sari Nusseibeh set up another notable channel, with David Is-shalom, an Israeli peace activist, acting as a go-between. Amirav met several times with Nusseibeh and, later, with Feisal Husseini, the senior Palestinian leader in East Jerusalem. Amirav's objective was to present his interlocutors with a Likud-backed initiative regarding an interim settlement that would be passed to and accepted by the PLO and, thus, bolster the prospects for a Likud victory in the upcoming 1988 elections.

Amirav also suggested that the circle of support for a Palestinian-Israeli interim agreement was quite wide within the ruling coalition. He told his Palestinian interlocutors that there was support for his views among senior Likud figures such as Dan Meridor, Meir Shitreet, Moshe Katsav, and even among hard-right representatives such as Benyamin (Benny) Begin and Ehud Olmert. A meeting with selected members of this group was to be arranged by Amirav, but was apparently aborted after a leak in the Israeli press. Ehud Olmert, however, met separately with Nusseibeh—albeit without raising issues of substance.

In subsequent meetings, Amirav delved into more details regarding the shape of a final settlement, including the establishment of a Palestinian state. As in most similar encounters, the Palestinian side was reporting directly back to the PLO leadership in Tunis. At one stage the latter was sufficiently encouraged by the discussions to consider a meeting between Amirav and Arafat—possibly in Geneva. At the last meeting in August 1987, Amirav produced a full-scale blueprint for a settlement. This blueprint included a detailed step-by-step proposal for direct PLO-Israeli negotiations, mutual recognition, and the establishment of an interim "Palestinian entity" with its "administrative capital in the Arab part of Jerusalem." It also included provisions for a comprehensive settlement dealing with Israeli settlements, the "return of Palestinians" and ultimate agreement on an "independent Palestinian State."

The Amirav-Nusseibeh channel, however, quickly came to a dead end. Amirav canceled the proposed Geneva trip on the grounds that he had not succeeded in obtaining a green light from then Prime Minister Yitzhak Shamir. Within a short period, Feisal Husseini was detained by the Israeli authorities on an apparently unrelated charge and was clearly in no position to pursue the initiative with any real vigor thereafter. Subsequently, Nusseibeh also suspended his dealings with Amirav. With the outbreak of the *intifada* at the end of 1987, the initiative was overtaken by events.

Most evidence, including the PLO's own postmortem, suggests that Amirav was acting largely on his own initiative and exaggerated both his influence with the Likud leadership and the latter's readiness to make a deal with the PLO. Amirav's position as a maverick within his own party also seems to be confirmed by his subsequent departure from the Likud and his virtual disappearance from the Israeli political scene. Nonetheless, according to Abu Mazin, the advantages of the Amirav exercise lay in the apparent recognition by the Israeli right (or at least significant segments within it) that the PLO was the ultimate address for any initiative. This was also seen as potentially the first step toward direct negotiations between the two sides. This perception was strengthened by the fact that Amirav had apparently briefed Shamir on his contacts with the Palestinian side without meeting any outright rejection to his enterprise. From the Palestinians' perspective, anything that contributed to the erosion of Israel's outright rejection of the PLO was relatively positive.

On the surface, the Amirav-Nusseibeh channel bore some of the characteristics of a classic Track-II exercise. It seemed to have "trusted" delegates on both sides reporting back to their respective leaderships and considering far-reaching creative proposals for conflict resolution. Amirav, Nusseibeh, and Husseini seem to have been ready to clinch a deal and to sustain the personal risks involved. The problem—as in many other similar instances at the time—was the asymmetrical engagement of the Israeli and Palestinian leaderships in the initiative. The Shamir government was neither willing to pursue the opportunity to establish an effective dialogue with the PLO nor was it ready to use the channel for anything approaching a mutually acceptable deal. Interestingly, however, Shamir never denied that he was aware of Amirav's contacts although he may not have been willing to endorse them. One possibility is that Shamir gave Amirav some leeway simply to explore what such talks could produce. Perhaps the only real surprise is that Shamir allowed Amirav to continue his efforts for as long as he did.

Pursuing Dialogue: The Kelman Harvard Project

Herbert Kelman, Professor of Social Ethics at Harvard University, orchestrated a more sustained effort focusing on "overcoming the barriers to a negotiation of the Israeli-Palestinian conflict."[12] Beginning in the mid-1980s, Kelman convened a number of meetings in an effort to explore whether there was sufficient common ground between the two sides. In the pre-Oslo era, the Kelman project provided Israelis and Palestinians one of the most extensive opportunities to exchange views and to understand each other's concerns. Participants shared the impressions they gained in these talks with a wider constituency.

In 1984 Kelman brought together five Israeli members of the Knesset and five Palestinians associated with the PLO and side-by-side opinion pieces were published in the U.S. press. The 1986 Israeli law outlawing meetings between Israeli citizens and members of the PLO later presented a major constraint to such exercises, and participants from both sides were also apprehensive about the wider implications of these meetings and the possible threat to their personal security that such talks entailed.

The Kelman talks passed through two phases: The first phase was largely concerned with an exchange of existential concerns, opinions, and ideas. It was assumed that the ideas generated by the group would be circulated among the leadership echelons and eventually spread to the public at large and other political groups on both sides. Although Kelman

---

12.　See Herbert Kelman, "Overcoming the Barriers to Negotiation of the Israeli-Palestinian Conflict," *Journal for Palestine Studies*, No. 61 (Autumn 1986). In the article, Kelman elaborates the objectives of his efforts and the methodology used.

was himself active in contacting the leaders of both sides, his success in penetrating the political process was limited.

The "existential" phase of the Kelman project lasted a number of years and involved meetings in the United States, Italy, Belgium and Austria. The Israelis taking part included scholars such as Shimon Shamir (a Tel Aviv University scholar, later appointed Ambassador to Egypt and then Jordan) and Yael (Yuli) Tamir (another Tel Aviv University scholar, appointed in 1999 to serve as Minister of Immigration in the Barak-led government), former defense and security officials Shlomo Gazit, Ephraim Sneh (appointed in 1992 to serve as Minister of Health in Rabin's government, in 1999 to serve as Deputy Minister of Defense in the Barak government, and in early 2001 to serve as Minister of Transportation in the Sharon-led national unity government), and senior defense analyst Zeev Schiff. The Palestinian participants included scholars and professionals such as Yezid Sayigh, Camille Mansour, and Leila Shahid from Europe, as well as Salim Tamari, Souad Ameri, Ziad Abu Ziad, and Ghassan al-Khatib from the West Bank, and others such as U.S.-based Palestinian academic Fouad Moghrabi.

The Kelman talks were informal and unrecorded by agreement, but all participants were free to keep their own notes. No written summaries were provided and no publications emerged directly from the talks. Although it is difficult to assess the degree to which the ideas generated by the Kelman project actually seeped into the broader political debate within and between the two sides, the project helped to educate and inform some of the more active Israeli and Palestinian opinion makers. For example, Shlomo Gazit conveyed his impressions and conclusions to senior Israeli leaders and government officials and received positive reactions to these reports from Shimon Peres, as well as from the Israeli Defense Force's (IDF) intelligence and planning branches. Zeev Schiff, Shimon Shamir, and Ephraim Sneh likewise informed Israeli officials of their participation.

On the Palestinian side, the PLO headquarters in Tunis was regularly kept abreast of the discussions, and Palestinian participants often traveled to Tunis to seek official sanction. Many among the Palestinian team involved in the Kelman project later joined the Palestinian delegation to the formal negotiations in Madrid and Washington, where they drew on their experiences in the project.

The first phase of the Kelman effort ended with the beginning of the Madrid-Washington talks in late 1991 and early 1992. Palestinian participants who were members of the negotiating team found it difficult to reconcile their simultaneous participation in both formal and informal tracks without compromising their official positions. A second phase was inaugurated soon after the Oslo agreement. This time the focus was on the "final status" negotiations agenda set out in the Oslo accords, including the future of Jerusalem, refugees, Israeli settlements, borders, and security arrangements. By late 1998 the first public output of the "second phase" Kelman group was made available.[13]

Kelman's exercise seems to have been most valuable when formal dialogue and contact between the two sides was difficult if not impossible. Its first phase had many of the characteristics of a "soft" Track-II exercise. Mere reporting back to the respective national leaderships or seeking their sanction in attending the talks was insufficient to elevate the discussions from a largely academic exercise into a more politically relevant channel. Nonetheless, the project provided a continuous forum for Palestinian-Israeli mutual familiarization and self-education.

---

13.   See "General Principles for the Final Palestinian-Israeli Agreement," Program on International Conflict Analysis and Resolution at the Weatherhead Center for International Affairs, Harvard University, September 1998.

Chapter 3

The Oslo Talks

Abu Ala' (Ahmad Qurei'), head of *Samed*—the PLO Economics Department—first put the idea of opening an informal Palestinian-Israeli channel to the Norwegian side during a visit to Oslo in January 1992. According to Terje Larsen, who later became the Oslo channel's Norwegian coordinator, the request for a secret Palestinian-Israeli conduit was also made by Feisal Husseini in mid-1992, just before the Israeli elections. Husseini, who was then active in the Palestinian delegation to the Washington talks, was evidently seeking a way to break the two-year-old deadlock in the formal peace negotiations.[1] But it was the Palestinian leadership in Tunis that finally succeeded in bringing the Oslo channel to fruition.

The Oslo process was launched in December 1992 during an impromptu meeting in London between Yair Hirschfeld, a faculty member of Haifa University, and Abu Ala'. Nine months later, in early September 1993, these talks produced the most dramatic breakthrough in Arab-Israeli peacemaking since the 1978 Camp David accord: an Israel-PLO Declaration of Principles (DOP).

The Oslo accords, and the associated letters exchanged, constituted a complete break from past Israeli and Palestinian approaches. The PLO accepted the deferment of vital issues such as the future of Jerusalem and Israeli settlements within a phased process whose end result was yet to be negotiated. This allowed for the implementation of interim arrangements without a prior Israeli commitment that these arrangements would

---

1. Zeev Schiff interview with Terje Larsen, mid-1997.

necessarily lead to independent statehood. At the time, the Palestinian leadership set aside its long-standing fear that such an approach would expose it to the risk that Israel might freeze negotiations half-way through the process—after the PLO abandoned its armed struggle and before its national aspirations were realized. In accepting this risk, the rationale of the Palestinian leadership was that the presence of a Palestinian authority on Palestinian soil would develop and propagate its own political and territorial dynamic that would inevitably lead to independence and statehood.

Israel's concessions at Oslo were no less significant. For the first time, Israel recognized the PLO as the representative of the Palestinian people and agreed—also for the first time—to transfer parts of what it considered to be the "Land of Israel" to Palestinian control. Israelis had long regarded the PLO as a terrorist organization determined to destroy their country and had viewed PLO Chairman Yasser Arafat as personifying such a commitment to violence. Yet in 1993 (and at least until early 2001) the Israeli leadership accepted the PLO as its primary Palestinian interlocutor and endorsed Arafat himself as its primary partner in peace and reconciliation.

The September 1993 Israeli-Palestinian DOP had monumental consequences. From Israel's standpoint, it initially transformed the PLO from an outright enemy to a part-rival, part-partner. This was to become especially relevant in the area of security. During this period, a similar dynamic began to affect the Palestinian side: After decades of armed struggle against Israel, a perception emerged within the Palestinian politico-security establishment and the public at large after the mid-1990s that controlling and preventing violence was in the Palestinian national interest. By mid-1995 and until the outbreak of the second *intifada* in September 2000, former Palestinian guerrillas commanded the Palestinian security and intelligence agencies cooperated with Israel's General Security Service (GSS) in an effort to prevent the opponents of the process from derailing it through violence.

Another significant consequence of the 1993 DOP was the opening it created for improved relations between Israel and other Arab states, primarily in the Gulf and the Maghreb. Beyond the Middle East, it at first helped to create a political environment conducive to better relations between Israel and Muslim states, from Pakistan to Indonesia. On the global level, it contributed to Israel's complete integration into the international community. Between the signing of the Oslo DOP in 1993 and late 1995, some 35 nations established or restored diplomatic relations with Israel.

The Israeli-Palestinian DOP also encouraged Jordan's King Hussein to defy conventional wisdom and to negotiate an early peace agreement with Israel. Most observers had expected Hussein to wait until an Israeli-Syrian accord was signed, but by 1994 Hussein seemed to have calculated that it was in Jordan's interest to strike a deal with Israel before any possible agreement with Syria was concluded. Very quickly, the Hussein-Rabin relationship assumed far-reaching dimensions; the two leaders seem to have accelerated the development of an Israeli-Jordanian strategic partnership. Notwithstanding some uneasiness on the part of some Jordanians and Palestinians, the Israeli-Jordanian relationship appears to have been consolidated despite all the challenges it has faced since Oslo.

Ripening

Why did the Oslo talks succeed? How could discussions between an Israeli academic and a Palestinian policy adviser produce such groundbreaking results? Why did this venue succeed in bringing the parties to an agreement where previous efforts had failed? The following sections attempt to trace some of the main international, regional, and domestic factors that affected the Oslo breakthrough.

THE FIRST INTIFADA

The causes and consequences of the first Palestinian *intifada* (1987–1989) had presented PLO chairman Arafat with a new challenge. Although the *intifada* brought renewed international attention to the Palestinian problem, the PLO was also concerned that events might be misinterpreted as showing that Palestinian youth in Gaza and the West Bank had taken matters into their own hands independent of the PLO leadership.

Yet the *intifada* invited Israeli repressive countermeasures, in turn resulting in the rapid deterioration of social and economic conditions in the West Bank and Gaza. By the early 1990s, it became increasingly clear that these conditions were not conducive to a quick resolution of the conflict. In addition, the PLO's limited ability to address the social and economic costs of the *intifada* only increased the appeal of its primary domestic rival—the Islamic movement Hamas. Indeed, Hamas made its breakthrough by proving better able to care for the welfare of the population of the territories (especially in Gaza), through its extensive network of health, education, and social facilities.

Gaining effective control of the West Bank and Gaza thus became imperative for the PLO. Although ever-present in a variety of ways in the occupied territories, the PLO leadership needed to reassert and demonstrate its authority publicly and quickly. Yet the slow-moving Track-I negotiations between Israel and the PLO's proxy delegation held in Washington since early 1992—in the aftermath of the 1991 Madrid Conference —had brought no prospects of relief for the Palestinians' predicament. A new, bold approach was required if the PLO was to consolidate its foothold in the territories and move closer to achieving its political objectives.

THE PLO'S 1988 "PEACE OFFENSIVE" AND THE SWEDISH INITIATIVE

The PLO leadership saw the first *intifada* as a valuable opportunity to convert the tactical and moral advantages gained from the daily confrontations with Israeli troops into some realizable political gains. The *intifada* provided the immediate backdrop to the development of a more realistic and programmatic Palestinian policy. The Palestinian National Council's (PNC) decision in Algiers in November 1988 based on the acceptance of a negotiated settlement and a partition of the historical Land of Palestine into two states was a major turning point in the political history of the movement, providing for a new diplomatic offensive to be built on the achievements of the *intifada*. Henceforth, the PLO was ready to demonstrate its willingness to participate in any agreed peace process and to depart from many of its previous ambiguous public positions on peace. The PNC's decisions had been aimed primarily at breaking the U.S. boycott of the PLO (based on Kissinger's 1975 commitments to Israel) as a necessary first step to international legitimization as a negotiating partner with Israel. Via a series of indirect contacts with the Reagan administration brokered in part by William Quandt and a U.S.-based Palestinian academic, Muhammed Rabie, the United States had been considering various ways of reviving the peace process.

In March 1988, Swedish Foreign Minister Sten Andersson had toured the occupied territories and had been deeply moved by the human cost of the *intifada*. A few months later, Andersson met with U.S. Secretary of State George Schultz and suggested a meeting between members of the U.S. Jewish community and Arafat to facilitate Palestinian-Israeli relations. Subsequently, Swedish diplomat Anders Bruner was dispatched to Tunis to convince the PLO leadership to accept the initiative.

Israel and the United States reacted coldly to the decisions of the November PNC meeting in Algiers. In response, Andersson invited a number of PLO figures, including Khalid al-Hassan, the head of the PLO's Foreign Affairs Committee and a senior founding member of the Fateh movement, to Stockholm meet with three members of the Jewish community to explain the significance of the PNC's resolutions and explore the possibilities it gave rise to. The three were Stanley Sheinbaum, Rita Hauser, and Drora Kass, all of whom were extremely well-connected in both Israel and the United States. The initial Stockholm meetings resulted in a joint statement outlining the PLO's readiness to attend a peace conference on the basis of UNSCR 242, its acceptance of Israel's existence as "a state in the region," and its condemnation of "terrorism in all its forms."

After further consultations with Secretary Schultz, Andersson quickly issued an invitation to Arafat to visit Stockholm in early December.[2] Abu Mazin records that the Palestinian side was pleased to be presented by Andersson with a draft letter from Schultz detailing the steps required of the PLO in order to begin the dialogue with the United States and to become a potential party to the peace process. With active Swedish mediation, negotiations over the Shultz draft continued for some time. Since Arafat was denied a visa to enter the United States, the UN General Assembly was specially convened in Geneva to hear him speak.

With Swedish help, the United States prepared a carefully formulated text. But when Arafat addressed the General Assembly on December 14, 1988, the United States perceived a number of departures from the agreed text. After twenty-four hours of intensive diplomacy led by Andersson and yet another explanatory statement by Arafat, the United States finally announced the commencement of a dialogue with the PLO the following day.

The 1988 experience was important for a number of reasons. First, the U.S.-PLO dialogue marked the first real step toward international legitimization of the PLO. Although it was subsequently suspended in May 1990 (after Arafat refused to clearly condemn an Iraqi-Libyan–inspired attack on Israel by Abu Abbas's PLO faction), the dialogue suggested to the PLO leadership that its post-Algiers diplomatic offensive was yielding results. This accelerated the transformation of the PLO away from armed struggle toward the adoption of purely political means to attain its objectives. Second, it put the Israeli government on the defensive, and helped to regalvanize Palestinian contacts with the Israeli peace camp that had been relatively moribund during the first phases of the *intifada*. Third, the decisive impact of the Swedish role in 1988 impressed upon the PLO the importance of third-party facilitation. It also opened the door for the development of a "Nordic" role both in Oslo in 1993 and again in Stockholm in 1994–1996. Indeed, it was Sten Andersson himself who encouraged Norway's then-Foreign Minister Stoltenburg to take over the role of facilitator after Andersson's Swedish Social Democratic Party lost power in Sweden's 1991 elections.

2. See interview with Sten Andersson, in *Majallat ad-Dirasat al-Filistiniyah* (Journal for Palestine Studies, Arabic edition), No. 1 (Winter 1991).

THE END OF THE COLD WAR AND THE GULF WAR

The end of the Cold War in the late 1980s and the dissolution of the Soviet Union had a decisive impact on both the Palestinian and Israeli sides. These changes eliminated Moscow's support for revolutionary national liberation movements like the PLO and for radical regimes that provided political and material assistance to such movements. This weakened the PLO's standing. Its standing was further weakened by what was widely perceived as Arafat's support of Saddam Hussein following Iraq's August 1990 invasion of Kuwait. Indeed, the PLO's financial supporters in the Persian Gulf—Saudi Arabia and the smaller Gulf Cooperation Council (GCC) states—saw Arafat's position as an act of betrayal. They suspended their financial assistance to the PLO, presenting the organization with its most severe financial crisis to date. Without such support, it was increasingly difficult to maintain its elaborate infrastructure in the Diaspora—with its headquarters in Tunis, its military units stationed from Libya to Yemen, and its now politically inaccessible population base stretched across the refugee camps of Lebanon, Syria, and Jordan.

By the early 1990s, a combination of international, regional, and domestic factors had also yielded a more flexible Israeli approach. The end of the Cold War and the dissolution of the Soviet Union—eliminating the Soviet strategic umbrella for Syria and Libya—reduced the magnitude of the strategic threats facing Israel. The Gulf War significantly reduced the military capabilities of Iraq, one of Israel's most vocal and potent adversaries. Moreover, Israel's partnership with the United States proved closer than ever, as illustrated during the Gulf War by the stationing of U.S. Army Patriot antimissile defense units on Israeli soil. Given the stability of its fourteen-year-old peace with Egypt and the serious weakening of Syria and Iraq, Israel's overall strategic position was now stronger than ever. Consequently, Israel now felt it could take risks that would have been difficult to contemplate only a few years earlier.

Despite his own deep misgivings, Likud Prime Minister Yitzhak Shamir found it impossible to rebuff the strong bid by the United States to capitalize on its greatly enhanced regional and international status by convening a full-scale Arab-Israeli peace conference in Madrid in late 1991. U.S. Secretary of State James Baker succeeded in dragging Shamir to Madrid via the deft adaptation of Shamir's own preconditions: no separate Palestinian delegation, no PLO presence at the negotiating table, no Palestinian representation from Jerusalem, no Palestinian Diaspora representation. By consenting to these positions, the PLO leadership in Tunis gave Shamir little room to maneuver.

The eventual acceptance by Syria of the U.S. invitation to the conference finally left Shamir with no way out. The Madrid conference locked the Israeli government into a process that was ultimately inescapable: the only real choices became that of exiting the process altogether and paying an exorbitant political price for "spoiling the peace," or finding the means for dealing with the PLO at an acceptable cost. Shamir's third way, based on a strategy of political attrition and prevarication, was simply not sustainable.

CHANGES WITHIN ISRAEL AND THE PLO

While the first *intifada* resulted in unprecedented hardships for the Palestinians in the occupied territories, it also eroded the long-standing Israeli illusion that its rule over the West Bank and Gaza could be maintained indefinitely at low cost. Suppressing the Palestinian uprising required many reserve-service days, as well as the willingness of Israeli reservists to continue to apply harsh measures against a civilian population—often comprising Palestinian children not older than their own. Moreover, such measures could not be hidden from the international mass media; hence, the *intifada* resulted in a serious erosion of Israel's image in the West. By the early 1990s, the willingness of Palestinians to carry the struggle into Israel's population centers—by knifing Israeli civilians in Jerusalem and Tel Aviv—only exacerbated the Israelis' fatigue. The result was rising Israeli support for a political "separation" between the two populations and for decisive steps to end the uncertainty engendered by the continuing conflict.

In the July 1992 elections, the odd mix of leftist and rightist supporters of "separation," and Yitzhak Rabin's appeal to this de facto coalition with a promise to conclude within six to nine months an autonomy agreement with the Palestinians, seems to have won Labor the narrow victory it needed. Yet one year later, Rabin was no closer to the promised agreement than he had been on the day of his inauguration. The Track-I negotiations in Washington were stalled by Rabin's perception of the need to maintain the facade of negotiating with Palestinians from the territories, and by his negotiators' obsession with insignificant detail.

It became increasingly clear to Rabin that only unconventional diplomacy might allow him to fulfill his promise of a Palestinian-Israeli breakthrough. This became even clearer after the Palestinians suspended the Washington talks in early 1993, following Rabin's ill-fated attempt to deal with the growing violence in the West Bank and Gaza by expelling 400 members and leaders of Hamas to South Lebanon.

Although Rabin knew that Jordan would not negotiate on behalf of the Palestinians, he needed evidence that the PLO could deliver what the "insiders" could not. Much of Rabin's dealings with the Oslo channel were designed to answer this basic question. And it was finally Arafat who ensured that Rabin receive the answer he desired, thus making the Oslo agreement possible: In March 1993 the Palestinian delegation to the Washington talks, which had been adamant in refusing to return to the talks before the deportee issue was settled, was ordered by Arafat back to the negotiations table. Unconvinced and unwilling, the delegation nonetheless acquiesced without exception. For Rabin, this seems to have been the final proof of the PLO leadership's political ascendancy over the "insiders."

As was the case with Israel, the PLO's own path to Oslo was facilitated by internal and external changes as important as those in 1988. After the Gulf War, when the United States seemed determined to put the framework for a comprehensive Middle East peace in place, the PLO fought a desperate battle to ensure that no such process could be brought to fruition without its active participation and consént. The PLO's tactical acceptance of a joint "non-PLO" Palestinian-Jordanian joint delegation to the Madrid Peace Conference of 1991 was never seen as more than a temporary expedient to be negated at the earliest opportunity. From the outset, it was designed merely to allow for a subsequent retrenchment of the organization's natural place in the process. As indicated by senior Arafat aides, the delegation of "insiders" from the occupied territories sent to the 1991 Madrid conference and to Washington in 1992–1993 was handpicked by Arafat and centrally directed from Tunis, and had little leeway for independent maneuver. The message was clear: no Palestinian delegation could act without the PLO, and no resolution of the conflict could be reached without the PLO's consent.[3]

This emphasis on form prior to Oslo was matched with a retreat on issues of substance at Oslo itself. Although long reconciled to the notion of a two-phased process (indeed, Palestinian participation in the Madrid process was premised on this basis), the PLO leadership had consistently argued for a clear understanding on the ultimate goal of negotiations: the creation of an independent Palestinian state. Nonetheless, given the stalemate in Washington and the "bonus" of direct Israeli recognition of the PLO obtained at Oslo, by late 1993 Arafat had committed himself to a transitional and phased process without any real guarantees as to its eventual outcome. This was crucial in making the deal palatable to the Israeli side. But it also sowed the seed for a great deal of subsequent

---

3. See Mamduh Nawfal, *Qusat Itifaaq Oslo* (*The Story of the Oslo Accord*) (Amman: Al-Ahliyyah, 1995), pp. 32–33. Nawfal was a former military commander of Nayyif Hawatmeh's Popular Democratic Front (PDF) and a close associate of its deputy leader Yasser Abed Rabbo, who was involved in the Oslo track. Both Nawfal and Abed Rabbo subsequently split from the PDF to form the new centrist group, FIDA.

misunderstanding and the ultimate breakdown of the Oslo process in 2000–2001.

Nevertheless, by mid-1993 an array of international, regional, and domestic circumstances propelled both Israel and the PLO to accept positions that they had long rejected. Yet the new political environment could not by itself produce the breakthrough concluded in Oslo. Without the unique characteristics of the Track-II approach, the Israel-PLO Declaration of Principles could not have been negotiated.

Participants

An important factor accounting for the success of the Oslo talks was the character, background, and connections of the individuals who conducted the discussions. The Israelis at Oslo, Yair Hirschfeld and Ron Pundik, fulfilled most of the requirements of successful Track-II participants: They were bona fide independent scholars attached to Israeli universities and so they initially provided the Israeli government with complete deniability. Had news of the talks leaked, the government could have credibly claimed that it was not connected to the discussions, let alone responsible for their results.

At the same time, the Israeli participants at Oslo enjoyed excellent access to some of Israel's top leaders. For a number of years, Hirschfeld had been a close associate of Yossi Beilin, who was serving as Deputy Foreign Minister when the Oslo talks were launched. Throughout the 1980s, Hirschfeld had acted as the main liaison between Beilin and Peres on the one hand, and key Palestinian leaders in the West Bank and Gaza, notably Feisal Husseini, on the other. In this capacity, Hirschfeld had arranged a number of meetings between the three leaders. Pundik, a journalist and former student of Hirschfeld, also enjoyed easy access to Beilin. Hirschfeld and Pundik's access was based on a three-step approach: First, from them to Beilin, then from Beilin to Peres, and finally from Peres to Rabin.

Hirschfeld and Pundik were committed to making progress toward resolving the Israeli-Palestinian dispute. At the same time, they were not seeking office and were therefore relatively free to refrain from considering what was acceptable and popular. Indeed, the talks in Oslo began on the same day that the Israeli Knesset repealed legislation prohibiting direct talks with PLO members. This is not to deny Hirschfeld and Pundik's ideological agenda. Both were ardent Zionists who believed that it was time for Israel to become a normal state while preserving its Jewish character. For this reason, they thought a solution of the Palestinian problem was imperative. They also believed it was possible.

Hirschfeld and Pundik were willing to accept a thankless task: they were ready to step aside and assume a minor role once it became clear that the Oslo talks might well result in a formal bilateral agreement. At that point, in mid-May 1993, the Israeli team was expanded to include Uri Savir, Director General of the Foreign Ministry and, a few weeks later, Joel Singer, a former military lawyer who was recruited from private practice in a Washington, D.C., law firm. Soon thereafter, Singer was named Legal Advisor to the Israeli Foreign Ministry. Singer claimed that when he was first instructed by Prime Minister Rabin to review the progress made in the Oslo talks, he was appalled by the unprofessional character of the draft Declaration of Principles (DOP) being negotiated. In his view, the academic background of Hirschfeld and Pundik did not prepare them for the task of formalizing a resolution of the Israeli-Palestinian dispute. The tension among the three was only exacerbated by the success of the Oslo talks when credit for the breakthrough was to be distributed.

Thus, like the initiators of a successful start-up company, Hirschfeld and Pundik were reluctantly willing to accept that their success would lead to a "take-over" of the Oslo talks by Track-I negotiators. Indeed, the two scholars had a limited role in the subsequent negotiations on Israeli recognition of the PLO and they were accorded no place in the Norwegian-Israeli ceremony that took place in Jerusalem on September 10, 1993, to celebrate this development. Similarly, a few days later, they were not invited to join the Israeli delegation that traveled to Washington, D.C., for the formal signing of the Oslo accords. Even their mentor and closest associate, Yossi Beilin, had neglected to verify that seats would be reserved for them on the prime minister's plane.[4]

No less significant was the nature and role of the Palestinian participants in the Oslo talks, Abu Ala', Hassan Asfour, and Maher al-Kurd. Although all three participants were official representatives of the PLO, their relative obscurity until the Oslo talks provided the PLO with a measure of formal deniability similar to that of Israel. For most well-informed observers of the Palestinian scene, the team would not have denoted a high-level exercise with the Israeli side. Abu Ala's position at *Samed* was politically marginal and his role within the leadership was largely the result of the losses by assassination and depletion of most of the other historical leaders of the Palestinian movement. Any leaks of contacts be-

---

4. Peres remained nonapologetic for the manner in which the original Oslo duo was treated. In private, he would later compare the lack of formal Israeli recognition of Hirschfeld and Pundik's role in Oslo to his own years of "thankless work" under Ben-Gurion.

tween Abu Ala' and the Israeli side would not have been taken seriously by the majority within the Palestinian camp. Indeed, when the composition of the Palestinian team was finally divulged, it was met with a great deal of incredulity, bordering on derision, in most Palestinian circles.

Abu Ala' seems to have been a comparatively unknown quantity to Israel; Israeli sources suggest that prior to Oslo his file with the Israeli intelligence community was sparse. Nonetheless, the Israeli side seems to have derived some comfort from the fact that none of the members of the Oslo team were known to have had an "operational" history within the PLO, and this may have contributed to the success of the enterprise.

Moreover, and also in contrast to their official Israeli counterparts, Palestinian officials such as Abu Ala' routinely participated in academic and other Palestinian-Israeli meetings by the early 1990s. Abu Ala's own mixed portfolio of international trade and responsibility for the multilateral track emanating from the Madrid process was both sufficiently diffuse and inconspicuous to draw little attention from either the Palestinian or the Israeli side.[5] This low profile offered both protection and relative freedom of action. Indeed, it could be argued that it was Abu Ala's relative unimportance before Oslo that helped to clinch the Oslo deal. A better-known figure on the Palestinian side might well have been more inhibited and more circumscribed in his dealings with the Israelis. Thus, within the PLO, Oslo propelled Abu Ala' from the second rank to the first. In effect, it was not Abu Ala's role that made Oslo important but Oslo that made Abu Ala'. By April 1996 he was the elected Speaker of the Palestinian Legislative Council and the constitutional—but not necessarily political—successor to Arafat.

Hassan Asfour and Maher al-Kurd were both middle-ranking officials whose role was largely defined by their patrons within the PLO. In 1993 Asfour was still a member of the Palestinian Communist Party (PCP), and was deputy director at Abu Mazin's Directorate of International Relations. An Iraqi-trained agronomist, he had been active in the Palestinian Students Union for some years prior to joining Abu Mazin's Directorate. Capable and then close to Abu Mazin, he was chosen to accompany Abu Ala' in order to maintain Abu Mazin's direct link to the talks. Asfour's presence in Oslo may have also been designed to ensure that other parties besides the mainstream Fateh—to which Abu Mazin and Abu Ala' belonged—were seen to be involved in the negotiations. Ultimately, however, when faced between a choice of loyalty to Abu

---

5.   A July 1993 report in the London-based Arabic daily *al-Hayat* about secret Palestinian-Israeli talks in Oslo passed almost without notice.

Mazin and loyalty to the PCP, Asfour chose Mazin and was expelled from the Party after Oslo.

Maher al-Kurd was attached to Abu Ala's Economics Department and was party to the initial phase of the talks because of his command of English and his competence in economics—an area that both sides had deemed important at Oslo. He later fell out with Abu Ala' when the latter discovered that al-Kurd was reporting back to Arafat separately. As a result, he was replaced for the later phase of the Oslo process by another middle-ranking official with economic expertise, Muhammed Abu Kush.

Most important was the readiness and willingness of the two teams to reach a deal. Rather than debate the past, or merely analyze the problems and challenges facing both sides, Abu Ala's primary objective— strongly backed by Abu Mazin and Arafat—was to seek the parameters of an acceptable settlement. Equally, Hirschfeld and Pundik—strongly backed by Yossi Beilin—were motivated by the desire to break the impasse and reach agreement on a broad package that could be sold to the two leaderships and their constituencies. As early as the first meeting in January 1993, Abu Ala' had outlined the components of such a package, and a common draft agreement was produced by the Israeli side soon thereafter.

One very important issue for the Israelis was the extent to which the Palestinian participants could be considered as authoritative and their word could be regarded as Arafat's word. This question was of central concern to Prime Minister Rabin, who devised a number of ways for verifying whether the Palestinians in Oslo were speaking on Arafat's behalf — including the March 1993 test over the return of the formal negotiating delegation to Washington. The Palestinian participants were also asked that the PLO refrain from embarrassing Israel by sending members of the Palestinian National Council as members of the Palestinian delegation to the Track-I multilateral Arab-Israeli negotiations. When the PLO responded by allowing the resumption of the Washington talks and by withdrawing the participation of PNC members in the multilateral talks, Rabin became convinced that the Palestinian participants in Oslo were both serious and authoritative.

Similarly, the Palestinian leadership in Tunis needed to know that the Israeli participants in Oslo were sufficiently authoritative. Given the existence of parallel Israeli-Palestinian contacts, Arafat was initially unsure whether he should regard the Oslo venue as the primary track for a PLO-Israeli exchange. Consequently, in February 1993, he instructed Abu Ala' to probe his Israeli interlocutors regarding the extent to which the discussions in Norway were "authoritative." Later, he also requested Egypt's President Mubarak to instruct his political adviser, Usama al-Baz, to ask Prime Minister Rabin about the extent to which he was informed about and involved in the Oslo effort.

Like the Israelis, the Palestinians also had some serious concerns about their Israeli interlocutors and their possible "operational" histories. But dealing with academics and then Israeli diplomats rather than military or security personnel helped to bridge initial fears and to facilitate confidence-building between the two sides. At first there were deep suspicions about Hirschfeld's and Pundik's credentials as free agents, and Abu Ala' was apparently initially convinced of their links to Israeli intelligence. Nonetheless, the Palestinian leadership viewed such links as an indication that the Israeli leadership was seriously engaged.

In May 1993, after five rounds of talks in Oslo, the Palestinian side suggested that a significant upgrading of the talks was necessary in order to confirm their real status. The next round at the end of May produced a decision by Rabin and Peres to send Israeli officials to the talks for the first time. Uri Savir, the Director General of the Israeli Foreign Ministry, joined the negotiations, thus producing the first formal face-to-face negotiations between Israel and the PLO. From the Palestinian point of view, this was a major if not decisive achievement; finally the Israelis seemed to be on the road to full recognition of the PLO as the Palestinian partner to the peace process. In this respect, Savir's attendance marked Oslo's shift from a Track-II exercise to formal if secret Track-I negotiations.[6]

Mentors: Beilin and Abu Mazin

While the nature of the Track-II participants seems to have been an important determinant of the success of the Oslo talks, even more significant was that these talks were directed by two individuals who were uniquely qualified to serve as mentors.

On the Israeli side, Deputy Foreign Minister Yossi Beilin had earlier become frustrated by what he regarded as the total futility of Track-I negotiations held in Washington. He later spoke of having become convinced that not much can be achieved in formal negotiations.[7] Beilin

---

6. Interestingly, Abu Mazin's account suggests that the PLO was not expecting this development when it happened, even though it had been seeking it for some time. See Mahmoud Abbas, *Through Secret Channels* (London: Garnet, 1995), p. 14.

7. In Beilin's words: "Track-II is actually the main avenue. Often it is the most influential route to progress. I do not believe that by formal negotiations alone it is possible to produce significant results. The only possible exceptions are negotiations focused on purely technical issues. I made every attempt to insure that the real effort would be made through the "bypass" and I often found that the "bypass" is the main road." Interview with Zeev Schiff, 1996.

personified an ideal Track-II mentor. He was dedicated to helping make progress in Arab-Israeli peacemaking. He was also convinced that the Rabin government was operating on "borrowed time"—that there was a small window for peacemaking and that time was running out. He regarded the domestic political circumstances—the credit enjoyed by Rabin among the Israeli public—as uniquely conducive to negotiating a deal. He was also convinced that it would be a national tragedy if the opportunity were lost.

Second, while Beilin's standing was one level below Israel's top leadership, he enjoyed complete access to Foreign Minister Peres and, to a somewhat lesser extent, to Prime Minister Rabin as well. For more than fifteen years, Beilin had been Shimon Peres's closest aid and political ally. By contrast, Beilin's relations with Rabin had been much rockier. As defense minister in the 1980s, Rabin had become furious with Beilin's campaign against Israel's defense ties with South Africa. Eventually, however, Israel's prime minister had come to respect the daring and tenacious Beilin.

Beilin's proximity to the top provided him with a first-hand understanding of the aspirations and constraints affecting the Israeli leaders' freedom of action. He was thus in a position to convey these notions to the participants in Oslo, so that they could better understand what, under some circumstances, might be acceptable to Israel's leaders and what would not. Moreover, once Beilin became convinced that the Oslo venue held real promise, his unique standing allowed him to persuade Peres—and ultimately Rabin as well—that the opportunity to reach an agreement with the Palestinians should be seriously explored.

Third, Beilin was a political risk-taker. With a strong conviction that a resolution of the Israeli-Palestinian dispute could not be found within the existing formal framework, he was willing to assume the risks involved in pursuing a more creative approach. Thus, he encouraged Hirschfeld and Pundik to engage their Palestinian counterparts in detailed discussions without informing Peres and Rabin that he had done so. Indeed, fearing that his seniors would compel him to terminate the effort prematurely, Beilin only approached Peres and Rabin regarding the Oslo talks in February 1993, some two months after the talks had begun, and only after the Oslo participants had already reached initial agreement on a draft document.

Also important was the Israelis' perception of the Palestinian mentor of the Oslo talks. Abu Mazin was well known to the Israeli intelligence community as a close political adviser of PLO Chairman Yasser Arafat. For over a decade, he had been in charge of supervising contacts between the PLO and Israelis. As a result, he had become knowledgeable about the different facets of Israel's cultural and political scenes. Equally important, Abu Mazin was seen as being committed to a negotiated resolution of the Palestinian-Israeli dispute. Thus, not only were the Israelis involved in the Oslo process supported by an effective mentor, they also regarded their Palestinian counterparts as benefiting from an equally effective and well-connected guardian.

Abu Mazin's role as a mentor of the Palestinian side was indeed vital. Since the early 1970s, the Palestinian leader had been convinced of the need to study and understand Israeli society and had been a strong supporter of the PLO's call in the late 1960s for a "secular democratic state" with equal rights for Arabs and Jews in Palestine. Recognizing Israeli hostility to this slogan, Abu Mazin later spearheaded the PLO's activities aimed at contact and dialogue with the Israeli side.[8] Abu Mazin also had a long-standing belief in the need to cultivate relations with the Sephardic (oriental) Jewish communities both in Israel and abroad. By the late 1970s, he was convinced that a two-tier approach—to the Israeli peace constituency on the one hand and the oriental Jewish community on the other—would eventually reap political results.

Abu Mazin's efforts to find Israeli interlocutors were not always viewed positively by other elements in the Palestinian leadership, and were often derided by the PLO rank and file. However, his support for the Sartawi-Peled channel in the mid-1970s and for other contacts was unwavering and was instrumental in ensuring their continuation over many years. Never a populist, and shying away from public appearances and political pronouncements, Abu Mazin's preference was for serious work away from the limelight. Paradoxically, his position in the PLO hierarchy as a veteran but less public figure also helped to insulate him from much of the political turmoil of the 1970s and the 1980s. The expulsion of the PLO from Beirut in 1982, and the virtual abandonment of armed struggle as an effective tool of policy, helped to give extra credence to his politico-diplomatic approach. By the early 1990s, and with the death of PLO front-rankers such as Abu Jihad and Abu Iyyad, Abu Mazin found himself thrust into positions of ever-growing responsibility.

During the 1991–1993 Madrid-Washington negotiations, Abu Mazin served as official head of the PLO committee overseeing the bilateral negotiations. In this capacity, he became thoroughly familiar with the issues and the impasses that developed out of the talks. Alongside Abu Ala'

---

8.   In private conversations with Hussein Agha in the mid-1970s, Said Hammami confided that his activities were supported directly by Arafat and Abu Jihad, as well as by Abu Mazin. Hammami voiced his greatest respect and admiration for Abu Mazin and his vision.

(who had been officially tasked with overseeing the Palestinian side on the multilateral track), Abu Mazin had become increasingly aware of the need to move beyond the extant Israeli peace constituency and the Sephardic community and reach out directly to the Israeli establishment. When the 1992 elections brought the Israeli peace camp into the government for the first time—represented by Meretz and Labor doves such as Beilin and Haim Ramon—the moment for such a direct approach seemed more opportune than ever.

Like Beilin, Abu Mazin can be seen as a political visionary. By late 1992–early 1993, he was willing to take the responsibility for pursuing the Oslo channel even when Arafat himself was not entirely convinced of its utility. Abu Mazin felt that Hirschfeld's first tentative contact with Abu Ala' in December 1992 could not have been held without some clearance from Beilin and Peres. Regardless of the accuracy of this instinctive response, Abu Mazin's readiness to pursue this perceived lead finally opened the door to an unprecedented opportunity.

Another characteristic of Abu Mazin's approach was his preference for discretion. Accustomed to keeping the full range of Palestinian-Israeli contacts out of the public eye, he was convinced early on that the Oslo channel would only succeed if knowledge of it remained within a very tight circle.[9] This was partly for security reasons, and partly to reassure the Israelis of the seriousness with which the PLO viewed the exercise. Secrecy also served to preempt any wide-scale political discussion within the PLO that could disrupt or abort the Oslo channel.

Although Abu Ala' subsequently bore the burden of the mechanics of day-to-day negotiations at Oslo, it was Abu Mazin's steadfast support that kept the Oslo channel going. Without Abu Mazin, the Oslo channel could easily have petered out, like the vast majority of contacts and exchanges that occurred at around the same time.

Leaders: Arafat, Rabin, and Peres

For Yasser Arafat, Oslo was a test of leadership. Fully on board by early 1993, Arafat was determined to prove his command of the Palestinian political scene. After Uri Savir appeared at Oslo in early May 1993 and throughout the spring and summer of 1993, Arafat pursued one supreme objective: to demonstrate that the Washington talks could not provide the Israeli leadership with an alternative.

---

9.   Abu Mazin records the flurry of contacts before and after the 1992 Israeli elections and his determination to preserve Oslo as the only agreed channel. See Abbas, *Through Secret Channels*, pp. 72–82.

With Abu Mazin's help, Arafat thus embarked on a series of steps that effectively scuttled what remained of U.S.-Israeli hopes of a Washington breakthrough. The Washington delegation was instructed to reject U.S. bridging proposals in June 1993 and was ordered to pull out of a previously agreed formula (one that the PLO itself had requested) for a tripartite U.S.-Palestinian-Israeli consultative committee. Frustration with Tunis reached a high pitch in the summer of 1993, as it appeared to the Washington negotiators that the PLO leadership was being deliberately negative and obstructive.

Arafat, however, was publicly dismissive of the delegation's concerns. Furthermore, by early 1993, the Palestinian leader had concluded that the United States was unlikely to sponsor any agreement that could be minimally acceptable to the PLO. On the contrary, the dominant perception in Tunis—as well as within the Washington delegation—was that the United States was more solicitous of Israel's concerns than Israel itself. Attempts by the United States in June and July to put forward bridging proposals seemed to confirm this. The conclusion was that the PLO was more likely to get a better deal from Israel by dealing with the Israelis directly—without the dubious merits of U.S. mediation.

Unlike Rabin, Arafat did not need to be convinced of the virtues of direct contact with the other side. In this respect, his only doubts were whether the initial Abu Ala'–Hirschfeld contact was the right one. Here, Abu Mazin played the role of consolidator and his desire to preserve the Oslo channel helped to convince Arafat of its worth. Like Abu Mazin, Arafat had long been convinced of the need for "secret" diplomacy, and was in the habit of complaining that no real work could be done in the very public style that had developed in Washington. To that end, Oslo suited his purposes perfectly.

The Oslo channel was thus successfully kept secret within the PLO, although the circle of those who knew about it in Tunis was larger than has been generally assumed. A small inner circle managed the talks, including Arafat, Abu Mazin, and Yasser Abed Rabbo—a close personal associate of Arafat and former political leader of the Marxist Popular Democratic Front (PDF) who had shed his previous allegiance. These three acted as an undeclared "cell" outside the PLO establishment and coordinated directly with the Oslo negotiators. Another occasional member of the cell was Palestinian poet Mahmoud Darwish, who was kept abreast of the talks and was sometimes called to help evaluate their progress. Bashir Barghouti, secretary general of the Palestinian Communist Party, was briefed by Abu Mazin and was also brought into the picture. Despite the agreed secrecy, Abed Rabbo shared Oslo's developments with his own close ex-PDF comrade, Mamduh Nawfal, and others in his political circle. None of this reached the outside world, although some in Tunis were suspicious that something was going on.

In overseeing the talks, Arafat did not concern himself with the minutiae of the Oslo negotiations and left these to other members of the cell. He was, however, on the same basic wavelength as Abu Mazin, and trusted him to oversee the details of the Oslo text.

Outside Tunis, Arafat was very keen to share the existence of the channel with his main Arab ally, Egypt, and he personally informed Egyptian President Hosni Mubarak of developments at Oslo after clearing this with the Israeli side. Arafat also used the Egyptians to test out ideas on Israel: in April 1993 he asked the Egyptians to float the idea of Israeli withdrawal from Gaza plus Jericho on the West Bank as a first step ("Gaza plus") to Rabin in Cairo. Surprisingly, this option had not yet come up in the Oslo talks themselves, but apparently, and without Rabin's knowledge, in November 1992 the idea had already been suggested to Arafat by Shimon Peres via the Egyptians.[10]

For Arafat, any serious move toward Israel required Egyptian consent and support as an essential prerequisite for obtaining a broader Arab consensus. Abu Mazin briefed the Tunisian and Moroccan governments, but Jordan was only provided with a deliberately garbled and unclear account by Arafat himself—a factor that exacerbated Jordanian suspicions after the deal was announced. Anticipating a Syrian-Israeli deal in the making and outright hostility from Syria under any circumstances, the PLO leadership did not attempt to approach Damascus with news of the Oslo connection until after the Oslo agreement was signed. Indeed, Rabin's own stated readiness to deal with Syria, and Arafat's conviction that the Israeli-Syrian agreement was already more or less complete, played an important role in pushing Arafat toward a "go it alone" approach at Oslo. Abu Mazin felt obliged to inform the Russians regarding the existence of the Oslo channel—a gesture of gratitude for Soviet support in previous years.

Critically important for pursuing the Oslo talks was the unique disposition of Israel's leaders—Peres and Rabin—and their complex relationship. Since the mid-1970s, Rabin and Peres had each regarded the other as his most serious competitor within the ranks of the Labor party. Having defeated Peres in the race for party leadership, Rabin initially attempted to deny Peres a central role in the government that he had formed after the 1992 elections. Eventually yielding to pressures from within his party, Rabin finally named Peres as foreign minister but ex-

---

10. David Makovsky, *Making Peace with the PLO* (Boulder, Colo.: Westview, 1996), p. 35.

tracted Peres's reluctant consent that the bilateral negotiations with the Arab states and the Palestinians—as well as Israel's relations with the United States—would be managed by the prime minister's office. Peres was left to deal with the less central Arab-Israeli multilateral negotiations, but even here was rarely given full rein by Rabin, who continued to control the sensitive Arms Control and Regional Security (ACRS) talks.

The Oslo venue presented Peres with a golden opportunity to return to center stage. Moreover, the effort was uniquely consistent with Peres's instincts: Since he had negotiated the alliance between Israel and France in the mid-1950s and throughout his political life, Peres had always preferred indirect approaches and secret diplomacy. Not surprisingly, once he gained Rabin's tentative consent to examine the Oslo option, he adopted it with all his political and intellectual might. Thus, beginning in February 1993, the Oslo venue became Peres's central project.

From the outset, it was clear to Beilin and the Israeli participants in Oslo that Rabin's support was a prerequisite to the talks' success.[11] Ultimately, only Israel's prime minister could "sell" an agreement of this kind to an anxious Israeli public. While Peres had conducted a lifelong love-hate relationship with Israeli voters, Rabin's long military career and his role as the architect of the Israeli victory in the 1967 War provided him with great credibility regarding all matters related to national security. While Peres's imagination was required for Israel to pursue the Oslo talks, the opening created in Norway could not have been brought to a successful conclusion without Rabin's backing.

Yet Rabin's support for the Oslo talks was by no means self-evident. On the one hand, Rabin shared Beilin's doubts regarding the ability of formal negotiations to achieve significant results. Indeed, the Track-II approach suited Rabin's preference for the secretive. At the same time, the Israeli prime minister was averse to anything intellectual. He regarded academics as divorced from the "real world," loose with words, fond of general formulations, careless with regard to detail, and undependable if not irresponsible when it came to matters of national security. Moreover, even as late as 1992, Rabin was still highly suspicious of Peres's political intentions and could not rule out an attempt by the latter to challenge his leadership sometime before the scheduled 1996 elections. Thus, he was highly unlikely to embrace a diplomatic effort conducted by scholars who were close to Shimon Peres.

Nonetheless, two considerations consistent with Rabin's character seemed to have made him receptive to the Oslo process. First, he re-

---

11. See Yossi Beilin's account of his peacemaking efforts in Yossi Beilin, *Touching Peace* (London: Weidenfeld and Nicolson, 1999).

garded his political credibility as a personal trademark. In the Israeli public's mind, credibility had become the main character trait distinguishing him from Peres. By mid-1993, Rabin had become particularly sensitive to the fact that he had failed to fulfill his 1992 campaign promise to conclude an autonomy agreement with the Palestinians within six to nine months. By this time, he also seemed to have become convinced that the Track-I negotiations were unlikely to result in such an agreement. In these circumstances he was prepared to consider alternatives to the futile exercise being conducted in Washington.

By the time the Oslo talks were brought to Rabin's attention in early March 1993, the discussions in Norway had been going on for some three months. Rabin must have been impressed that complete secrecy was maintained throughout this period and that neither details from the talks nor the fact that they had been taking place had leaked to the press. This was particularly important in addressing Rabin's doubts about the ability of academics to keep a secret. The importance attached by Rabin to maintaining total secrecy was clear throughout the Oslo process: He did not share information about the talks—even just their existence—with anyone in his office.

While these considerations played a major role in persuading Rabin to give the Oslo talks a chance, Beilin and Peres also addressed his reservations about a process conducted by academics. For this purpose, Uri Savir and Joel Singer—both highly experienced individuals—supplemented Hirschfeld and Pundik. Singer's involvement was particularly important because as a successful former military attorney who was intimately involved in the legal aspects of most Israeli-Arab negotiations since the late 1970s—including the Camp David Accords and the abortive May 1983 Lebanese-Israeli Agreement—he could be trusted by Rabin to pay close attention to every detail discussed at Oslo. Rabin could also be particularly confident that Singer, a former senior officer in the Military Prosecutor's office, would not overlook any issues or stipulations that might have a negative effect on Israel's security.

To address the fact that the Oslo team was spearheaded by individuals who were not close to him and for whom he did not have high regard, Rabin opened a separate channel of communications with the Palestinians through someone he trusted and respected: Haim Ramon. At the time, the charismatic Ramon was one of the younger generation of Labor leaders very close to Rabin, and was a strong supporter of a political accommodation with the Arabs. Ramon had developed a close relationship with Ahmed Tibi, an Israeli-Arab gynecologist who had become a confidante and political advisor to Yasser Arafat. Through Ramon, Rabin conveyed to Tibi in July–August 1993 a set of questions to be explored with Arafat, mostly related to the responsibility for security during the interim phases of an Israeli-Palestinian accommodation. When Tibi returned with answers that were consistent with the spirit of the discussions in Norway, Rabin became convinced that the PLO was serious about the Oslo talks.

Finally, regarding at least one important matter, Rabin used another Track-II venue to check the information and assessments he received from the Israeli participants in Oslo. Through Israeli participants in talks that were hosted by the American Academy of Arts and Sciences (see Chapter 4) he received confirmation that the Palestinians were prepared to accept the "Gaza-first" option and assume control over Gaza in the first stage of the phased process. This added to Rabin's mounting evidence that the Oslo talks were serious.

Sponsors

The Norwegian government played a decisive role in making the Oslo process successful. During a visit to Oslo in January 1992, following the fall of the Swedish Labor government in late 1991, Abu Ala' had first raised the possibility that Norway might succeed Sweden as a third-party mediator. Feisal Husseini had also approached Terje Larsen, then Director of Norway's Institute for Applied Social Science (FAFO).

FAFO had been established in the early 1980s to conduct research on social, political, and economic issues. Strictly speaking, FAFO was not a nongovernmental organization (NGO). It received considerable government support and was very sensitive to the Norwegian government's agenda. Nonetheless, it retained academic respectability and a measure of distance from any overt official capacity. Larsen developed an interest in Middle East affairs during an extended stay in Cairo, where his wife, Mona Juul, a young diplomat, had served in the Norwegian Embassy. Marianne Heiberg, wife of Norway's Defense Minister Johan Jurgen Holst, was also a senior researcher at FAFO when the talks were initiated.

When Abu Ala' first suggested to Larsen that Norway host secret talks with Israel, Larsen was initially concerned that this might undermine FAFO's work—then nearing completion—on social and economic conditions in the occupied territories. When this work approached its final stages, Larsen decided to act. In consultation with the Norwegian government, he began to consider the modalities of possible talks. Judging the PLO ready to engage in such talks due to its post–Gulf War financial crisis and the apparent challenge of a new "insider" leadership, Larsen was convinced that the time was ripe for a productive back channel. For its part, the Norwegian government decided to stay out of the proposed channel and delegate its management to FAFO. The government's view was that "a different type of mediation" was needed to contrast with the U.S. role since the 1991 Madrid conference, since the United States was perceived as biased.

Secrecy would be the key to these contacts. The Norwegians decided to convince both sides that their delegations should be small, not exceeding three each. They further decided that they should initially push for "prenegotiations" as a confidence-building preliminary stage and were surprised when the two sides eventually opted to begin negotiations immediately, without any preliminaries.

Norway's interest in the talks was cemented in late May 1992 at a lunch conversation between Larsen and Israel's then-Deputy Foreign Minister Yossi Beilin. Larsen suggested to Beilin that FAFO would host back-channel meetings between Israelis and Palestinians after Israel's June 1992 elections. While the conversation did not lead to any specific steps, in September 1992 the idea of holding such talks was presented to the Israelis again, this time by the visiting Deputy Foreign Minister Jan Egeland. On behalf of Foreign Minister Thorvald Stoltenberg, Egeland promised that Norway's Ministry of Foreign Affairs would fund the meetings hosted by FAFO. The stated purpose of the discussions was to overcome the obstacles blocking progress in the Track-I negotiations held in Washington. Initially, no one had suggested that the FAFO channel would become an alternative to the U.S.-sponsored official negotiations.

By December 1992, Larsen was sure that Abu Ala's proposition was feasible. He therefore flew to Tunis to meet with Arafat regarding this issue. According to Larsen, it was at this meeting that Abu Ala' suggested that the Norwegian side contact Beilin to elicit his response. Concurrently, Peres's attention had been drawn to a paper on future regional economic cooperation prepared by Abu Ala' for the multilateral talks that seemed to echo much of Peres's own views on the subject. For Beilin, Peres, and the Norwegians, the stage was now set. It was this series of developments that led to Abu Ala's meeting with Yair Hirschfeld in London later that month; and it was there that Abu Ala' formally proposed to Hirschfeld that Norway should host the talks.[12]

Norway's concept of the talks was based on "the importance of personal contact." The Norwegians believed that they should refrain from intervention except in *extremis*. They did not want to appear to be acting as an international witness to the talks and felt that they should encour-

---

12. Zeev Schiff interview with Larsen in mid-1997.

age the two sides to deal with issues incrementally rather than attempt to reach immediate solutions. According to Larsen, "when a crisis arose because of an external event we decided to stand on the side and not get involved, and to wait until the sides decided that they should go forward."[13]

Aside from its critical role in initiating and funding the meetings, the Norwegian government provided key logistical and security services that made the talks' success possible. It provided private and government facilities for holding the discussions and did everything possible to maintain complete secrecy, with a high degree of success. With one exception, no two meetings were held in the same location. At first, the hosts were careful not to inject themselves into the talks. Moreover, the Norwegian leaders were sensitive to the two parties' needs and conferred closely with them regarding Norway's potential role and the extent to which they should brief the U.S. government about the progress made at Oslo.

Finally, and despite their initial caution, Norway's leaders were prepared to assume the role of mediators when circumstances required their intervention. Beginning in May 1993, newly appointed Foreign Minister Johan Holst became increasingly involved in the Oslo talks. In July, he traveled to Tunis for discussions with Yasser Arafat in an attempt to bridge the gap between the parties' positions. Following the meetings in Tunis, Holst sent Larsen and Juul to Jerusalem for discussions with the Israeli Oslo team, its mentors, and leaders. The two Norwegians then returned to Tunis for additional talks with Arafat, and, following these discussions, they traveled to Jerusalem again for another round of talks with the Israelis. On July 20, Holst, Larsen, and Juul held yet another meeting with Arafat in Paris, and, following that meeting, Holst reported his impressions to Peres. He conferred with Beilin by phone after the unsuccessful round of the Oslo talks on July 25. And, at Beilin's suggestion, he wrote Peres again, urging that Israel adopt a more flexible position in the talks.[14]

The Norwegian mediation effort reached its peak in mid-August. Peres left for an "unrelated" visit to Sweden and Norway. Holst secretly traveled to Stockholm on August 17 for an all-night meeting with Peres, resulting in the final breakthrough that allowed the Oslo agreement to be signed. Holst held nine rounds of phone conversations with Arafat dur-

---

13. Ibid.

14. See Beilin, *Touching Peace,* pp. 108–113.

ing that night, with Abu Mazin, Abu Ala', and Hassan Asfour at Arafat's side. At the same time, Peres consulted continuously with Beilin and Rabin. By the early hours of August 18, the Norwegian mediation effort in Sweden had succeeded. The Israeli-Palestinian Declaration of Principles (DOP) was signed in Oslo two days later.

Norway's role was even more pronounced in the subsequent negotiations between Israel and the PLO on mutual recognition. By that time Holst seemed to have completely forgotten that he was not a mediator, and the phone calls to Tunis and Jerusalem never stopped. On September 4, Holst sponsored negotiations in Paris between Savir, Singer, and Abu Ala'. These discussions resulted in a historic understanding on mutual recognition: Arafat would write Rabin a letter that would stipulate the PLO's commitments and Rabin would respond by announcing Israel's recognition of the PLO as representing the Palestinian people.

The Israeli side generally, and Foreign Minister Peres in particular, had a positive attitude toward the Norwegian efforts for peace. Israel regarded Norway's espousal of the Oslo channel as indicative of its balanced attitude and understanding for the plight of both sides in the conflict. The Norwegian role was also highly appreciated by the Palestinian side. The PLO felt generally comfortable with the Norwegian role and was impressed by the efficiency of Larsen and his staff and their dedication to the channel's success. Abu Mazin records the Norwegian team's readiness to adapt to Middle Eastern ways (such as late night meetings) and their willingness to learn and understand both sides.

U.S. Involvement

The United States was of vital importance at Oslo. Since early 1992, official talks had been taking place in Washington under the auspices of the U.S. government, which saw itself as the main architect of the Middle East peace process. Although the Washington talks were predicated on excluding the PLO, the United States could not adopt a negative response to Oslo, as it would have been hard pressed to justify a harder line against the PLO than that taken by the Israeli government itself.

Nonetheless, the Clinton administration was surprised by the success of the Oslo talks. Although the administration was not entirely unaware of the discussions being held in Norway, only one of its senior officials was regularly briefed about the talks, and the briefings he received were far from complete. Yossi Beilin had conferred with Deputy Assistant Secretary of State Dan Kurtzer just before the talks began in December 1992. Kurtzer was not opposed to the effort but insisted that it should not become a substitute for, or otherwise damage, the Washington Track-I negotiations.[15]

In March 1993, Norway's Foreign Minister Stoltenberg briefed Secretary of State Warren Christopher about the existence of the Oslo talks but did not convey to him the substance of the drafts that had been exchanged and discussed at Oslo. After Holst replaced Stoltenberg, Deputy Foreign Minister Egeland continued to brief Kurtzer about the talks, using the secure communication system at the U.S. Embassy in Oslo. But Egeland was asked by his U.S. interlocutors not to come to Washington to brief the administration formally about the talks. At that time, the Clinton administration was still prohibited by law from conducting any direct contact with the PLO, and such a briefing could have been interpreted as a violation of the law.

While informing the United States of the talks, the Norwegians and the Israelis continued to mislead the Clinton administration regarding the seriousness of the discussions held at Oslo. For example, when Foreign Minister Holst briefed Secretary of State Christopher in late May 1993, he failed to mention that Uri Savir had joined the talks and that with such official involvement the talks had now become a venue for back-channel Track-I negotiations. Not surprisingly, Holst was impressed that Christopher did not attribute much significance to the talks and regarded them as an academic seminar.

Similarly, Beilin concealed Savir's involvement from Dan Kurtzer when the two officials met in Washington in early June. When Kurtzer asked Beilin who had been sent by him to Oslo in addition to Pundik and Hirschfeld, Beilin responded that Joel Singer was now also involved in the talks. At that point, Singer was still a private attorney practicing in Washington, D.C. Clearly, Beilin did not wish to deceive Kurtzer but he was also cautious about letting Kurtzer know that the discussions with the PLO had now become official. Nevertheless, Beilin did lead Kurtzer in the right direction by adding that "he [Beilin] was no longer in charge of the sending and that the matter was now in the hands of the highest echelons."[16] With Beilin's knowledge, Hirschfeld also briefed Kurtzer periodically about the Oslo talks, but the depth and accuracy of these briefings remain unclear.

On another occasion, Kurtzer was surprised to find Foreign Minister Holst in the State Department waiting room. In Washington for a few

---

15.   Beilin, *Touching Peace*, pp. 76–77.

16.   Ibid., p. 113.

days, Holst had apparently decided to drop in unannounced to preserve the secrecy of the Oslo channel. Holst briefed Kurtzer on the progress of the Oslo talks, but whether Kurtzer fully shared the information he received with the secretary of state and his colleagues in the U.S. peace team remains unclear.

Prime Minister Rabin also played an active role in deceiving the United States about the importance of the Oslo talks. When visiting Israel in the summer of 1993, Christopher asked Rabin about the exchanges being held in Norway. With his typical wave of hand, Rabin dismissed the subject as not worthy of further discussion.

Yet these incomplete briefings and deceptive communications cannot explain the depth of the Clinton administration's surprise. It is not clear why the partial information obtained by the administration officials—including the secretary of state—did not lead them to request that the U.S. intelligence community gather additional information about the talks.

The most likely explanation is that the U.S. intelligence community was not asked to target the Oslo talks because the administration failed to attribute any significance to this venue. During the first year of the Labor-led government, most U.S. government officials tended to center their attention on Prime Minister Rabin, often ignoring Peres. Israel's foreign minister was viewed as being "out of the loop" regarding significant bilateral Arab-Israeli talks, especially between Israel and Syria. The result was that senior administration officials tended to downgrade the importance of Peres's efforts. Rabin's reaction to Christopher's questions merely reinforced the Clinton administration's predisposition to regard any initiative led by Peres as relatively insignificant and nonauthoritative. Based on this assumption, it failed to make gathering information about the Oslo process a priority. The administration remained misled about the depth of Rabin's involvement and commitment to the Norwegian-led discussions.

Summary

The Oslo talks can be considered "the mother of all Track-II talks" in the Middle East. They played a crucial role in bringing about one of the most dramatic developments in the history of Arab-Israeli peacemaking, and despite subsequent developments, they best illustrate the potential utility of Track-II talks for conflict resolution.

Yet it would be a mistake to use the Oslo talks as a yardstick for judging the success and failure of Track-II venues. First, the talks were intended from the outset as a "hard" venue—to help bridge the gaps that plagued the Track-I negotiations then being conducted in Washington. Clearly, it would not be fair to compare "soft" Track-II discussions intended only to provide a framework for communicating threat perceptions and security concerns with the achievements of the Norwegian venue. Indeed, most Track-II talks do not result in a political breakthrough because it is not their purpose.

Second, these talks never comprised a pure Track-II venue. From the outset, the Palestinians taking part in the talks were PLO officials. Once an initial breakthrough in the talks was achieved, Israeli officials took control over their country's participation in the talks, thus transforming them into a Track-I venue.

All this does not diminish the significance of the initial phase of the talks. The breakthrough reflected in the first draft DOP at Oslo had eluded the official Track-I negotiators in Washington in 1993 for very good reasons: Arafat was not ready to allow a delegation not directly representing the PLO to negotiate an agreement on his behalf. In turn, Rabin was not about to run the domestic political risks involved in engaging the PLO directly without proof that the engagement would result in a breakthrough. It was crucial that independent Israeli scholars—"classic" Track-II participants—conclude the initial draft DOP before Rabin could decide that the venue was valuable, justifying that a senior Israeli government official—the director general of the Ministry for Foreign Affairs —be sent to join the Israeli participants in Oslo. Thus, without the preparatory work achieved at Oslo at the Track-II level, the discussions in Norway would have never become Track-I negotiations.

The ultimate failure of the Oslo *process* to deliver a final and stable resolution of the conflict over time should not be confused with the effectiveness of the Oslo Track-II talks as a breakthrough *mechanism* in 1993. At the time it was agreed, the Oslo DOP provided a glimpse into a better future based on mutual recognition and a roadmap to peace, but the political realities on the ground between 1993 and 2000—the mutual misreading of Oslo's "spirit" as well as the continuous violation of its text— eventually destroyed the political process and brought about an almost total reversion to pre-Oslo attitudes on both sides.

The violence that broke in September 2000 was seen by the Palestinians as a product of Israel's refusal to implement Oslo's territorial provisions, its unremitting post-Oslo settlement policies, and its violation of some of Oslo's most vital provisions regarding the release of Palestinian prisoners, the sanctity of Palestinian institutions, and the lifting of Israeli strictures on the Palestinian economic and daily existence. For the Palestinians, Oslo's promise was subverted by Israel's unwillingness to reach a real historical compromise based on the two-state solution along the boundaries of the cease-fire lines of June 4, 1967.

Conversely, Israel saw the outbreak of the second *intifada* as a violation of one of the most basic concessions made by the Palestinians in the framework of the Oslo agreement—namely, to abandon violence. Israelis now saw Palestinian conduct as proof of a prevailing Palestinian culture of violence and a readiness to resort to arms and terror for political purposes against a backdrop of apparent major Israeli concessions at the Camp David summit of July 2000 and after.

With the formation of a new Israeli national coalition government with Likud leader Ariel Sharon at its helm in early 2001, many on both sides began to see Oslo irrelevant at best and dangerous at worst. Within the Israeli establishment, a significant body of opinion came to the conclusion that Oslo (and in particular its security provisions) had been a strategic mistake, and that it was necessary to undo its most threatening manifestations by direct military means. Equally, a new Palestinian view emerged, seeking to break out of Oslo's legal and political strictures and end the occupation by armed struggle and by carrying the conflict right into the Israeli heartland.

But the breakdown of the Oslo agreements, and the loss of faith in the sincerity and credibility of each side as a partner in peace, are not true measures of the value of Oslo as a Track-II exercise. Whereas the implementation of the Oslo agreements may have been fatally flawed and full of misperceptions and delusions, the fact remains that the Oslo Track-II put in place a pathway to ending the conflict. Ultimately, only a return to this Oslo legacy is likely to provide the basis for a lasting settlement.

Chapter 4

The American Academy of Arts and Sciences

The American Academy of Arts and Sciences (AAAS), based in Cambridge, Massachusetts, hosted one of the most significant of the Israeli-Palestinian Track-II venues. The main purpose of the talks was to reach a better mutual understanding regarding the security concerns and measures associated with Israel's possible withdrawal from the West Bank and Gaza.

Drawing on its previous experience in the domain of East-West relations, the AAAS had launched a series of Arab-Israeli conferences in 1989, designed to examine various aspects of the Middle East political and strategic landscape and to explore the security issue in depth. In Cairo during December 1990, several weeks before the Gulf War, the AAAS hosted a conference attended by Nabil Shaath from the PLO and by Israeli interlocutors. The bilateral Israeli-Palestinian track was an outgrowth of these conferences, during which the parties had come to appreciate the serious, low-profile approach of the Academy. In 1992, the AAAS decided to put together a joint Palestinian-Israeli effort to look at security issues. The objective was to publish a joint report that would ascertain each sides' goals and concerns across a wide range of issues: the establishment of a Palestinian state, Israeli withdrawal from the occupied territories, the establishment of a Palestinian security force, control over the borders of Gaza and the West Bank, the future of Israeli settlements, and the role of third parties.[1]

Beginning in October 1992, AAAS hosted a set of seminars and meet-

---

1. The main findings of the project were subsequently made public in Jeffrey Boutwell and Everett Mendelsohn, et al., *Israeli-Palestinian Security: Issues in the Perma-*

ings designed to bridge the gap between the positions of Israelis and Palestinians regarding important dimensions of their dispute. What was unique and different about the AAAS meetings was that they brought together for the first time a PLO security official with Israeli experts who had operational security experience. The mixture of academics, senior journalists, and security professionals provided a sound basis for serious discussions that continued into 1994 over six formal sessions.

The AAAS talks came in the wake of an exercise initiated by a British NGO and Israeli-based NGOs. This meeting, held in June 1992 between Israeli and Palestinian participants, was hosted by Stan Windass of the Foundation for International Security (FIS) based at Adderbury near Oxford, England, in June 1992. Based on the Adderbury discussions, which focused on the security issue, Palestinian participants concluded that any useful further debate required the attendance of PLO security officials. By October 1992, yet another initiative on security issues launched by the Jerusalem-based Israel Palestine Center for Research and Information (IPCRI) had coincided with the AAAS venture, and a first meeting was held in London under the joint auspices of AAAS and IPCRI. After October 1992, AAAS assumed sole sponsorship of the project.

Political Environment

A number of factors contributed to the utility of the Academy talks: Most importantly, the political environment provided a "real" context and framework within which the talks could be conducted. The political conditions propelling the post-Madrid Track-I Israeli-Palestinian negotiations in Washington implied that sooner or later Israel was likely to transfer at least some of the territories it had controlled since the 1967 war to the Palestinians.

For the Israeli side, the AAAS talks attempted to address the most significant Israeli concern associated with such a withdrawal, concerns that remained constant throughout the 1990s and into the new millennium: the possibility that the PLO would fail to establish order in these territories and would not stop Palestinian factions from pursuing a violent campaign against Israelis in the West Bank and Gaza as well as inside Israel itself. After a withdrawal from the West Bank and Gaza, Israel was expected to lose some of the intelligence assets it employed when it controlled the territories. More generally, there was an Israeli concern that inter-Palestinian violence could spill over into Israel proper as a re-

nent Status Negotiation, Report of a Study Group of the American Academy of Arts and Sciences (Cambridge, Mass.: AAAS, 1995).

sult of a "Lebanonization" of the Palestinian entity. It was also feared that in the absence of a single address to which deterrent messages could be effectively directed, Israel might have no choice but to reoccupy the territories *in extremis*. The Israeli side saw a common interest with the Palestinians in avoiding this scenario.

For the Palestinian side, the AAAS talks provided an unprecedented opportunity to present Palestinian security concerns to a specialized Israeli and U.S. audience. Then as now, the Palestinians viewed Israel as dominating the security debate and perceived a need to inject some balance into the prevailing Israeli (and U.S.-Western) views on Middle East security. The Palestinian participants presented their concerns, describing past and current threats to Palestinian "existential security," the territorial threats emanating from Israeli settlement policies, and the dangers facing the Palestinian side, given the vast asymmetry in the balance of power between the two sides.

The Palestinian participants also examined possible future Israeli threats to a Palestinian state, including the threat from right-wing revanchism. Palestinian security needs were posed as a parallel prerequisite to Israeli needs in any possible settlement. At the same time, the presence of a PLO official was seen as an opportunity to project a responsible PLO image. Part of the Palestinian participants' tacit brief from Tunis was to impress upon the Israeli side the validity of the PLO as a political and security interlocutor. The presence of a PLO security official at the talks was thus as much political as it was professional.

Participants

The full AAAS plenary consisted of U.S. academics as well as representatives from the two sides. Alongside Professor Everett Mendelsohn of Harvard University and Jeffrey Boutwell representing the Academy were Shibli Telhami, then Associate Professor and Director of Middle East Studies at Syracuse University, and Middle East expert Naomi Weinberger from Barnard College, New York. The Israelis taking part in these talks were Joseph Alpher, Deputy Head of Tel Aviv University's Jaffee Center for Strategic Studies; Maj. Gen (Res.) Shlomo Gazit, a Senior Research Associate at the Jaffee Center and a former Director of Military Intelligence; and Zeev Schiff, military editor of *Ha'aretz*. The Palestinians involved were academics and security specialists Ahmad Khalidi and Yezid Sayigh, Khalil Shikaki, Director of the Center for Palestine Research and Studies in Nablus, and Nizar Ammar, a PLO security official delegated from Tunis especially for the project. None of those involved in the AAAS talks were aware of the discussions then taking place in Norway.

In addition to the main effort undertaken by the Academy—to help participants negotiate a document addressing the security problems associated with Israel's possible withdrawal from the West Bank and Gaza—the AAAS talks provided a setting for informal meetings among a subset of the participants: effectively a Track-II within a Track-II. On the Israeli side, Gazit, Schiff, and Alpher, and on the Palestinian side Khalidi, Sayigh, and Ammar took part in these talks. The AAAS hosts were aware of these discussions but did not take part in them; nor were they briefed about their contents. After each round of talks, Gazit and Alpher reported their impressions in writing to Israeli leaders and top officials, as well as to a small circle of their colleagues, primarily at the Jaffee Center. Schiff shared his impressions from these talks verbally in meetings with Israeli leaders, including Prime Minister Rabin. Ammar reported in detail back to the PLO leadership, including Arafat and Abu Mazin. He also prepared a series of briefing papers and circulated them within a select circle of security and political officials.

The subjects discussed in these "inner" Track-II talks ranged beyond the specific agenda of the Academy-sponsored talks. For example, it was through this more intimate channel that the Israeli participants learned from Nizar Ammar in March 1993 that the PLO leadership was willing to consider the "Gaza first/plus" option. This referred to the transfer of control over the Gaza Strip from Israel to the PLO before an agreement on the transfer of control over the West Bank was to be concluded. A message to this effect was conveyed by Israeli participants to Prime Minister Rabin and allowed him to verify the information he was receiving from the Israelis taking part in the Oslo talks. Thus, without the knowledge of the participants involved, one Track-II venue reinforced the other.

From the Israeli participants' standpoint, the AAAS talks helped to make the Palestinians more aware of the security problems that were likely to be associated with Israel's withdrawal from the West Bank and Gaza. The Israelis taking part in the talks also gained insights into how the Palestinians perceived these likely security problems. Later, in October 1994, they were gratified when their Palestinian counterparts were able to convey and utilize directly the lessons gained through the Academy venue: Ammar, Khalidi, and Sayigh became advisers to the Palestinian delegations in the formal PLO-Israeli talks in Cairo and Taba, and participated in the initial security negotiations over the post-Oslo "Gaza and Jericho" agreement.

The professional background of the Israeli and Palestinian participants also aided the utility of the Academy talks. The three Israelis who took part in the talks had extensive experience in security affairs: Gazit had a long career in military intelligence and had served as coordinator of operations in the territories under Defense Minister Moshe Dayan; Alpher had spent twelve years in the Mossad before joining the Jaffee Center; and Zeev Schiff—with a long career as a defense journalist and editor—was well-versed in the concerns of Israel's security establishment. The backgrounds of the three Israeli participants also allowed them access to Israel's leaders and to the top officials in Israel's defense and security bureaucracies. They knew how to convey the impressions they gained in the talks effectively.

As a prominent defense editor, Schiff enjoyed easy access to Rabin, who served as prime minister and defense minister, and could share his impressions from the talks with him. Such contacts helped to facilitate an AAAS tour of the Israeli politico-military establishment in June 1993. Schiff's participation in the AAAS talks was productive in yet another way. As a defense journalist he frequently wrote about subjects related to the issues addressed in the talks. Although he was careful not to reveal specific information gained in these discussions or the sources of his insights, he found ways to communicate to the public some of the conclusions he reached as a consequence of these talks.

On the Palestinian side, Khalidi and Sayigh were both academics with professional qualifications in the field of strategic studies and a long-standing political affiliation with the Palestinian movement and its leadership. Ammar, who had been trained in Egypt, had served with Fateh intelligence branch *(Jihaz ar-Rasd)* in Jordan and Lebanon in the 1970s, and had served as aide-de-camp to Fateh intelligence chief Abu Iyyad in Beirut and Tunis until his assassination in 1991. At the time of the AAAS meetings, Ammar was deputy director at Abu Mazin's Directorate of International Relations, but he was not in on the Oslo secret. As with their Israeli counterparts, the Palestinian side was accorded easy access to the PLO leadership as the situation required. Ammar was also able to organize extensive briefings with senior PLO officials in Tunis during an AAAS tour of the region in the summer of 1993. Khalidi, Sayigh, and Shikaki equally contributed to the security debate on the Palestinian-Arab side through their writings and interviews in Arabic journals and the press, often reflecting the lessons learned at AAAS meetings.

Each side in the AAAS track perceived its counterpart as equally professional. The Israelis knew that the Palestinian participants had conducted much research and analysis of defense affairs, and Nizar Ammar had operational experience managing security and intelligence for the PLO. The Palestinians saw Gazit, Alpher, and Schiff as well-established people whose views were generally received with due seriousness. The backgrounds of the participants allowed them to isolate the security issues from the more sensitive and complex political subjects discussed in

Washington. Thus they were able to produce practical suggestions for managing the Israeli-Palestinian post-withdrawal security agenda.

Yet in contrast to the "risk-takers" who took part in the Oslo channel, the AAAS participants generally followed a more conventional approach. Although the Israeli law against talking with the PLO had been rescinded in 1991, Israeli participants felt the need for an "academic" buffer to protect them against the possible domestic political fallout of dealing with the PLO. This issue came to the fore in the spring of 1993, when Ammar tried to arrange a visit by the Israeli team to Tunis. After some hesitation, the Israeli side suggested instead a meeting with Abu Mazin in Cairo. Ammar obtained Abu Mazin's consent but even this proved too problematic for the Israeli participants, who eventually declined on the grounds that the meeting could compromise their political and professional standing at home. Gazit, Schiff, and Alpher held back for different reasons. Gazit was informed that his safety was at risk, and Schiff was concerned that he would be "labeled" by key members of Israel's defense community with whom he needed to interact as defense editor of *Ha'aretz*. More generally, the Israeli participants were reluctant to exceed significantly the Israeli national consensus that still rejected dealings with the PLO. The failure of the AAAS participants to grasp the opportunity to meet with the PLO leadership illustrates the limitations of the exercise as a potential deal-making venue.

Mentors

The AAAS talks lacked an Israeli or Palestinian mentor who could play the critical role that Yossi Beilin and Abu Mazin filled in the Oslo process. On the Palestinian side, none of the participants actively sought a mentor, and none emerged as the talks proceeded despite the evident interest in Tunis in the ongoing debate with the Israeli team. Ammar's leadership contacts were direct and personal and did not pass through the mediating agency of a committed mentor.

On the Israeli side, there was no one close to Rabin and Peres who was ready or willing to persuade them of the possible utility of the AAAS talks for advancing Israel's security interests. Given their more-than-full agenda and the multiplicity of messages being received from the PLO at the time, it was unlikely that Israel's top leaders would have been sensitive to the possibilities opened by the AAAS channel unless someone close to them alerted them. Consequently, Gazit was never asked to brief Peres or Rabin directly regarding the substance of the AAAS talks. Nonetheless, the AAAS talks did affect other members of the Israeli security establishment, since both Gazit and Alpher made a point of circulating the results of their discussions within the security establishment. Indeed, Deputy Defense Minister Mordechai Gur announced to the Knesset after the Oslo accords had been signed that the AAAS talks had substantially contributed to the Oslo breakthrough.

Leaders

It is not clear whether the AAAS-sponsored talks had much direct impact on Israeli thinking and conduct during this period. An official close to Prime Minister Rabin did not recall that the reports provided by the Israeli participants in the talks received much attention in his office. Thus, it would be difficult to associate any specific policy decision with any particular development in these talks.

The reasons why the AAAS talks failed to leave a greater imprint on Israeli decision-making during this period seem complex. The question is particularly puzzling insofar as it relates to Prime Minister Rabin and in comparison with the Oslo talks. None of the individuals involved in the Oslo process were particularly close to Rabin. Moreover, with the exception of the legal adviser Joel Singer, all were quite close to his political rival, Shimon Peres. In contrast, Gazit had a long-established military record and had served as Director of Military Intelligence during Rabin's first term as prime minister (1974–1977). In addition, the Academy talks were focused on the security implications of an agreement with the Palestinians—a subject that was very dear to Rabin. Indeed, Beilin later testified that in the final stages of negotiating the Oslo package, Rabin feared that insufficient attention was given to obtaining a Palestinian commitment to prevent terrorism. Why then did he neglect a channel that focused on the issue that he cared about most?

It seems that other considerations led Israel's leaders to regard the Oslo talks as the main venue, and to downgrade the Academy effort by comparison. First, the AAAS talks were not intended to create a breakthrough in Israeli-Palestinian relations. Neither side perceived them as a "deal-making" exercise. The participants in these talks did not seek a political agreement and the nature of each side's engagement with its leadership reflected this. For its part, the PLO leadership also did not treat the AAAS as an alternative to Oslo. The AAAS talks were designed to suggest a way of managing the consequences of such a "hypothetical" political breakthrough rather than achieve the breakthrough itself. Hence, under the best of circumstances the AAAS talks were unlikely to produce the drama that was created in Oslo.

The PLO leadership treated the AAAS talks largely as an "academic" exercise and did not fully engage itself in their substance. Although the Israeli participants were well known and considered to be of some influence within Israel, Abu Mazin in particular seems to have been unconvinced of the utility of the AAAS talks and gave them relatively little credence as a conduit to the Israeli side. This was at least partly due to his own preoccupation with the Oslo channel and the PLO's decision, after Savir joined the Oslo talks in May 1993, to consider Oslo as the sole authorized direct channel to Rabin and Peres. Equally important, Abu Mazin's relationship with AAAS participant Nizar Ammar was less close than that with Hassan Asfour, Ammar's colleague at Abu Mazin's International Affairs Directorate who attended the Oslo talks. Asfour was a close aide and political confidant of Abu Mazin.

Despite this, Arafat was well aware of the importance of eliciting qualified Israeli responses on security issues, and he attentively received frequent briefings from Ammar regarding the AAAS deliberations. Arafat's interest can be gauged by the fact that he allowed Ammar to attend an AAAS meeting in Rome in January 1993 despite the fact that he had suspended all Israeli-Palestinian contacts in the wake of the Israeli deportation of 400 Hamas activists to South Lebanon in December 1992. In addition, the AAAS delegation that came to Tunis in June 1993 was received by a large number of PLO political and security officials, and the delegation's report on its findings in Israel was received with great and serious interest.[2]

An important consideration that affected the Israeli leaders' attitude toward the AAAS talks concerned the likelihood of maintaining secrecy. From Rabin's standpoint, too many people knew of the AAAS talks and were being informed of their proceedings. This reduced the chances that serious business could be conducted through this channel without being leaked. For example, while the Israeli Track-I negotiating team in Washington was not aware of the Oslo talks, it received copies of the reports written by an Israeli participant in the AAAS talks. One report conveyed strong criticism of the conduct of the Israeli Track-I delegation in Washington expressed by the Palestinian interlocutors in the AAAS talks. This triggered a sharp written reply from the head of Israel's Track-I delegation, Elyakim Rubinstein. Attempting to defend his record, Rubinstein

---

2. Mamduh Nawfal, who was one of the PLO security officials most closely engaged with Ammar on the AAAS channel, attests to Arafat's sustained interest in its proceedings. See Mamduh Nawfal, *Qusat Itifaag Oslo* (*The Story of the Oslo Accord*) (Amman: Al-Ahliyyah, 1995) p. 34.

distributed his reply to a number of leaders and government officials. To put it mildly, the exchange was quite inconsistent with Rabin's modus operandi. Clearly, such an exchange could not have taken place in the Oslo process given the secrecy with which the participants, mentors, and leaders surrounded the Norway talks.

Another possible reason for the absence of greater receptivity to the AAAS talks by Israel's leaders may have been that they, like Abu Mazin, had become too deeply involved in the Oslo talks by March 1993. They may have wished to refrain from confusing Arafat by operating through more than one Track-II channel. Such confusion had already developed as a result of conversations held between Labor Knesset member Ephraim Sneh and PLO leader Nabil Shaath. Since Sneh was a political ally of Rabin, these conversations led the Palestinian participants in Oslo to ask which of the two tracks was authoritative. Rabin may have been persuaded by this experience that it would be a mistake to communicate with the PLO through more than one Track-II venue simultaneously.

Nonetheless, the AAAS venue seems to have provided—even if for-tuitously—an important measure of reinforcement to the Oslo channel. As early as the first AAAS meeting in October 1992, well before the Oslo talks, the Israeli side had raised the idea of "Gaza first" in the inner group discussions. The Palestinian side reported this back to Tunis. Coinci-dentally, another set of unrelated meetings of the FIS at Adderbury had generated enthusiasm for a follow-up discussion dedicated to "Gaza first" to be attended by the same inner group that was involved in the AAAS track. The result was a preliminary paper prepared by Gazit and Alpher that was forwarded to the Palestinian participants in January 1993.

Although the proposed FIS symposium on the "Gaza first" idea never took place, by early 1993 Palestinian thinking had begun to take the "Gaza first" option seriously. In a visit to Tunis in March 1993, Khalidi and Ammar debated the issue extensively and prepared some internal papers on the advantages and disadvantages of this option. These thoughts were shared with both Abu Mazin and Hassan Asfour—both of whom divulged nothing about the Oslo track. Abu Mazin outlined his ideas of a preliminary transfer of powers in Gaza with subsequent elec-tions for a Legislative Council in Gaza and the West Bank as a mechanism for linkage between the two parts. The result was an understanding that "Gaza plus" would be needed if "Gaza first" was to be acceptable. Inter-estingly, these debates seem to have preceded Arafat's presentation of "Gaza plus" to Rabin (via Egypt) or any discussion of this formula at the Oslo talks. Ammar presented the "Gaza plus" option to Gazit, Schiff, and

Alpher at an AAAS inner group meeting in Rome in March 1993. By that time, the Oslo channel had moved onto the subject and briefings reaching the Israeli side from the AAAS may have finally consolidated Rabin's interest in the formula.[3]

While the AAAS venue did not engage Israel's top leaders and did not produce a drama equivalent to Oslo, it had positive effects that were lacking in the Oslo process. For example, Israel's defense establishment, which was kept in the dark regarding the discussions held in Oslo, was generally well informed of the Academy talks. Indeed, at least one participant in the talks received numerous positive reactions to his briefings from Israel's defense community. Such briefings appear to have helped prepare the community for the post-Oslo negotiations dealing with the implementation of Israel's withdrawal from Gaza and Jericho.[4]

On the Palestinian side, the security discussions at the AAAS highlighted the importance of the internal security issue for the first time. Commencing with the first FIS (pre-AAAS) meetings at Adderbury, the Palestinian leaders in Tunis had slowly been made aware of the dimensions of this issue and the kind of demands and expectations the Israelis would have in any handover of security functions to the PLO or related agencies. Prior to the early 1990s, little thought had been given to this issue within the PLO, but over the next few years it became the subject of increasingly serious work.

The AAAS discussions also pointed to an Israeli readiness to countenance the entry of PLO security personnel into the occupied territories as part of a security agreement between the two sides—albeit not on the scale seen after Oslo. Arafat had long been dedicated to this "return," and reports of the AAAS discussions may have strengthened his belief that this was possible.[5] The AAAS exercise may thus have provided a direct input into PLO thinking—notwithstanding the still rudimentary capability of the organization to institutionalize and systemize such thought. What is also worth noting here is the complex interaction between the

---

3. David Makovsky suggests that in April Rabin was initially hostile to the idea because it had not been raised at Oslo; he thought that the PLO was playing games with the Egyptians. *Making Peace with the PLO* (Boulder, Colo.: Westview, 1996), pp. 37–38.

4. Joel Singer was apparently handed the AAAS file as part of his briefing for the Oslo talks.

5. As early as 1990, Arafat privately told Ahmad Khalidi that he foresaw the deployment of the Palestine Liberation Army (PLA) Ain Jalut brigade from Egypt into Gaza as part of an interim agreement on security—an idea that seemed farfetched to Khalidi at the time.

AAAS, FIS, and Oslo initiatives, and the potential each seemed to have to affect or reinforce the other.

Sponsors and the U.S. Role

The AAAS's prestige as an academic body provided a suitable umbrella for the talks, and the formal Academy talks benefited from the excellent navigation provided by its sponsors. Everett Mendelsohn and Jeffrey Boutwell, who orchestrated the talks on behalf of AAAS, were wise to define an agenda that was both practical and important. They also managed the project and moderated the discussions with care and sensitivity. The AAAS staff facilitated the discussions with no overt agenda and allowed the two sides to engage in serious debate without preconditions or preconceived direction.

In allowing the "inner" discussions to develop, the AAAS was consciously providing a political service, but one that both sides were seeking. Thus, while nominally playing a politically neutral role, the AAAS project directors were indirectly facilitating Israeli contacts with the PLO that were designed to help break the logjam in the peace process. This was also evident when a delegation of AAAS participants visited Israel in June 1993. The Israeli participants in the talks arranged for the delegation to meet with Deputy Defense Minister Mordechai (Motta) Gur. The AAAS delegation was also able to meet a wide range of Israeli political and security personnel including Major General Uri Saguy, then head of Israeli Military Intelligence. Saguy was particularly forthright on Israeli security needs being potentially accommodated in a political agreement with the PLO. The AAAS delegation later shared their assessment of what they had heard in Israel with PLO officials in Tunis, thus indirectly helping to bolster mutual confidence in the possibility of a deal.

The AAAS staff also played an indirect role between the PLO and the Clinton administration. Mendelsohn and Boutwell briefed State Department officials on the group's deliberations, emphasizing the evolution of security thinking on the Palestinian side. These briefings were received politely and with interest in Washington, but without any visible effect on the official U.S. stance. However, members of the AAAS staff could only convey their impressions of the plenary meetings and could not pass on any full or first-hand assessment of what was going on in the more intensive and informal inner side-meetings that they did not attend. Therefore, it would have been difficult for the AAAS facilitators to have credibly alerted the Clinton administration regarding the growing feasibility of the "Gaza first" option.

Summary

The AAAS talks were unique in that they consisted of two connected yet different venues: an "inner" Track-II channel within Track-II discussions. The latter comprised talks between a number of Israelis and Palestinians convened by AAAS to discuss the security arrangements that would be needed following Israel's withdrawal from the West Bank and Gaza. The staff of AAAS navigated the discussions and later wrote and published a summary of the exploration's results. The "inner" channel constituted meetings among a small subset of Israelis and Palestinians—excluding their U.S. hosts—to explore specific but broader political issues. It was within this smaller circle that the twin issues of "Gaza first" and "Gaza plus" were discussed.

These discussions point to one of the advantages of Track-II frameworks, namely that leaders can use them to verify information received from other sources, including Track-I negotiators and participants in other Track-II venues. In this case, the information obtained through the AAAS talks was probably used to verify information received from Oslo.

At the same time, the AAAS talks highlight two potential sources of weakness of Track-II venues. First, in the absence of a mentor who was capable of bringing the results of the talks to the attention of Israel's leaders, the channel could not hope to have an impact similar to that of the Oslo talks.

Second, the AAAS talks fell victim to the success of the Oslo talks. To avoid confusion, the PLO decided that it would not converse with Israel through more that one venue. For various reasons, the PLO decided that the Oslo talks would be the only authoritative informal venue. Thus, the significance of one Track-II channel seems to have eroded the potential significance of the other.

The Palestinian-Israeli security debate took a different turn after 1994 and the establishment of the Palestinian Authority (PA). Large numbers of PLO security personnel were brought into Palestinian areas by agreement, and the PA's nascent security apparatus established a framework for cooperation with its Israeli counterpart that went far beyond the boundaries envisaged during the AAAS talks.

The Palestinian-Israeli security issue, however, remained highly vulnerable to external political events. Without a real resolution of the underlying political causes of the conflict, the attempt to build common ground on security became increasingly difficult, leading to serious PA-Israeli violence in 1996 and calamitous breakdown and large-scale military confrontation between the two sides after September 2000.

The salience of the security issue for both sides was reinforced by the second Palestinian *intifada* and ensuing Israeli military actions against PA areas. Many of the fears and concerns voiced by both sides during the AAAS talks—at one stage seemingly in abeyance—were revived. The AAAS achievement in launching a serious debate on security still stands, but the distance to be traversed before any real and sustainable understanding is reached remains considerable.

Chapter 5

The Stockholm Talks

A year after the Oslo Declaration of Principles (DOP) was concluded, another set of Israeli-Palestinian Track-II talks was launched in Sweden between the original Israeli participants at Oslo—Yair Hirschfeld and Ron Pundik —and two of the co-authors of this book, Hussein Agha and Ahmad Khalidi. Until terminated following the assassination of Prime Minister Rabin in November 1995, these discussions were potentially as significant as the Oslo talks.

While the Oslo DOP and the associated Israeli recognition of the PLO broke the psychological barrier dividing the Israelis and Palestinians and set in motion an interim process, the purpose of the Stockholm talks was even more ambitious: to chart a course for the final resolution of the most difficult issues in dispute between Israel and the Palestinians, and to prepare for a permanent peace agreement between the two parties. The Stockholm talks concentrated on the "final status" issues identified in the Oslo DOP: the nature of the future Palestinian entity and its borders with Israel; the future of Jerusalem; the "right of return" of Palestinian refugees; security arrangements; and the future of the Israeli settlements in the West Bank and Gaza.

Concealed and protected by the Swedish security service, the Israeli and Palestinian interlocutors held some twenty-one secret meetings. By late October 1995, the talks produced an unprecedented working paper that was intended to serve as the basis and starting point for more detailed negotiations aimed at resolving the numerous and highly sensitive final status issues. The hope was that these intensive negotiations might be completed by May 1996, which was stipulated by the Oslo DOP as the last date for opening the Israeli-Palestinian "final status" negotiations.

The Stockholm talks' initial purpose was to complete a draft for a full "final status" agreement covering all issues in detail. This objective was modified over the course of the discussions. As the possibility of early Israeli elections became more likely during 1995, it was agreed to work toward a less ambitious goal: an understanding that could be tailored for Israeli electoral purposes. This agreed shift was intended as a temporary measure and was not meant to divert the project from its original purpose. At the time, Yossi Beilin, the Israeli mentor of these talks, had moved slightly away from Peres, and closer to Rabin. This was presented by the Israeli team as a potentially positive development in helping to "sell" the understanding to Rabin, although it was also clear that Rabin would not go forward without Peres's consent. In any case, it is difficult to believe that Peres would have rejected any concession that was acceptable to Rabin.

By early November 1995, the two teams had reached some potential if incomplete understandings regarding a framework agreement. Beilin, serving as Minister of Planning was scheduled to meet with Foreign Minister Peres on November 8 to present him with the working paper. Beilin had hoped to solicit Peres's support in persuading Prime Minister Rabin to adopt the document as a basis and a starting point for more intense and detailed negotiations. In Beilin's view, if he took the understandings first to Rabin, the prime minister would have asked him to solicit a response from Peres first. In addition, Beilin felt that going to Rabin first would have been seen by Peres as an attempt to bypass him or "fix a deal" behind his back. Beilin estimated that while a positive response from Peres could facilitate a similar reaction from Rabin, a negative reaction would not have been sufficient to prevent Rabin from looking favorably on the results of the Stockholm talks.

These hypotheses were never put to the test. On November 5, 1995, only days after it was decided to present the document negotiated at Stockholm to the Israeli leadership, Rabin was assassinated. When Beilin finally briefed Peres on November 11 about the results of the Stockholm talks, Israel's newly appointed prime minister was noncommittal and unenthusiastic about the understandings reached.

The Stockholm Understandings

The Stockholm talks produced a consensus that the final status of the emerging Palestinian entity would be independent statehood, and that this was to be agreed at the outset as part of the overall package. It was also agreed that the Palestinian state would be demilitarized but that there would also be an Israeli acknowledgement of Palestinian self-defense needs to be negotiated over time. Relative to the June 4, 1967, lines, the border between the two states was to result in Israel's annex-ation of the approximately 4–5 percent of the West Bank where the vast majority of Israeli settlers reside—some 100,000 Israelis in about 50 settle-ments. The understanding incorporated a land swap between the two sides on a one-to-one basis. The Palestinian state would be partly com-pensated for its land loss by the addition of an equal amount of territory in the Negev, allowing for a necessary expansion of the Gaza Strip, or of other areas of Israel to be agreed. An intensive Israeli-initiated develop-ment program for the areas newly attached to the Gaza Strip was to com-pensate for the difference in the "quality" of the exchanged territories. In addition, the Palestinian State would also be granted control of an extra-territorial land link between Gaza and the West Bank. The Palestinian state was to be in full control over its borders, and movement of people and goods in and out of Palestine was to be free and unimpeded.

The understandings also stipulated that Israeli settlements located beyond the areas annexed would come under Palestinian rule and would lose their status as exclusive Israeli enclaves. Israeli citizens opting to stay in these settlements were to be given the choice between receiving com-pensation and moving or remaining under Palestinian sovereignty. Those remaining under Palestinian sovereignty were to have the choice of Pal-estinian or Israeli citizenship and the right to vote in Knesset elections if opting for the latter. The Palestinian side would maintain the principle of the "right of return," but Israel would only agree to absorb within its pre-1967 borders a limited number of Palestinian refugees; the number remained to be negotiated. Any Palestinian refugees wishing to live in the new state of Palestine would be permitted to return without precon-ditions. The refugees were also to be offered a free choice of different options for moral and material compensation and additional funding for relocation and rehabilitation. As part of this process, Israel was to contribute certain unspecified sums to an international organization that would be set up to oversee the implementation of the agreement on refugees.

The understandings also stipulated that no Arab military forces would be stationed on Palestinian soil west of the Jordan River. Without compromising Palestinian sovereignty, Israel would be permitted to sta-tion a military unit and two logistical bases in unspecified locations in the Jordan Valley. Israeli-Palestinian joint patrols were to guard the Palestin-ian-Israeli border. Israel would maintain early warning facilities and air defense units east of the central mountain range. All these arrangements were subject to terms of agreement consistent with Palestinian sovereignty and valid for a specific and limited period of time. An international force would help to monitor and verify the agreement.

Possibly the most innovative aspect of the Stockholm talks was the framework suggested for addressing one of the most sensitive of all "final status" issues—the future of Jerusalem. The approach separated the sovereignty and municipal dimensions of the city's future. The understanding suggested the maintenance of an open unitary city, with free unimpeded access to all parts of the city by citizens of both states, and with security checkpoints at the point of *exit* rather than *entry* into the two states. Jerusalem's current municipal boundaries would be redrawn to include adjacent areas that the Arabs regard as part of "al-Quds," where the Palestinian entity could initially establish its government institutions. Municipally, the city was to be divided into a number of boroughs, conducting their affairs autonomously and separately with very strong local powers including full zoning, building, education, health, and taxation rights. The "green" areas of East Jerusalem would thus revert to full Arab municipal jurisdiction, to be used by the sub-municipality for housing or other purposes as it saw fit. The "unified" city council was to comprise three elected bodies: two would govern the overall affairs of the Jewish and Arab boroughs separately, and a joint body—reflecting the relative size of the two populations in Jerusalem/al-Quds—would provide a mechanism for the coordination and resolution of inter-urban problems.

Palestinian sovereignty would apply to the newly added Arab parts of Jerusalem, while Israeli sovereignty would be applied to West Jerusalem and to the city's Jewish suburbs. The Palestinians were also to obtain extraterritorial control of the Muslim and Christian Holy places in the Old City. The Old City would also have its own regime: the Jewish neighborhood and Jewish Holy places would fall under the Israeli sub-municipality, and the Arab neighborhoods and Holy sites would be placed under the Arab submunicipality. A Joint Parity council would oversee the coordination of overall administrative matters pertaining to the Old City.

Final sovereignty over East Jerusalem—including the Arab and Jewish neighborhoods extending beyond the Old City—was to be phased in a manner to be decided by a bilateral committee to be established for this purpose the moment the agreement went into effect. It was clearly understood in Stockholm that all-Arab areas of East Jerusalem would revert to Palestinian sovereignty and all-Jewish areas to Israeli sovereignty. The Stockholm understandings constituted a clear common commitment to implement agreed infrastructural and other policies on the ground designed to ensure that this would be achieved in a programmatic and well-defined manner. Further detailed work by the Stockholm teams was to clarify and finalize this issue, but the work did not take place.

Although it was never formally adopted by the two sides, the significance of what was misnamed as the "Abu Mazin–Beilin agreement"—after the two mentors of the Stockholm talks—has been far from lost. After the Likud-led government was formed following the 1996 elections, the agreement became the basis for extensive talks between a number of Labor leaders led by Beilin and a number of Likud leaders led by Michael Eitan, the chairman of the Likud party members of Knesset. The talks, aimed at creating a new Likud-Labor consensus on final status issues, resulted in January 1997 in the so-called "Beilin-Eitan document." Together with other important developments in 1996–1999—notably the commitment undertaken by the Netanyahu government to implement "further redeployments" in the West Bank as agreed under the terms of the October 1998 Wye agreement—the Stockholm understandings contributed to diminishing the Likud-Labor divide over the future of the Land of Israel. Thus, the Stockholm talks left a lasting imprint on the Israeli internal ideological debate about the future of the territories and became a major factor in helping to create a new bipartisan Israeli consensus on a partition of the Land of Israel.

The Stockholm understandings may yet prove even more important to the future of the peace process. The understandings set the limits of a durable and acceptable settlement that met the basic political, moral, and strategic requirements of both sides. During the final status Israeli-Palestinian negotiations at Camp David and Taba in 2000 and 2001, the Stockholm blueprint was the only common framework for the talks, and it served as the basis of the Clinton bridging proposals in December 2000.[1] Any future agreements that deviate substantially from this standard are unlikely to stand the test of time and the challenges of constant change in the local and regional environment. Indeed, as the only extant political framework for a comprehensive final settlement forged jointly by the two sides, the work done at Stockholm remains the benchmark against which any future agreement is most likely to be measured.

The Political Environment

The euphoria prevailing in the immediate aftermath of the Oslo accords had an important role in making the Stockholm talks possible. The dra-

---

1.　It is instructive to note that senior Likud figures initially showed great interest in the Stockholm understandings and asked for detailed briefings on the talks.

matic breakthrough achieved in Oslo created an impression that nothing was impossible in the realm of conflict resolution in the Middle East. In Israel, many leaders who had opposed making any concessions to the PLO now accepted the Oslo accords as a reality. This led Deputy Foreign Minister Yossi Beilin to conclude that a unique moment of goodwill existed, and that it should not be lost.

By late 1994, there was also a growing sense of urgency about peacemaking—a sense that progress in the Israeli-Palestinian peace process should be made quickly. The difficulties involved in translating the Oslo accords into operational agreements—such as the Gaza-Jericho accords—had already made it apparent that the high hopes associated with the Oslo and Washington ceremonies could not be sustained indefinitely. Moreover, the Rabin government now had less than two years to complete its first term in office. It was clear that the window of opportunity for creating further breakthroughs in Arab-Israeli peacemaking was very narrow.

From the Palestinians' standpoint, it was thus eminently sensible to make every attempt to create a breakthrough on "final status" issues. With less than half a term of the Rabin government left, the Palestinian leadership faced the prospect that its worst fears might materialize: If some understanding with the Israelis on the array of "final status" issues could not be reached before the 1996 elections, and if the Labor party lost these elections, the process could be jeopardized and Arafat might find himself functioning as no more than the de facto mayor of Gaza. Consequently, the PLO leadership showed great interest in reaching an agreement with Israel on "final status" issues while Rabin was still in power and while he remained politically strong enough to begin the implementation of such an accord.

Moreover, during 1994–1995 there were periodic rumors of an impending breakthrough in the Track-I Israeli-Syrian negotiations. Although some on the Palestinian side viewed such a breakthrough as helpful for resolving the Israeli-Palestinian conflict, other Palestinian leaders thought that Israel would exploit a peace agreement with Syria by freezing any further implementation of the Israeli-Palestinian Oslo accords. When the PLO first debated the Oslo agreement, Arafat's opponents—even within Fateh—had warned against such a development. In these circumstances, it seemed that the Palestinians would be motivated to reach an understanding with Israel on "final status" issues before a breakthrough in the Israeli-Syrian talks could occur.

The Stockholm discussions on "final status" issues were held when nothing else even remotely comparable was taking place. Unlike in 1992, before the Oslo accord—when a number of channels were working on similar and overlapping lines—the Stockholm talks were the only venue where the two sides were jointly and seriously examining the whole range of vexed "final status" issues. In that sense, the talks enjoyed the advantage of a virtual vacuum on issues of substance. The potential of the Stockholm talks to serve as a shortcut to "final status" was evident to both sides.

But the Palestinian team at Stockholm had concerns that were not necessarily identical to those of the PLO leadership. For the team, there was growing concern that the Oslo-B negotiations, which finally produced a full interim agreement in September 1995, would lead to a new political-territorial reality that would make it very difficult to redraw the boundaries of the proposed Palestinian state. In particular, the "bypass" roads for the Israeli settlements agreed upon in Oslo-B, were seen by the Palestinian team at Stockholm as allowing for an even closer integration of the settlements into the Israeli security and infrastructure network of roads and facilities already pervading the West Bank. The Palestinian team viewed the interim process as leading to a consolidation of some of the most problematic aspects of the Israeli occupation. From their perspective, while agreement on a starting point and a framework for "final status" would serve Palestinian interests and would meet Rabin's electoral purposes, it would also help to short-circuit the dangers presented by the interim process and speed up the attainment of a permanent settlement. Beilin was also sympathetic to this Palestinian concern.

The Stockholm channel can thus be seen as seeking to overtake the concurrent formal talks on interim issues. Paradoxically, these talks were seeking to result in a different end-state than the official PLO-Israeli negotiations and perhaps even undo some of the perceived damage done by the official agreements. In this respect, the Stockholm talks were clearly different from the Oslo venue, but in another sense they were similar: the objective was to attempt to construct a bypass around official Track-I talks.

Participants

The Stockholm talks developed out of a chance meeting between Ahmad Khalidi and Ron Pundik at a conference held in the United Kingdom in May 1994. The two full teams, including Hussein Agha and Yair Hirschfeld, later met in London in the summer of 1994 to consider how to develop their project.

Initially, the group intended to find an external academic sponsor for the project. In September 1994, Agha was attending a meeting of the Washington-based Search for Common Ground, which was then engaged in building a regional dialogue in the Middle East in Stockholm, and informally suggested a Swedish sponsorship of the project. This was almost immediately agreed upon, and the talks were launched in Stockholm shortly afterward. This genesis of the Stockholm talks provides another example of how Track-II talks can interact and build upon each other.

The Palestinian participants in the Stockholm discussions better fit the definition of Track-II participants than did the participants in the Oslo process. The Palestinian participants in Oslo had been PLO officials led by Abu Ala'. In contrast, both Agha and Khalidi were Oxford-trained political analysts and long-time Fateh activists. While they enjoyed close connections and easy access to the PLO's top leaders, they had no official status, as did Abu Ala' and other members of the Oslo team. The Stockholm channel was thus free from any direct official PLO presence throughout its deliberations until Oslo veteran Hassan Asfour joined the Palestinian side for the last two rounds of talks. In that sense, there was a symmetry between the members of the two Stockholm teams that had been absent at Oslo.

Soon after obtaining the go-ahead from the Swedish sponsors, Agha and Khalidi contacted the PLO leadership and informed Arafat and Abu Mazin of the project with their Israeli counterparts. Both Abu Mazin and Arafat were convinced that Hirschfeld and Pundik could not be acting without a clear green light from the Israeli leadership and were interested to find out how far the Israelis would go. Again, based on the Oslo experience, the two Palestinian leaders requested that the Palestinian team keep the exercise very confidential. Some aspects of the Stockholm work were shared with a few associates, and exceptionally, Feisal Husseini attended one round of talks in Stockholm focusing on the future of Jerusalem; Yossi Beilin was also present. At the strict request of the Palestinian leadership, however, the full range of the discussions was not divulged to any wider audience on the Palestinian side.

At one stage, the Palestinian team attempted to probe for alternative Israeli interlocutors. Toward late summer of 1995, the Palestinian team was increasingly unsure whether Hirschfeld, Pundik, and Beilin could ensure a positive response from Rabin. The Palestinian team began a series of contacts with new potential Israeli interlocutors considered to have a closer and more credible connection to Rabin. Initial tentative contacts with Zeev Schiff led to some exploratory talks under Schiff's auspices with Major General (res.) Danny Rothschild, the former Military Coordinator for the occupied territories, and Brigadier General (res.) Gadi Zohar, then leading the Oslo-B formal negotiations on the transfer of civilian authority to the Palestinian side. This alternative line of pursuit petered out, largely through inertia and inconclusive contact between the two sides.

On the Israeli side, Hirschfeld and Pundik remained committed to furthering the prospects of resolving the Israeli-Palestinian dispute, despite having been slighted by their own leaders in the final stage of the Oslo process. In Oslo's immediate aftermath, they were gratified by the attention given by the Israeli and international media to the positive role they had played in reaching a historical breakthrough in Israeli-Palestinian relations. They were thus able to view their role as Track-II participants as not entirely thankless, and were willing to take a similar mission again.

In 1994, the Economic Cooperation Foundation (ECF)—the Tel Aviv–based nongovernmental organization that Hirschfeld and Pundik directed—became engaged in considerable efforts to support the peace process by initiating Israeli-Palestinian people-to-people exchanges, particularly related to social and economic development. With Beilin's participation, during 1994–1995 they also conducted a series of seminars in Israel focused on the "final status" issues. Some of these seminars took place before the Stockholm talks began, while other meetings were held parallel to the discussions held in Sweden. Israeli experts were asked to contribute their thoughts on the different issues involved but were not told that they were providing intellectual ammunition for a new Track-II venue.

By the time the Stockholm talks began, Hirschfeld and Pundik had become seasoned Track-II participants. Most important, the Oslo process provided them with important insights regarding the manner in which the Israeli political system worked and the constraints facing the implementation of any policy change. Consequently, they became aware of the critical importance that must be attached to the domestic marketing of such a change. Two other Israelis were aware of the Stockholm channel. In early 1995, Beilin had consulted with the author Amos Oz regarding different solutions for "final status" issues being discussed in Sweden. He later held similar consultations with Major General (ret.) Amram Mitzna, Mayor of Haifa and a former commander of the IDF's Central Command. Mitzna's advice focused on the security dimensions of the understandings being discussed.

At one point, Nimrod Novik, a long-time associate of Beilin, joined the talks in Sweden alongside Hirschfeld and Pundik. Novik had been a senior researcher at Tel Aviv University's Jaffee Center for Strategic Studies when Beilin recruited him in 1984 to become foreign policy adviser to Prime Minister Peres (1984–1986). He continued to work with Peres in a similar capacity when Peres became foreign minister (1986–

1988). Novik's role in the Stockholm talks was to consider the implications of the various ideas discussed in terms of the ability to "sell them" to Prime Minister Rabin and to the Israeli public.

Mentors: Beilin and Abu Mazin

In a conversation with PLO Chairman Yasser Arafat in Tunis in October 1993, Yossi Beilin, then deputy foreign minister, initiated the preliminary moves that led to Israeli participation in the Stockholm talks. Beilin was convinced that it was important to exploit the post-Oslo atmosphere of goodwill. The recent success of the Oslo format persuaded him that Track-II talks are an extremely useful tool in conflict resolution. He therefore suggested to Arafat that the Oslo method should be used to try to resolve the Israeli-Palestinian "final status" issues, and he received Arafat's approval for having Hirschfeld and Pundik serve once again as the primary Israeli interlocutors.[2]

Beilin attempted to repeat the success of the Oslo format in yet another fashion: he refrained from reporting to Peres and Rabin that he had discussed with Arafat a possible opening of a Track-II venue for deliberating the final status issues, and that Arafat had agreed to appoint representatives to such talks. Beilin later testified that his decision to refrain from informing Peres about this aspect of the meeting resulted from his understanding that Peres would be bound to brief Rabin about the matter. He feared that Rabin would not wish to enter into "final status" discussions at that early stage and that he might well veto the proposed effort.

When the talks began a year later, Beilin avoided telling Peres and Rabin of this development. Indeed, he informed Peres about the existence of the venue only after Rabin's assassination. Thus, there is no direct evidence that Beilin briefed Rabin about the Stockholm talks. The Palestinian side, however, suspected that Rabin knew about the channel from his own separate intelligence sources. This suspicion was reinforced during Rabin's last three months by the repeated coincidence between the position he expressed publicly on "final status," and the work being done in Stockholm.[3]

---

2. Yossi Beilin, *Touching Peace* (London: Weidenfeld and Nicolson, 1999), p. 171.

3. During a meeting with Arafat in the summer of 1995, Agha and Khalidi were told by the PLO chairman: "Do you think that Beilin is so stupid as to jeopardize his position as government minister by concealing his involvement in the Stockholm channel from Rabin?"

The distinction between participants and mentors was far less clear in the Stockholm process than at Oslo. While Beilin did not participate directly in the Oslo negotiations, he took an active interest in the Stockholm channel. In June 1995, Beilin and Feisal Husseini took part in a meeting of both mentors and participants in Sweden. Two meetings between Beilin and Abu Mazin took place in Israel after the latter had relocated from Tunis, but these did not involve any direct negotiations over the Stockholm understandings.

Beilin does not appear to have been totally dedicated to the four-sided Stockholm talks as the sole channel for a "final status" agreement. While the Stockholm talks were in full swing, he sought to keep his options open elsewhere. He held discussions with other senior Palestinian leaders regarding possible solutions to the various "final status" issues. One discussion also took place in Sweden in mid-February 1995 between Beilin, Nabil Shaath, and General Abd al-Razzak Yihya, the PLO's chief military adviser and negotiator. Another meeting among the three took place in Jerusalem on April 11, in the presence of Sten Andersson and Pierre Schori from Sweden. But these single meetings did not develop into a process. It became more difficult to arrange meetings between Palestinian leaders and Beilin outside Israel once he became minister of planning in July 1995. In his new capacity, he was required to obtain the government's authorization for any trip abroad.

Abu Mazin's role as mentor of the Stockholm channel differed from that of Beilin and was also different from his role at Oslo. He was now driven by a sense of historical purpose: from his perspective he had started an incomplete process at Oslo and he now wanted to see it through to fruition. He felt that this was both his duty and his political legacy to the Palestinian movement.[4] Unlike Beilin, Abu Mazin did not see the need for the involvement of a wider outside circle, nor did he feel the pressure to consult with any "Party" constituency. Since the Stockholm talks were not in any way formal negotiations, Abu Mazin also did not feel it incumbent upon himself to put his weight behind every item in the discussions. Also unlike in the case of Oslo, no inner "cell" within the PLO leadership was developed or designated to follow and supervise the Stockholm talks. This was also meant to preserve some leeway for the leadership and to maintain a credible buffer of deniability.

Whereas Hirschfeld and Pundik worked with and under Beilin, Agha and Khalidi worked largely independently and without constant refer-

---

4.   This was made clear by Abu Mazin to Agha and Khalidi in private talks in early 1995: "After this I will retire from politics, " he said.

ence to Abu Mazin or others in the Palestinian leadership. Not operating formally on behalf of the PLO, the Palestinian team thus had a wider mandate and was often able to develop its lead positions without the need for continuous consultation or supervision by the leadership. This was in part a function of the implicit trust between the Palestinian team and its command, but it also reflected Abu Mazin's hands-off style: interested and well-informed about the details but willing to micromanage negotiations only when absolutely necessary (which did not happen in this case).

As the Stockholm talks progressed, the mentors' standing with regard to the final product was crystallized. Although the understanding was later labeled the "Abu Mazin–Beilin agreement," the two mentors never negotiated, drafted, wrote, or planned to sign the working papers. Instead, they intended to take what had been agreed upon by the four participants to their respective leaders—Peres and Rabin on the one side, and Arafat on the other—in order to persuade them that the ideas could be adopted as the basis and starting point for further intense negotiations. This procedure provided the mentors with a measure of deniability, as neither Beilin nor Abu Mazin were formally committed to the content of the document. The status of the paper was intended to be similar to that of the draft negotiated in Oslo in February 1993, just prior to the involvement of Peres and Rabin in the Oslo process. In Norway, it had taken six additional months of detailed negotiations to translate the February draft to the agreement initialed in Oslo on August 18 and signed in Washington a few weeks later.

Leaders: Arafat, Rabin, and Peres

As of late 1993—just after Oslo and before the Stockholm talks—Rabin and Peres both evinced interest in developing some of the ideas that were put to the Palestinians at Stockholm, and they were party to Yossi Beilin's internal deliberations on these issues.[5] Certainly, many of Rabin's public pronouncements regarding the contours of a final settlement during 1995 seemed to echo the discussions at Stockholm. As a number of late-1995 interviews in the Israeli media indicate, Rabin had already begun to enunciate publicly his position on the need to maintain settlement blocs (mentioning specifically Gush Etzion and Ma'ale Adumim, but interestingly not the major settlement of Ariel) and to preserve the Jordan River

---

5. See the detailed report by Steve Rodan in the *Jerusalem Post Weekly*, October 10, 1993.

valley as a "security" border (but not necessarily as Israeli sovereign territory), as well as the "unity" of Jerusalem. His position on a Palestinian state was deliberately noncommittal, leaving room for maneuver. For the Palestinian leadership and Stockholm team, this seemed to corroborate their assumption that Rabin affected and was influenced by the discussions held in Stockholm.

It remains unclear whether Israel's intelligence community alerted Peres and Rabin about the Stockholm talks. Given the recurring visits to Israel made by the two Palestinian participants in the talks, it is highly unlikely that the Stockholm process remained totally unnoticed by Israel's General Security Services (GSS). It cannot be demonstrated for certain that Rabin was informed of the talks, but there is sufficient circumstantial evidence to suggest that he may have decided to allow them to proceed with the option of embracing or rejecting their results at a later stage. Be that as it may, Rabin's assassination aborted the Stockholm process before a critical stage of negotiations regarding the "final status" issues could take place. While the psychological breakthrough created by the Oslo accords produced a political environment that was conducive to the success of the Stockholm talks, Rabin's assassination altered the domestic Israeli political environment, preventing the hope embodied in the Stockholm document from being materialized.

Shimon Peres, who succeeded Rabin as prime minister, did not believe he enjoyed the support of the Israeli public for another daring move *vis-à-vis* the Palestinians. He preferred to focus on implementing the interim agreement with the Palestinians and to explore the possibilities of reaching a declaration of principles with Syria as a step toward resolving the two countries' dispute. Consequently, Peres did not embrace Beilin's suggestion that the Stockholm understandings could be used as the basis for accelerated Israeli-Palestinian final status negotiations.

Instead of forging ahead toward another dramatic breakthrough in the peace process, Peres now preferred to proceed cautiously and to adopt a tougher line that might reestablish his credibility as a leader who could be entrusted with Israel's security. He soon became engulfed by a series of suicide bombings carried out by Islamic militants in Tel Aviv and Jerusalem, as well as by an ill-conceived Israeli military operation deep inside Lebanon ("Operation Grapes of Wrath"). His defeat in the June 1996 elections was a final blow to the chance that the Stockholm understandings would serve as a readily available basis for negotiations aimed at resolving the Israeli-Palestinian dispute.

When Beilin gave Prime Minister Peres a detailed account of the Stockholm talks on November 11, 1995, Peres objected to the substance of what he heard on several grounds.[6] First, he argued that the Jerusalem issue remained unresolved and could thus lead to future tensions between the two sides. Furthermore, Peres' own vision of a Jerusalem settlement was based on a religious rather than political formula and was centered on the Islamic holy sites. Second, he objected to the fact that no role had been allocated to Jordan—this at a time when Peres was very keen to involve the Jordanians in a final peace settlement based on the notion of a confederation between Jordan and the West Bank. Third, the Israeli leader viewed the security arrangements along the Jordan Valley as unsatisfactory. Fourth, he seems to have believed that a better deal could be achieved for Israel through other channels. Peres believed that working with his own preferred team, he could get a more favorable deal for Israel.[7]

Beilin's relations with Peres became somewhat less intimate after Rabin had appointed him as a full cabinet minister in the summer of 1995, and Peres was also upset that Beilin had not informed him of the Stockholm track before. His ire was compounded by the revelation—after taking office—that Rabin had shut him out of developments on the Syrian track. He had only just been informed that the slain Israeli leader had apparently communicated his readiness to make sweeping territorial concessions on the Golan in return for a full peace treaty with Syria, including normalization and security arrangements. Peres therefore believed that the Syrian track was potentially close to fruition. In such a context, he may have felt that a "final status" accord with the Palestinians could wait, especially given the certain controversial and internally divisive effect it would have. In the aftermath of Rabin's assassination, it may have seemed unwise to deepen the already dangerous rifts in Israeli society.

Finally and perhaps most importantly, Peres did not believe that accepting the Stockholm understandings would enhance his prospects of victory in the upcoming Israeli elections, thus largely negating the purpose for which the understandings had been designed. Despite his efforts, Beilin was unable to convince Peres that a Labor Party adoption of such a program would appeal to the Israeli public by ending the uncer-

---

6. See Beilin.

7. During the period 1994–95 (i.e. contemporaneously with the Stockholm channel), Peres had been working through Oslo negotiator Uri Savir with King Hassan of Morocco, in an attempt to develop a religious formula for the Holy sites acceptable to three Arab Kings: Hassan of Morocco, Hussein of Jordan, and Fahd of Saudi Arabia. This was meant to pre-empt any attempt by Arafat to push for a political solution to Jerusalem. See report by Akiva Eldar in *Ha'aretz*, July 26, 1999.

tainty about the future with the Palestinians and posing a clear alternative to the negative visions of Likud.[8] Whatever the underlying calculations, Peres effectively shelved the Stockholm understandings and proceeded to give utmost priority to a Golan settlement. Soon after he took office, Israeli-Syrian talks resumed at Wye River under U.S. auspices, and continued throughout late 1995 and early 1996. This process finally ground to a halt with the Hamas bombings in March and the killing of Lebanese civilians who had taken refuge in a UN compound in Qana, Lebanon, in April 1996, during Operation Grapes of Wrath.

On the Palestinian side, Abu Mazin and Arafat knew about the Stockholm channel from the start. Arafat insisted that the channel be entrusted to the exclusive direction of Abu Mazin and that its existence be kept highly confidential. For his part, Abu Mazin checked and verified developments in the channel throughout its work. By November 1995, after a briefing by the Palestinian team and the Swedes, the PLO leadership considered the work done at Stockholm as an adequate starting point for subsequent formal negotiations. The PLO was thus awaiting news of a go-ahead from Rabin and Peres when Rabin was assassinated.

The Stockholm understandings addressed the needs of the Palestinian leadership. From Arafat's point of view, the understandings provided for a number of vital achievements: First, up-front Israeli recognition of the establishment of a fully sovereign independent Palestinian State with full control over its own borders. Second, a political presence in Jerusalem and eventual full sovereignty in the Arab areas of the city. Third, no net loss of land. The 5 percent of the West Bank that was to be annexed by Israel would be compensated by the addition of an equal area of Israeli territory to the Palestinian state. Fourth, the establishment of territorial integrity and continuity between the two Palestinian areas: An extraterritorial passage was to be created between Gaza and the West Bank, while there was to be no Israeli extraterritorial presence or settlements in Palestinian areas. Fifth, an acceptable resolution of the refugee issue was to be implemented, with no renouncement of the "right of return" and an unhindered return of refugees to the Palestinian State. Finally, the immediate transfer of responsibility over the Christian and Muslim Holy sites in Jerusalem to the Palestinian state.

The PLO was also well aware that the Stockholm understandings had been formulated so as to be acceptable to Rabin and form the basis of the Labor Party's political platform for the 1996 elections. The Israeli side be-

---

8.   It is worth recording, however, that in briefings on the Stockholm understandings after the elections, senior Netanyahu advisors voiced their belief that the understandings could have helped Labor win the elections, had they been adopted at the time.

lieved that the understandings would satisfy Rabin's declared "red lines" in the following manner: First, the understanding provided for Israeli annexation of approximately 5 percent of the West Bank along the Green line and thus would meet Rabin's pledge not to return to the 1967 lines. Second, Jerusalem would remain physically undivided. Third, the Jordan Valley would be retained as the security borders of Israel—namely, military forces would not be stationed west of the Jordan River—and Israel would maintain a military presence—but not sovereignty—along the Jordan Valley for an agreed limited period. Fourth, Israeli settlements would not be uprooted forcibly and the settlements where a majority of the settlers reside would be annexed to Israel. Finally, the refugee problem would be settled and the refugees would be dealt with in an international context with Israeli participation.

The muted reaction of the Palestinian leadership to Israeli press reports about the Stockholm talks in February 1996, and their denial of the existence of any agreement with Israel, was largely due to the nature of the product itself. First, the understandings were formulated as a working paper that was not finalized and that needed extensive further work and elaboration. Clearly, the document had no formal or official status and in no circumstances could it be construed as an agreement. Second, the understandings were intended to serve as the basis for a Labor Party election platform to which the Palestinians did not object. This platform could then constitute the starting point for future negotiations. In this sense, the Stockholm understandings—as they stood in November 1995 —were seen by the PLO as more of an Israeli than a Palestinian concern.

But there were other reasons for the Palestinians' silence after the Stockholm understandings were reported in the press. The Palestinian leadership was especially concerned about the manner in which Beilin subsequently seemed to be appropriating the talks for his own political purposes. Abu Mazin in particular was unhappy with any suggestion that the so-called "Abu Mazin–Beilin agreement" had received official PLO sanction of any kind. Abu Mazin was also deeply disturbed by any suggestion that the PLO was ready to accept the Arab suburb of Abu Dis as a substitute for Arab East Jerusalem as its capital—as implied by Beilin. Perhaps more than any other, this issue served to devalue the potential utility of the Stockholm talks in Palestinian eyes and increased the pressure on Abu Mazin and other members of the PLO leadership to formally distance themselves from the understandings.

Nonetheless, Abu Mazin refrained from any overt attack on Beilin or the Stockholm channel. For one thing, it was felt that such attacks would only give credence to the growing speculation about the Stockholm talks and would merely lead to mutual recriminations and public disagreements between the two sides. Given Abu Mazin's polite public persona and his genuine appreciation for Beilin's political courage and his vital role in leading the peace camp within the Israeli Labor Party, it was felt that such attacks would be self-defeating and counterproductive. The fact that as a Track-II exercise the Stockholm understandings did not commit either side to anything also allowed the Palestinians to avoid reacting to Beilin's assertions. A possible unilateral Palestinian endorsement or even comment on the talks—at a time when the Israeli side had shunned the understandings—would have been both gratuitous and politically foolhardy. Finally, it was felt that the understandings would in any case retain their value until a credible Israeli interlocutor appeared. Without such an interlocutor, the elaboration of any further public position on Stockholm was unnecessary.

Sponsors

The initial decision to sponsor the Stockholm talks was made by Sweden's Minister of Foreign Affairs Margaretha af Ugglas. Ann Dismorr, then assisting af Ugglas at the Ministry, was charged with overseeing the talks. Af Ugglas had rapidly approved the project after Eliot Goldberg of the Search for Common Ground had arranged for Hussein Agha to approach Dismorr on the fringes of a Search meeting on the Middle East, sponsored by the Swedes in Stockholm in June 1994. Following this approval, the government of Sweden agreed to arrange for the meetings of the two teams. Indeed, the government took every precaution to ensure the participants' safety and the secrecy of the talks. Upon their arrival in Sweden for each round of talks, the participants were met at the plane and were taken directly to the location of the talks. Located mostly outside Stockholm, the facilities were surrounded by security personnel.

One of the first agreements reached between the participants stipulated that the Swedish hosts would be briefed periodically regarding the progress made in the discussions. The reports received by the highest echelons of the Ministry of Foreign Affairs later contributed to their assessment that the progress made would allow the talks to become the main venue for Palestinian-Israeli "final status" negotiations.

There were a number of contrasts between the role of the sponsors in the Oslo and Stockholm talks. In Oslo, FAFO, a nongovernmental organization, provided the initial umbrella for the talks, but the talks were largely hosted by Norway's Ministry of Foreign Affairs. In Sweden, the reverse took place. While the project was initially sponsored solely by the Ministry of Foreign Affairs, the Stockholm-based Olof Palme International Center, headed by former Foreign Minister Sten Andersson, later assumed cosponsorship of the talks. This happened after the 1994 Swedish general elections and the resulting change in government.

The second difference was that the role of the Swedish government in the talks never surpassed that of a sponsor. Because of their informal nature, the Stockholm talks never suffered the repeated "official" crises experienced by the Oslo talks. Nonetheless, there were occasional strong disagreements resulting in sharp and heated exchanges. During such moments of tension, the Swedish sponsors played an inestimable role in clearing the atmosphere and reestablishing confidence between the two sides. Still, their involvement was much less intense than their Norwegian counterparts' had been.

The Swedish team's dedication and consummate diplomatic skills allowed for the management of even the gravest crisis in the talks. Sten Andersson's experience and commitment to Middle East peace was a source of constant reassurance to the two teams. His strong personal relations with Arafat also was a vital reinforcement for the talks. Ann Dismorr (later to become Swedish ambassador to Lebanon and then Turkey) was also to play a crucial role as coordinator of the project and was always ready to suggest ways out of perceived difficulties. Experienced diplomat Mikael Dahl also played a supporting role at the earlier stages. Sven-Eric Söder, a veteran of Palestinian-Swedish NGO relations and director of the Palme Institute (and later state secretary for Nordic cooperation) brought his experience to bear to ensure the success of the later stages of the project.

But vital as it was, the Swedish role never exceeded its agreed brief and remained primarily one of moral and material support and facilitation. In contrast to the role of Johan Holst in the Oslo process, Sweden's top officials never intervened as mediators on issues of substance and never attempted to impose their views or preferred solutions on the two sides. As hosts and sponsors, the Swedes were exemplary and left a lasting positive impression on both the Israeli and the Palestinian Stockholm teams and their respective leaderships.

Although the experience of 1988 (which led to the U.S-PLO dialogue) was important in engaging the Swedes in 1994–1995, other considerations also played a role in leading to their involvement. Sweden had a traditionally high moral and political profile in the Middle East and a history of involvement in Middle East mediation dating back to Count Bernadotte's UN reconciliation mission and his assassination in 1948. The Swedish Labor Party's support for Israel; its strong links with the Israeli Labor Party; and its support for a resolution of the Palestinian-Israeli conflict based on recognition of Palestinian rights and an Israeli dialogue with the PLO placed the new Swedish government in a strong position to play a constructive role with both sides after 1994. Having passed the baton to Norway after 1991, Sweden was now ready to resume its natural role.

The Stockholm project required a constant Swedish presence with the mentors on both sides. Andersson, Dismorr, and other officials were frequent visitors to the Palestinian and Israeli leaderships as the project progressed. As part of the broader strategy for ensuring the project's success, it was envisaged that the Swedes would play a crucial part in mobilizing support for any agreement reached and that they would take the lead in briefing and eliciting a positive response from major players such as the United States and the European Union. Although this aspect of the Swedish role was never put to the test, it was evident that the sponsor's role would exceed mere facilitation once an agreement had been reached, and that it was to comprise a direct and important part of the implementation process. For instance, both sides understood that Sweden would be invited to take a leading role in the international effort to resolve the Palestinian refugee problem once the parties reached a formal understanding on such a resolution.

Summary

The Stockholm talks constituted a pure "hard" Track-II venue. It was "pure" in that it was conducted on both sides by scholars who were independent and well connected to their respective leaderships. It was "hard" in the sense that it aimed to reach closure on the most difficult and hypersensitive issues at dispute between Israelis and Palestinians, such as the future of Jerusalem, Israeli settlements, and the fate of the Palestinian refugees.

The Stockholm talks also provided the most telling testimony of the potential utility of Track-II venues for conflict resolution: in the prevailing circumstances of 1994–1995, such a far-reaching understanding on the most contentious issues still dividing Palestinians and Israelis would have been very difficult to achieve in formal negotiation sessions. The exercise also demonstrated the significance of mentors—Yossi Beilin on the Israeli side and Abu Mazin on the Palestinian side—who proved their critical importance in guiding the talks. To the extent that the so-called "Abu Mazin–Beilin agreement" became the basis for the later "Beilin-Eitan document," the Israeli mentor proved critical to transforming the results of the Stockholm talks to a new consensus supporting the peace process within Israel.

Yet the Stockholm talks also illustrated the limitations of Track-II venues. As with other aspects of the Arab-Israeli peace process, the talks were susceptible to the impact of external developments—primarily, in this case, the assassination of Israel's Prime Minister Rabin. Because of the informal nature and standing of the exercise, the Stockholm talks were exceptionally vulnerable. Newly appointed Prime Minister Peres refused to accept the understandings reached as the basis for further progress and thus essentially blocked the potential of the talks as another dramatic milestone in the Arab-Israeli peace process.

Moreover, since the results of the talks were never fully published in an authoritative form, it is difficult to ascertain what their impact might have been had the exercise come to fruition. This is primarily due to the ambiguity surrounding some of the understandings reached. The Palestinian interpretation is that their Israeli interlocutors agreed that Israel would accept some responsibility for the refugee problem; and that although sovereignty over parts of East Jerusalem would be phased over a period of time, the Palestinians would eventually regain sovereignty over all parts of "Arab Jerusalem." It is not certain that Rabin would have accepted these concessions as a basis for "final status" negotiations.

Chapter 6

Project "Charlie": Israeli Settlers and the Palestinians

One of the most interesting of the bilateral Middle East Track-II talks that took place during the past decade was the discussions held in 1994–1995 between Israeli settlers in the West Bank and senior officials of the Palestinian Authority and the PLO. Joseph Alpher, then director of the Middle East Office of the American Jewish Committee, organized the project, which was code-named "Charlie." The American Jewish Committee thus became the first mainstream U.S. Jewish organization to become involved in Arab-Israeli Track-II talks. Held in Europe and Jerusalem, the meetings were funded by concerned individuals contacted by Alpher. Altogether, seven meetings were held within this framework, mostly in mid-1995.

To the Israeli public, members of the settlers' community—who were widely viewed as holding the most extreme views on Israeli-Palestinian affairs—were the least likely candidates for such talks. Not surprisingly, press reports revealing that the talks had taken place were met with general astonishment and with sharp criticism within this community.[1] In-

---

1.   First details of the talks were published in April 1996. The Israeli participants refused to comment, but according to Alpher: "The project involved an effort to establish some acquaintance between senior members of two populations that circumstances have transformed into neighbors. The talks did not comprise political negotiations but rather an effort to understand one another's ideological motivations. The purpose was to explore each party's room for flexibility as the Palestinian auton-

deed, the settlers who took part in the talks did not inform the leaders of the political parties closest to them—the Likud and the National Religious Party (NRP)—that such discussions were being held. Driven by compelling reasons of their own, the Israeli participants "bypassed" their political leaders and made direct contact with their archenemies: officials of the PLO and the Palestinian Authority (PA) who had been previously regarded as terrorists. The Israeli government was not involved in Project "Charlie." However, the talks' sponsor provided written reports on the progress made to Rabin's military secretary, Major General Danny Yatom. Copies of the reports were also distributed within Israel's intelligence community.

The Political Environment

The Oslo Declaration of Principles shocked the Israeli settlers' community. Project "Charlie" could not have taken place had the Israeli settlers in the West Bank and Gaza not felt themselves to be under severe pressure as a consequence of the Oslo agreements. When the first phase of the process was implemented in 1994 and Yasser Arafat established his headquarters in Gaza, many settlers became convinced that the peace process was gaining momentum and that the agreement would soon be implemented in the West Bank as well. This new reality forced these settlers to think the unthinkable: that control of the territory on which their settlements are located might be transferred to the PA.

At the same time, the settlers involved in the talks felt that they could not depend on the leaders of the right-wing political parties such as Likud and the NRP to address their concerns in a satisfactory way. Hence, they concluded that they should explore some issues with Palestinian officials directly. As a result, they took a step that the right-wing political leadership was not willing to take prior to the 1996 elections: direct talks with the PA. Clearly, the settlers involved did not expect the Labor party to lose the 1996 elections. They seem to have assumed that the party that achieved the Oslo accords would retain power and would form Israel's next government for the following four years.

One purpose of the Israeli participants in the talks was "to get to know the enemy"—to ascertain for themselves the plans of the Palestinian Authority and to explore whether it was possible to form continuous

---

omy is taking roots and when different possibilities related to the "final status" negotiations must be considered." See *Ha'aretz*, April 7, 1996.

contact with PA officials despite the ideological divide. The settlers were also interested in assessing whether it was possible to reach some understanding with the PA on "red lines"—limitations that both sides would adopt in the event that clashes between them may occur, with the purpose of preventing their spread and minimizing the damage incurred. The settlers wanted to know whom to speak to in the PA so that they would not be dependent on the Israeli government or the IDF after its expected withdrawal from the territory was implemented.

The settlers taking part in the talks knew that reactions within the settler community would be extremely sharp and that a heated debate would result were the talks with the PA to be revealed. They knew that many of their comrades—committed to Israel's right to settle in all parts of the "land of Israel," would regard the decision to communicate directly with PA security officials as a sell-out—an act bordering on ideological treason and as a sign of willingness to accept an "immoral reality" that had been forced upon them.

For their part, the Palestinians regarded the Israeli settlements as one of the most significant obstacles to peace and as an ever-growing danger to the emergence of a territorially and politically viable Palestinian entity. With the possible onset of final status talks slated to commence in May 1996 according to the Oslo accords, the Palestinian side was aware of the need to find practical solutions to the settlement problem in both the short and long terms. The Palestinians were also aware that any Israeli government that attempted a forced evacuation of settlements might be faced with severe internal divisions, possibly leading to serious civil disturbances and bloodshed, and that though many Israelis were critical of the settlers and their behavior, they would be opposed to their forcible displacement. Consequently, the Palestinian side seems to have concluded that it was possible that some Israeli settlers would remain within the territory of the Palestinian entity or state even after a peace treaty was signed and the IDF's withdrawal was implemented.

The PA representatives were additionally concerned that friction between the settlers and the Palestinian population might increase as the IDF began to withdraw from the West Bank before a final settlement. Indeed, a number of Israeli press reports at the time indicated that the settlers were prepared to obstruct the implementation of the agreements reached between Israel and the PA and to attack PA personnel and members of the Palestinian police forces. Given these circumstances, the PA was interested in becoming acquainted with the settlers and in ascertaining what they intended to do and how they intended to behave during the next phases of the peace process. The PA also wanted to find out whether there was some basis for an ongoing dialogue with the settlers and to explore the limits of such a dialogue.

In sum, the anxieties of both the Israeli settlers and the PA during the initial phases of implementing the Oslo agreements created a shared perception that there was ample reason to meet. Moreover, the settlers and the PA had a common interest in exploring whether there was a basis for ongoing engagement on tactical issues to prevent bloodshed and superfluous clashes, a reflection of post-Oslo optimism later largely destroyed by the second intifada of 2000.

The Project "Charlie" talks made clear that the existing Israeli settlements were a major bone of contention between the two sides, and that they were a major obstacle facing the implementation of the Oslo DOP and any Israeli-Palestinian peace agreement. At the time, the Palestinian participants did not oppose the notion that Israeli settlers could reside in territories *as individuals* under the control of the PA after a peace settlement, but they strongly rejected the possibility that settlements could remain there as exclusive blocs or *extraterritorial enclaves.* They were also willing to accept the continued existence of towns such as Kiryat Arba, near Hebron, with the vital precondition that they not remain purely Jewish residential areas. Instead, they argued that such towns should be integrated as mixed towns with Arab municipalities. The Palestinian side also raised the issue of reciprocity and asked whether Israel would accept the right of Palestinians to reside in Israel *as individuals,* as part of a final status agreement.

The Israeli settlers rejected the Oslo accords, arguing that the Israeli government, not the Israeli people, had signed the accords. The settlers argued that were the Palestinians to win sovereignty over the territories it would be necessary to take measures to defuse the "traumatic situations" that might develop between Israelis and Palestinians and possibly within Israel as well. Some of the settlers stressed their desire to coexist with the Palestinians peacefully but only under Israeli sovereignty. But it was of particular interest to the Palestinian side to hear from their interlocutors of the possibility that some may be willing to accept staying within a Palestinian state as long as they could live a "Jewish life" under Palestinian rule. From this perspective even the "ideological" settlers did not appear homogeneous.

Nonetheless, the settlers noted an ideological motivation to engage in the talks: the need to explain Israel's "moral right" to settle in Judea and Samaria—not only the political, economic, and security rationale for establishing such settlements. In addition, they were moved by the desire to hear "the other party's story" and to ascertain whether the other side understands the Israelis' own "moral story" and their right to a sovereign state.[2] Also of note was the deep antagonism shown by the settlers toward the Israeli left-liberal peace camp and their perception of an internal ideological war with the left, not only over the fate of the territories occupied in 1967 but over the very ethos of the state of Israel.

On the practical side, at the prompting of Alpher the parties discussed the possibility of establishing a "hot line" that would connect the PA leadership with leaders of the settlers' community. The "hot line" would be used to save lives by helping to avoid incidents that might result from misunderstandings and by preventing the escalation of such incidents. But this idea failed to elicit the support of either side; both preferred to maintain indirect means of contact and to regard Alpher himself as an adequate if ad hoc "hot line."

The settlers also raised the issues involved in travel arrangements for Israelis within the territory that would be transferred to the PA's control.

Another possibility discussed was that representatives of each party would be given the opportunity to appear in public forums of the other party in order to explain their points of view. The Palestinian participants accepted this suggestion. However, Alpher's attempt to draw up an agreed code of conduct between the two sides was not met with any enthusiasm by either side.

The meetings between the Israeli settlers and the representatives of the PA stopped in December 1995. Although there was no formal agreement to end the talks, they were never resumed. This was less the result of either side's deliberate decision to disengage, and more a reflection of three developments that affected the prospects of reviving the talks: First, the election of a Likud-led government in May 1996 made the settlers less anxious about their future and hence no longer convinced that a dialogue with the PA was an urgent imperative. Second, the Israeli participants in the talks were embarrassed by the newspaper reports of the talks. Indeed, the revelation that talks between Israeli settlers and representatives of the PA had taken place sparked a sharp debate within the settlers' community as well as within the "Council of Judea, Samara, and Gaza," the umbrella organization of all Israeli settlements in the territories. Finally, the wave of suicide bombings carried out by Hamas in Tel Aviv and Jerusalem in February and March 1996 created an atmosphere that was not conducive to the continuation of such talks.

---

2. See Joseph Ben-Shlomo's subsequent account of the meetings in *Ha'aretz*, July 2, 1997.

Participants

In preparing themselves for the talks, the settlers took care to ensure that they would minimize their exposure and vulnerability should the talks become known. This required, first, that the composition of the group be as representative as possible of the settlers' community at large. Second, it was felt that the group should include people of high standing in the community and some spiritual leaders, including a rabbi. Third, it was felt that the group should include "men of action" who could not be labeled by other settlers as "soft."

The Palestinian participants initially included non-officials linked to the PLO, and PA officials at a later stage. By contrast, the Israelis taking part in the talks were private individuals who were linked neither to the official establishment nor to the party in government. Rather, they belonged to a community considered "in opposition" to Israel's elected government. This representation did not change throughout the talks—at no stage were party or government officials involved on the Israeli side. Moreover, while the Palestinian participants in the meetings spoke authoritatively about the PA's approach and plans, the Israeli participants represented the settler community only in a general sense. They were not authorized by the official governing bodies of the settlements to engage in such a dialogue. Although they acted as a group, they spoke as private individuals. Nevertheless, given their high standing in the settler community, their views carried considerable weight.

The process of choosing Israeli representatives to the talks was complex. Those who first agreed to take part insisted on expanding the circle of participants so that if the talks were revealed they could claim that the initiative did not represent the private whims of a few individuals. They also wanted to ensure that if the exercise was exposed, they would not be portrayed as a small rogue group that was seeking publicity at the expense of the settlers' cause.

One of the main architects of the talks was Israel Harel from the settlement of Ofra. Harel was one of the founders of Gush Emunim (the original settlers' movement), and a former chairman of the Council of Judea, Samaria, and Gaza, as well as a former editor of the settlers' journal, *Nekuda*. Other Israeli participants included Uri Elizur, then editor of *Nekuda*; Professor Joseph Ben-Shlomo from the settlement of Kedumim, another founder of Gush Emunim and one of the ideologues of the first settlers; Rabbi Avraham Waldman from Kiryat Arba, a member of Gush Emunim who was widely considered by the settlers as a rabbinical authority; and Professor Ozer Schild of Kedumim, a former president of Haifa University.

Following the Likud victory in the 1996 Israeli elections, and a few months after the first newspaper report of the talks was published, Ben-Shlomo published a detailed account of the talks. By then, the settlers viewed the political environment as having changed dramatically, making talks with representatives of the PA less urgent. The account revealed that the settlers taking part in the talks were promised that reports of their discussions would be conveyed only to Prime Minister Rabin and his military secretary. This implies that the settler-participants were not interested in the transmission of such reports to the leaders of Likud. It probably also reflected their assessment that they were better able to conduct the talks—especially to represent the ideological thinking that led to the establishment of the settlements—than was Likud itself. Clearly, they were also convinced that they could represent their interests better than Israel's Labor-led government could.

The Palestinian participants in the talks were motivated by their own desire "to get to know the enemy." Previously, the Palestinian side had considered the settlers as off-limits. Although many Palestinians were employed in the settlements as laborers, there had been no prior *political* contacts between the settler leaders and senior Palestinian or PA representatives. For the majority of Palestinians, the settlers were perceived as the most vocal opponents of the Oslo process; they represented the most extreme elements in Israel and favored the continuous occupation, annexation, or both, of the West Bank. They were also seen as the most dangerous pressure group—perfectly capable of resorting to violence to achieve their aims. Many Palestinian civilians had been shot by settlers—armed and free to travel the roads of the West Bank—who had taken matters into their own hands.

The Palestinians initially taking part in the talks included non-officials Yezid Sayigh, Ahmad Khalidi, and Khalil Shikaki, all of whom had taken part in the AAAS talks. Soon after these first contacts, and despite the virtues of an exchange of existential and ideological concerns, the initial Palestinian participants felt that Project "Charlie" would be of very limited utility if there were no direct exchange and dialogue between the settler representatives and the PLO and the PA. Hence, the non-officials contacted the PA and suggested that the matter be pursued on a more formal basis and with greater relevance to the situation on the ground.

The PA responded positively by sending Sufian Abu-Zaydeh, head of the PA's Israel affairs department, to the first meeting outside Israel. Later, Hassan Asfour, a participant in the Oslo and Stockholm talks who was then director of the PLO's negotiations department, and Colonel Muhammed Dahlan, director of Palestinian preventive security in Gaza, attended other meetings in Israel as a token of the PA's seriousness and its readiness to test the other sides' credibility. Once the non-officials completed their role as participants in the initial phase of the talks, they voluntarily withdrew from the project once it began to center on political practicalities.

Sponsors

At the margins of the AAAS talks on Israeli-Palestinian security arrangements, two Palestinian participants accepted a suggestion by Israeli participants Joseph Alpher and Zeev Schiff that they visit settlements and meet with settlers. At first, the leaders of the settlers who were contacted to arrange such visits and meetings expressed fear of a political trap—a leak that would embarrass the settlers by showing that they were doing what they vowed never to do. Eventually, the curiosity of the settler leaders overcame their fear, but to diminish the risks entailed they decided that the settlers participating in the meeting should be second-echelon leaders. Project "Charlie" grew out of this meeting, which took place in April 1994 in Kedumim.

Kedumim is one of the first Israeli settlements in the urban areas of the West Bank and was the focus of a dramatic struggle between the settlers and the first Rabin government (1974–1977). It was there that the settlers registered one of their greatest victories when the Rabin government —under pressure from its then-hawkish Defense Minister Shimon Peres—accepted their demands and allowed them to stay where they had settled without permission.

The first meeting clearly aroused the curiosity of both sides. The conversation was held primarily between the Palestinian side and the settlers who hosted the meeting. Gazit, Alpher, and Schiff—the three Israeli participants in the AAAS talks—deliberately kept a low profile in order to let the two sides exchange views without interruption, as did the U.S. representatives of the AAAS. The discussion focused on each party's perceptions of future relations between them; on exploring whether there was any mutually acceptable resolution of the conflict; and whether either side had a realizable political plan. However, the meeting did not have any concrete results.

A follow-up to the first encounter appeared useful to both sides. In 1994, Alpher had become head of the Middle East Office of the American Jewish Committee. Given the further progress made in the peace process and the expected transfer of Israeli control over the West Bank to the PA, Alpher became convinced that meetings between Israeli settlers and PA leaders had become even more urgent. Based on his experience in helping arrange for the first settlers' meeting, he persuaded the Committee leadership in New York to grant him the unprecedented permission to host more meetings between Israeli settlers and PA-associated Palestinians.

The initial meeting under Alpher's direct sponsorship, which eventually led to Project "Charlie," took place in Israel in June 1994 between Yezid Sayigh and Israel Harel. At first, Alpher did not report to the Israeli authorities his intention to hold meetings between settlers and senior Palestinian officials. Nor did he inform them that the first such meeting had taken place. The June meeting resulted in a decision to attempt an expanded meeting between representatives from the two parties in November. However, the projected November meeting was postponed after a suicide bombing carried out in the center of Tel Aviv by a Hamas militant made it untenable.

The process was relaunched a few months later. Most of the meetings took place at the Jerusalem offices of the American Jewish Committee but the first formal contact between the settlers and a PA official took place in England, at the Foundation for International Security premises at Adderbury, near Oxford—the same venue used earlier in Israeli-Palestinian security contacts sponsored by AAAS. The American Jewish Committee funded the meetings in Jerusalem, while the meetings in England were financed by FIS. The meetings between the Israeli settlers and the representatives of the PA took place under conditions of strict secrecy. The code-name given to these talks—Project "Charlie"—was used in all correspondence and reports related to the talks, such as those provided to General Yatom.

Mentors and Leaders

In contrast to other Track-II talks described in this volume, Project "Charlie" had no political mentors or leadership input. The Israeli leadership was informed about the venue but remained unengaged. The PLO leadership was aware of the contacts, approved them, and was interested in their results, but did not see the settlers as potential partners in any real political sense. Dealing with the settlers was thus not the same as dealing with the Israeli government or its unofficial representatives in Oslo or Stockholm. The PLO did not seek recognition or acceptance as an interlocutor; indeed, it was very wary of being seen to confer such "legitimacy" on the Israeli settler community. Nonetheless, it was felt that contact with the settlers could help to manage the situation on the ground, impress upon the settlers the changing post-Oslo reality, and cause an ideological split among the settlers or between the settlers and the Israeli "right." For some on both the Israeli and Palestinian sides, these goals were largely achieved; indeed, it could be argued that having made contact with the PA, the settlers found it increasingly difficult to sustain credibly their political and ideological objections to subsequent dealings between the new Likud government and the PLO, which led to the Hebron accords in early 1997 and to the Wye River Memorandum in late 1998, which resulted in additional land being handed over to the PA.

Summary

Project "Charlie" was a classic "soft" Track-II exercise, since the participants did not enter the talks with a view to reaching a political deal, although a number of PA officials later joined the discussions, thus effectively transforming them into a Track-I½ venue. The purpose of the talks was to exchange views in order to better understand the other side and thus develop a more effective future policy toward it. There was also hope that increased understanding among the parties regarding their different perspectives might help them better manage their relations.

Clearly, in 1994 both parties approached the talks with the purpose of "know thine enemy" in mind. At most, the sponsors may have hoped that some tactical arrangements could be agreed upon that would prevent uncontrolled escalation and unnecessary violence. Some of the arrangements discussed were related to the settlers' ability to travel through the territories following their transfer to Palestinian control. Another issue concerned the settlers' behavior during the elections to the Palestinian Council. The Israeli settler community is widely perceived as the most radical, sharpest, and vocal opposition to the Israeli-Palestinian peace process. Hence, their willingness to engage responsible Palestinians in general, and officials of the PA in particular, was a revelation to both sides' constituencies.

The primary lesson of Project "Charlie" was that a modicum of self-interest may be sufficient to bring together even those parties that are deeply antagonistic toward each other. The establishment of a Track-II channel between opposite poles and sworn enemies such as the Israeli settlers and the Palestinian Authority demonstrated the potential use of Track-II talks for conflict management—if not conflict resolution.

Conversely, the talks also demonstrated that Track-II talks between sworn enemies are extremely vulnerable to media exposure. Given both sides' constituencies, the mere willingness to engage may be considered a major concession if not outright treason. Under such circumstances, support for the talks may be thin at best, exposing participants to extensive criticism. Thus, if Track-II discussions between two extreme poles are leaked, the resulting political turmoil and pressures can lead to an imme-diate termination of the talks.

Finally, the Project "Charlie" talks provide a good illustration of the importance of context. From the settlers' standpoint it made sense to con-duct the talks as long as Labor remained in power. In that setting, the working assumption of the settlers was that the peace process would con-tinue and that, consequently, they were likely to soon find themselves di-rectly affected—if not actually controlled—by the PA. As long as this seemed to be the dominant trend, it made sense to engage the PA in a quiet dialogue, if only to ascertain the latter's intentions and views re-garding possible developments.

Once Likud returned to power, this context—at least in the settlers' eyes—changed completely. During its first two years in office, the Netanyahu government did not seem to be interested in any further transfer of West Bank territory to Palestinian control. It seemed, at least temporarily, that the settlers' worst nightmare would not materialize. Since it was this nightmare that prompted the settlers to engage the Pal-estinians in dialogue in the first place, the changed context meant that it was no longer necessary to continue the exercise. Once the talks were leaked, the new context led to their immediate termination.

While the political environment of 1995–1996 may have allowed for an initial if limited Palestinian-settler dialogue, subsequent develop-ments have made it unlikely that such a dialogue will be resumed in the near future. The continued expansion of Israeli settlements after 1993 led to a virtual doubling of the settler population by the outbreak of the sec-ond *intifada* in late 2000, aggravating Palestinian grievances against the settlers and the Oslo process as a whole. Indeed, for many Palestinians the continued expansion of settlements ultimately seemed to negate the positive achievements of the entire Oslo process.

After September 2000, Palestinian-settler clashes and a mounting Pal-estinian armed campaign against West Bank and Gaza settlers helped to raise mutual hatred to new heights. With the second *intifada*, the settle-ment problem took on yet sharper and more intractable dimensions, and Palestinian attitudes hardened considerably toward any form of settler presence on Palestinian soil. The settlers' sense of besiegement and Pales-tinian hostility have been exacerbated, suggesting that the settlement is-sue will be much less amenable to future Track-II exercises, and may only be resolvable—if at all—within the framework of an overall political so-lution to the Palestinian-Israeli conflict.

Chapter 7

Israeli-Syrian Talks under Search for Common Ground

Israeli-Syrian discussions held from 1992 to 1993 proved to be one of the most difficult of Middle East Track-II talks. This reflected the general intractability of the two countries' dispute. Not surprisingly, the gap manifested in the Israeli-Syrian Track-I negotiations, launched in Madrid in late 1991, left much to be bridged in Track-II discussions.

Given Syria's centralized political system, it proved difficult to sustain a stable framework of meetings between Israelis and Syrians without the specific approval of the Syrian government's highest echelons. It was thus difficult to identify a Syrian individual—a scholar or other person of some stature—who would agree to meet Israelis on a regular basis, even in the framework of a conference that included representatives of other countries. Syrians who were invited to participate in meetings hosted by international research centers, where Israelis might also be present, made sure to receive permission from senior government or party officials (if they were members of the ruling Ba'th party). High-level backing was important to reduce the danger that the participant would later be accused of having "deviated" from the official or party line.

This attitude did not change after the 1991 Madrid Middle East Peace Conference, despite the participation of a large Syrian delegation headed by Foreign Minister Faruq as-Shara'. In fact, the difficulties involved in holding Israeli-Syrian Track-II talks increased as the Syrian side rejected suggestions that the two countries implement some confidence-building measures (CBMs). Syria was adamant that CBMs should not substitute for or precede the resolution of the basic issues dividing the two countries—primarily the future of the Golan Heights. Syria's position has been consistently opposed to cooperative action with Israel before an agreement is reached in the bilateral Israeli-Syrian track. For the Syrians, such an arrangement required an explicit Israeli commitment to withdraw from the Golan to the lines of June 4, 1967. This is also the reason why Syria rebuffed invitations to take part in any of the Middle East multilateral negotiations established by the 1992 Moscow Conference, including the Arms Control and Regional Security (ACRS) talks. Informal discussions between Israelis and Syrians were perceived in Damascus as merely another CBM that was unacceptable under the prevailing circumstances. A related Syrian concern has been that news of such meetings might be leaked, undermining its stance and the consistency of its position.

As a result of these difficulties, sponsors of Track-II talks were most often compelled to seek the participation of Syrian individuals who did not reside in Syria but were well informed regarding the Syrian dimension of the Arab-Israeli conflict. Yet even these individuals often canceled their participation in such meetings at the last moment. Thus, the considerable difficulties that arose from attempting to address the Israeli-Syrian conflict in a Track-II setting was only partly a product of the intractability of the problem; it also reflected the difficulty of obtaining authentic Syrian participation in any such effort.

The 1991 Madrid Conference and the subsequent Track-I Israeli-Syrian negotiations in Washington did create a small crack in Syria's position. In August 1992 Professor Aziz Shukri, Dean of the University of Damascus Law School, was permitted by the Syrian government to address the Washington Institute for Near East Policy—a research center known for its pro-Israeli approach.[1] Shukri provided an optimistic assessment of the changes that Syria was experiencing and of the chances of moving the peace process forward. Some Syrians were also permitted to participate in conferences and meetings in which Israelis took part, but these were mostly one-time efforts conducted by various universities and research centers.

The only organization that succeeded in creating an ongoing framework for meetings between Israelis and Syrians was the Initiative for Peace and Cooperation in the Middle East (ICPME)[2]—a special Middle East project of Search for Common Ground—a Washington-based nongovernmental organization. The project comprised a number of subgroups, including one devoted to security issues. It was within this sub-

---

1. See Muhammad Aziz Shukri, "Syria's Approach to the Peace Process", Peacewatch No. 38, The Washington Institute, Washington D.C., August 3, 1992.

2. Now known as Search for Common Ground in the Middle East.

group that discussions were held regarding possible ways to resolve the Israeli-Syrian dispute.

The first meeting addressing the problems of the Golan Heights and South Lebanon took place in Airlie House, Virginia, in February 1992. The participants were two Israelis, a Syrian strategic analyst residing in Europe, a Lebanese, and a number of Jordanians and Americans. Participants were asked to present position papers on the Golan Heights, South Lebanon, and the relations between Israel and Jordan. However, most of the time was devoted to seeking ways to resolve the Israeli-Syrian conflict. The point of departure for the theoretical discussion was that Israel would repeal the application of Israeli jurisdiction over the Golan Heights, that it would ultimately withdraw from the area, and that Syria would accept an Israeli military presence on the Golan for a limited period. Suggestions were also made for resolving the conflict in South Lebanon, with Syrian participation in the security arrangements to be implemented there.

Subsequently, participants produced the first written report presenting each party's positions and approaches to the Golan and South Lebanon. The report also summarized the points of agreement and the issues on which the parties remained divided. For example, the parties agreed that it might be possible to apply small-scale interim CBMs in South Lebanon. It was also agreed that discussions of these issues should continue, focusing on expanding the points on which agreement could be reached.

The second meeting took place in London in May 1992. Participation was expanded to include a Saudi scholar and a senior Egyptian retired military officer. Progress was made in addressing the problem of South Lebanon, later resulting in a monograph written by Hussein Agha and Israeli military analyst Aharon Levran. The publication addressed Syria's central role in Lebanon and suggested the application of CBMs by Israel, Lebanon, and Syria.[3]

Participants also made a major effort to elaborate further the points of agreement regarding the Golan Heights and to explore whether the proposed CBMs could be applied in the Golan as well. At that early stage, the Israeli participants did not accept the idea of a complete Israeli withdrawal from the area as a basis for discussions. Instead, participants analyzed different hypothetical situations "among states." One focus of the discussions was measures that Israel and Syria might undertake to reduce mutual fears of a surprise attack. These involved complex security problems as well as issues related to the sources of water in the area. One

---

3.   Hussein J. Agha and Aharon Levran, Common Ground on Lebanon, (Washington, D.C.: Search for Common Ground in the Middle East, August, 1992). No. 1.

suggestion made during this meeting was that if participants could reach agreement, a joint document would be made public.

The third meeting took place in September 1992 in Salzburg, Austria. A larger number of participants of more varied backgrounds took part in this meeting, including a senior military officer from Turkey and a former Iraqi diplomat. The meeting agenda was also expanded to include discussions of Iraq after the Gulf War, and the relations between Israel, Jordan, and the Palestinians. Most of the time, however, was devoted to the Israeli-Syrian conflict. It was agreed that at the next meeting the participants would attempt to prepare a first draft of a document summarizing their points of agreement, and that the aim would be to make this document public eventually.

The fourth meeting, held in January 1993 in Rome, was a watershed in Israeli-Syrian Track-II talks. The gathering was preceded by a more intimate meeting between two Israelis, the Syrian, and a Lebanese, for the purpose of preparing the first draft of the agreed document. In contrast to the Israeli-Syrian Track-I negotiations then being held in Washington, participants in this meeting permitted themselves the liberty of examining ways to address the most sensitive issues involved in the two countries' dispute on a "what-if" basis. Since they were not concerned about committing their countries in any way, or conceding tactical positions in formal negotiations, participants were ready to explore various options for reciprocal concessions. Disagreements were also clarified regarding a number of issues, notably those related to water resources and to the future of Israeli settlements on the Golan. Most importantly, the Rome meeting explored some possibilities that had not been discussed in the Washington negotiations then taking place.

One such proposal, made by an Israeli participant, was that some areas of the Golan would be restored to Syrian sovereignty but would be leased to Israel for a long period. The Syrian participant rejected this proposal, especially once it became clear that there was considerable opposition on the Israeli side to the possibility that Syrian farmers, who fled the area during the 1967 War, might return to cultivate their land during the lease period. The Syrian rejection became even firmer when the Israeli participants could not agree to refrain from establishing new settlements in the Golan during the lease period, or even to stop from expanding existing ones. More generally, there was a wide gap between the parties' positions about the future of the Israeli settlements on the Golan as well as about the length of time that an Israeli military presence would be allowed to remain there. For its part, the Syrian side emphasized that a peace treaty with Israel could only be signed after Israel concluded similar agreements with other Arab states.

Despite these sharp disagreements, it became apparent that the parties could reach some common ground regarding key issues. First, both parties agreed that the Golan is sovereign Syrian territory. Second, it was agreed that both Israel and Syria have legitimate security concerns associated with the Golan, such as the fear of surprise attack. Third, and despite Syrian protestations, an understanding was reached that Israel's withdrawal from the Golan Heights would be carried out in stages, and that a defensive Israeli military presence would remain in areas from which there would be no withdrawal during the interim period. Fourth, again with Syrian reservations and subject to approval from Damascus, there was a discussion of Israel's requirement to maintain observers and early warning stations in the Golan for a limited period. Finally, it was agreed that the United States would play some role in completing the agreement and in verifying the parties' compliance with its stipulations. Obviously, as a Track-II exercise, none of these understandings had any official or formal status for either side.

The draft prepared by ICPME staff at this meeting already referred in considerable detail to the security arrangements that would form part of the agreement between the two countries. These arrangements involved verification and transparency, ground-based early warning stations, aerial patrols, and the possible role of satellites in verifying compliance. In addition, a preliminary discussion was held regarding the force structure and deployment of the two countries' armed forces and the need to reduce their orders of battle. The Syrian side emphasized the need to take into account both sides' military doctrines and they opposed, as a matter of principle, Israeli intervention in what they defined as their "internal affairs." It was also emphasized that Syria would insist on the principle of reciprocity in every realm, and that Israel would be expected to adopt any arrangements that Syria would be asked to implement. Nevertheless, it was clear that both sides were willing to consider trade-offs between security measures, and it was understood that without such willingness it would be very difficult to proceed.

The fifth and sixth rounds of talks were held in Athens and Istanbul, respectively. Slow but considerable progress was made in the fifth meeting, and afterwards it became clear to the participants that the different drafts and details of the talks were being brought to the attention of ranking Syrian officials. In May 1993, prior to the Istanbul meeting, an interim working draft was distributed to members of ICPME's Security Group. The draft was expanded and improved at this meeting and many of the hypothetical assumptions noted in the earlier drafts were replaced by the parties' specific demands from one another. Although the disagreements remained considerable, those who later read it regarded this "secret" draft as extremely impressive. It was clear that at the very least, the document would assist the formal negotiators in understanding one another's positions and concerns.

At Istanbul, both sides emphasized that an agreement between Israel and Syria must include some understandings regarding Lebanon. It was also agreed that once the IDF withdrew from the Golan, the Israeli settlements in the area would also have to be evacuated. An understanding was also reached that no new Israeli settlements would be established during the interim period and that the construction of new housing in existing settlements would be limited to the requirements of natural population growth.

The new draft further elaborated the security arrangements that should be implemented following Israel's withdrawal from the Golan. Israel's fear of surprise attack was accepted with some understanding by the Syrian side, which, in turn, emphasized its fear of an Israeli surprise attack on Damascus, given the proximity of Syria's capital to the border. In addition to the principles that could guide any changes in both sides' force structures, Israel's demands regarding limitations on specific weapon systems were detailed. The Syrian side stressed that certain weapon systems in its arsenal were not intended to threaten Israel, but rather provided some balance against extant Israeli systems, particularly the Israeli air force.

At this stage of the discussions it became evident that the parties—the Israelis, Syrians, Jordanians, Palestinians, and Americans—had all been briefing officials in their respective governments and leaderships regarding the content and progress of the talks. The Syrians repeatedly emphasized that the draft represented no more than an interim consensus that had no standing until it was approved in Damascus. It was clear that, at the very least, semi-approval by government officials was required. It was also made apparent that despite the progress made in the discussions, the Syrian government was not likely to approve the publication of the document as a joint paper, even if only unofficial Syrian participants were involved in its drafting. For the Syrians, it was not acceptable that academics and other private individuals adopt positions on matters relating to national security that were not in line with the positions held by the government.

The seventh and final meeting took place in Oslo, coincidentally just after the signing of the Palestinian-Israeli Oslo accords. Two Israelis and a senior Syrian representative who had not taken part in any of the previous discussions were invited to the meeting. As a result, issues that had been agreed upon in earlier meetings were now reopened for discussion. The parties agreed to adopt a three-paragraph set of clarifications of matters that had been originally included in the expanded draft. It confirmed Syria's sovereignty over the Golan Heights but also the obligation to establish "full peace" with Israel. Israel's commitment to complete withdrawal from the Golan was also restated but it was stipulated that this would be implemented in phases. The future of the Israeli settlers in the Golan Heights would be discussed in the formal negotiations between the parties. Another paragraph noted that Syria would normalize its relations with Israel in parallel to the IDF's withdrawal from the Golan. Security arrangements, which were not elaborated in the one-page document, would be implemented in the Golan following Israel's withdrawal.

The short document negotiated at Oslo represented another achievement in a long process. Israeli Prime Minister Rabin seems to have shown some initial interest. He was given a copy of the one-page document, and reportedly folded it and placed it in one of the drawers of his office desk. Later, he showed it to the head of Israel's delegation to the Track-I Israeli-Syrian negotiations in Washington, Ambassador Itamar Rabinovich. However, Rabin refrained from making any further effort to exploit the utility of the document.

Be that as it may, the achievement proved to be short-lived as the talks were completely derailed by a set of leaks to the press.[4] The Syrian participants in the talks were stunned by these revelations. They were called in "for consultations" with government officials, as well as with officials of the Ba'th party. Shortly thereafter, a second wave of press reports appeared. This led the head of Syria's delegation to the Track-I negotiations in Washington to ask his government whether it allowed private individuals to conduct parallel negotiations that could undermine Syria's position in the official talks. As a result, the Syrian government issued directives prohibiting Syrians from engaging in exercises similar to the IPCME talks. They also warned Lebanese individuals not to take part in such efforts. This ended all hope that the Israeli-Syrian Track-II talks might be resurrected.

It is interesting to note that an earlier and more extensive leak of the more substantive document, detailing the security arrangements that would be implemented following Israel's withdrawal from the Golan,

---

4. The first reference to talks held by Israelis and Syrians that attracted wide attention appeared in the London-based Al-Hayat, on December 31, 1993. Datelined Washington, the report was the day's main's headline. A more significant leak appeared later in the now defunct Israeli daily *Hadashot* in a column by Amnon Barzilai on October 22, 1993. The article named a number of Israelis who took part in the Oslo meeting as well as one of the Syrian participants—Professor Aziz Shukri, Dean of the University of Damascus Law School and a former Legal Advisor to Syria's Ministry of Foreign Affairs and the Arab League.

failed to have much impact. The leak was datelined Tunis (headquarters of the PLO at the time) and took place in late August 1993.[5] One possibility is that upon examining the document, the PLO leadership concluded that the Syrian-Israeli track was far advanced toward a peace agreement. The PLO may then have leaked the document to expose the "secret talks" between Syria and Israel and prepare the way for the Palestinians' acceptance of the Oslo agreement, which came only a few weeks later, on September 13. It is unclear why this initial and more substantive leak had little discernible impact and did not galvanize the Syrians into ending their participation in the IPCME talks.[6]

Participants

Unlike other Track-II exercises, the Syrian-Israeli talks included a permanent external presence and input—there was a third-party presence and participation during all the Initiative for Peace and Cooperation in the Middle East discussions on the Golan issue. At different junctures, Jordanians, Palestinians, Iraqis, Saudis, Lebanese, Turks, and others joined the discussions, thus reinforcing the academic nature of the talks. Thus, the talks were more multilateral than bilateral. The only partial exception was a meeting in Rome in February 1993, which was attended by two Israelis, a Syrian, and a Lebanese. It was at this meeting that the foundation and fundamentals of a potential agreement were seriously discussed for the first time.

Unlike their Israeli counterparts, none of the Syrian participants in the IPCME talks had any particular expertise in security affairs. While this did not prove to be a major obstacle in the discussions, it reflected Syria's approach to the talks—as a general political reconnaissance, rather than as a detailed debate about security provisions. Thus, as in other meetings, it was clear to the Syrian participants that they were not negotiating nor were they mandated to do so. Their brief required them to solicit Israeli reactions and answers to a set of Syrian inquiries in an unofficial context. The object was to allow for a general evaluation of Israeli intentions and test how far the Israeli side was willing to go to meet Syrian requirements. Such probing would have been impossible in the official Track-I talks in Washington. The Syrian side was less interested in

---

5. See the Saudi international Arabic-language daily *Asharq al-Awsat*, August 1993.

6. In February 1994, another story appeared on the cover of the London-based Arabic weekly al-Wasat. The report reproduced in translation the Agha/Levran paper on South Lebanon. This came at a time when the Syrian side had decided to suspend its participation in the IPCME exercise.

elaborating on its own positions, or in indicating how far it was ready to go to meet Israeli concerns, than it was keen on eliciting Israeli responses to the issues raised.

The Israeli side similarly refrained from negotiating since it was not mandated to do so. On many occasions, Israeli participants in these talks stressed that the discussions were theoretical and that they would have liked to explore different "if-then" options and scenarios. Whereas the Syrian participants were only interested in discussing the option of a full Israeli withdrawal from the Golan even on the theoretical level, the Israeli side was keenly interested in considering other scenarios involving partial withdrawal and long-term leasing. But discussion of these scenarios never materialized as the IPCME initiative was aborted as a consequence of the press reports.

Sponsors

The Syrian-Israeli talks were the direct result of a sustained IPCME initiative over a year and a half. Without IPCME's sponsorship, these talks would never have taken place. Indeed, the organization's success in initiating the talks remains a tribute to its overall approach and provides conclusive testimony to the potential role of nongovernmental organizations in Track-II diplomacy and conflict resolution.

In the context of a sharp bilateral conflict, in which the two major parties concerned had little prior contact with each other (unlike the very active history of Israeli-Palestinian contacts), IPCME's multilateral formula diluted the bilateral Syrian-Israeli frictions and created an environment that served to dissipate possible tensions between the two sides. In most of the discussions, participants representing the two sides were joined by participants from other countries, thus reducing the impression of direct talks and adding useful third-party input to the exchanges.

In addition, the role played by IPCME's senior staff was vital. Under the very able leadership of the late Peter Constable (formerly U.S. ambassador to Pakistan and head of the Multinational Force and Observers in the Sinai), the prospects of a successful Track-II exercise emerged seamlessly from the discussions. Constable's light hand and subtle facilitation helped to nourish the discussions without appearing to manipulate or push the debate in any particular direction. Balanced and careful to give the discussions their due without arousing any side's fears as to their possible negative ramifications, Constable assiduously avoided giving the impression that the two sides were engaged in anything that resembled "negotiations." Indeed, it was not even evident to many participants that the talks had taken on the aspect of a "hard" Track-II exercise, or that a potential groundbreaking achievement was within reach. Without Constable's experience and instinct, the IPCME forum could well have drifted without any real direction or productive output. Other IPCME members, such as Dov Zakheim and Eliot Goldberg, also provided vital intellectual and practical input.

After the May 1992 meeting, IPCME staff members briefed U.S. State Department officials regarding the progress made in the talks. These officials included Director of the Bureau of Policy Planning Ambassador Samuel Lewis; Special U.S. Representative to the Middle East Peace Process Ambassador Dennis Ross; and, at a later stage, Deputy Assistant Secretary for Intelligence and Research Dan Kurtzer. Members of the U.S. peace team then in charge of the Track-I Israeli-Syrian negotiations were reportedly impressed by the briefing and encouraged Search for Common Ground to continue its efforts.

Summary

The talks between Israelis and Syrians sponsored by IPCME provide an excellent illustration of the extent to which the original purpose of a Track-II venue may change over time. While the sponsors of this venue initially intended it to allow a "soft" exchange of views on the various dimensions of an Israeli-Syrian agreement, the exercise was later seen by Israeli and U.S. participants as a "hard" effort to agree on security measures that would be implemented following an Israeli withdrawal from the Golan Heights.

This transformation was even more dramatic from the Syrian participants' standpoint. The Syrians had entered the discussions to conduct a "soft" fact-finding expedition intended to explore Israel's positions on matters that were not sufficiently thrashed out in the Track-I negotiations then taking place in Washington. Soon, however, the Syrian participants found that they had been taking part in what was later perceived to be a "hard" exercise aimed at formulating an agreed text of a Syrian-Israel Declaration of Principles.

The venue also demonstrated the vulnerability of Track-II talks to four problems: The first was the lack of sufficient expertise among Track-II participants; clearly, the Syrians taking part in the discussions did not have the professional expertise required to reach agreement on security measures. The second was the extreme vulnerability of Track-II talks to leaks: When Track-II talks are conducted on behalf of a regime that is almost obsessive about maintaining control over the policy process, any significant untimely leak may lead to an immediate end to the exercise.

The third was asymmetry between participants: Since the Israeli participants in the talks had no formal position or attachments, they were less vulnerable to the consequences of the leaks. The Syrians involved were less independent—their participation in the talks required the approval of the highest echelons of the Syrian government. Consequently, their exposure to the leaks was much greater. Thereafter, they were forbidden to take part in any additional Track-II activities and venues.

Finally, in the absence of clearly identified mentors to the talks—or some other way to inform leaders of the progress achieved in Track-II activities—such venues cannot become an effective tool for conflict resolution.

Nonetheless it is worth noting that subsequent Israel-Syrian Track-I talks at Wye Plantation in 1996, Shepherdstown in 1999 and the May 2000 Geneva summit between U.S. President Bill Clinton and Syrian President Hafez al-Assad not only confirmed the effectiveness of the IPCME forum in accurately transmitting the Syrian position, but also emphasized the clear requirements for a solution on the Golan: a solution that IPCME itself had helped to develop.

Chapter 8

The Multilateral ACRS-Related Talks

While the previous chapters describe five bilateral Track-II talks, this chapter surveys various security-related Middle East multilateral Track-II venues.[1] In contrast to the talks that were designed to help resolve the Israeli-Palestinian and Israeli-Syrian disputes, the multilateral Track-II talks addressed issues related to the prospects for regional security and arms control in the Middle East at large. A number of the venues were specifically designed to support the Track-I negotiations conducted in the framework of the Arms Control and Regional Security (ACRS) working group of the Middle East peace negotiations, launched in Moscow in January 1992. Israel, the Palestinians, and thirteen Arab states took part in these talks during 1993–1995.

Some multilateral Middle East Track-II talks preceded and anticipated the ACRS process. Most notable and productive among them was a venue directed by Geoffrey Kemp at the Carnegie Endowment for International Peace. Another was a series of meetings organized by the Geneva office of the Friends International Service Committee and orchestrated by Brewster Grace, the Committee's Middle East representative. PUGWASH and the Institut Francaise des Relations Internationales (IFRI) in Paris also held useful Track-II talks before the ACRS process began. Other multilateral Track-II talks were launched in late 1990 by Steven Spiegel through the University of California's Institute for Global Conflict and Cooperation (IGCC).

---

1. Although strictly speaking the IPCME talks were also multilateral, the focus in Chapter 7 was on the Israeli-Syrian bilateral dimension of these talks.

Additional NGOs and research centers joined the effort after the Track-I ACRS negotiations were launched. These included the Mershon Center at Ohio State University, the Search for Common Ground, the American Association for the Advancement of Science, the University of California at Los Angeles (UCLA), and the United Nations Institute for Disarmament Research (UNIDIR). Later, the Stockholm International Peace Research Institute (SIPRI), De Paul University in Chicago, and the International Institute For Higher Studies in Criminal Sciences (ISISC) in Siracusa, Italy, also launched ACRS-related Track-II talks.

The Strategic Environment

The international and regional developments that provided the setting for the ACRS negotiations also created the conditions for the ACRS-related Track-II talks. The first was the end of the Cold War and the dissolution of the Soviet Union. Instead of superpower rivalry—manifesting itself in the two superpowers' race to arm their allies in the Middle East with greater quantities of more advanced weapons—by the late 1980s, Russia and the United States seemed disposed to cooperate in placing some controls on the regional arms race.[2] It was symbolic of this change that one of the first major Track-II discussions of the prospects for regional security and arms control in the Middle East took place in Moscow in October 1991.

The 1980–1988 Iraq-Iran War may have provided another inducement to proceed toward arms control. The war, with its massive use of ballistic missiles and the first significant use of chemical weapons since World War I, was interpreted as demonstrating the dangers of the regional arms race. The potential implications of these developments for the stability of a region that provides critical energy resources to the United States, Europe, and Japan were considerable.

Iraq's invasion of Kuwait in August 1990 was the third major development that motivated serious exploration of the prospects for regional security and arms control in the Middle East. During the 1980s, Iraq had acquired huge quantities of conventional arms and a significant arsenal of chemical weapons and ballistic missiles, and it had developed an infrastructure for the production of nuclear and biological weapons. These efforts could not have been sustained without financial support from the Gulf states and without technology transfers by U.S. and West European

---

2. This development was reflected in 1986 in Gorbachev's admonition to Syria's President Assad that Syria should cease seeking strategic parity with Israel and should instead aim at a negotiated resolution of the two countries' dispute.

firms, which hoped to gain financially from Iraq and to strengthen Iraq's defense against Khomeini's regime in Iran.

Clearly, the confidence gained by Saddam Hussein as a result of the acquisition of these huge arsenals led him to believe that he could invade Kuwait with relative impunity. Hence it was not surprising that U.S. Secretary of State James Baker noted the need to explore the prospects for arms control as one of the imperatives for U.S. policy in the Middle East in the post–Gulf War era. It was even less surprising that the subject became one of the five items of concern for the U.S.-Russian cosponsored multilateral Middle East peace negotiations launched in Moscow in early 1992. Consequently the ACRS working group was established.

The Track-I ACRS Negotiations

From the outset, there was a considerable gap between the Israeli and Arab approaches to the Arms Control and Regional Security process. Egypt in particular emphasized that the talks should deal with Israel's nuclear capability first, stressing that nuclear weapons are the most destructive and hence the most destabilizing weapons. Conversely, Israel argued that the evolution of arms control in Europe demonstrated that sensitive issues involved in strategic deterrence could be addressed only after the parties develop a considerable degree of security, confidence, and mutual trust. Hence, Israel emphasized the need to apply regional confidence- and security-building measures (CSBMs) before nuclear arms control could be applied in the Middle East.

Early in the evolution of these talks, the Clinton administration brokered a compromise that stipulated that the ACRS talks would produce a conceptual framework for structural arms control, including in the nuclear realm, but that implementation of this framework would proceed "step by step, brick by brick." The steps proposed were to comprise CSBMs that would enhance security, predictability, and mutual trust in the region. Eventually, this dual-track approach resulted in a shifting of emphasis in ACRS to intersessional meetings and to the division of these meetings into two "baskets": a "conceptual basket" and an "operational basket."

By late 1994 the parties had made some progress in the operational basket of the ACRS talks. Agreements were reached to implement two maritime CSBMs: measures to avoid incidents at sea and cooperation in search and rescue operations. The parties also agreed to establish a regional communication system and to adopt procedures for the exchange of military information and the prenotification of major military movements and exercises. In addition, a mandate for the establishment of a Regional Security Center in Amman, Jordan, with related facilities in Tunisia and Oman, was adopted in the conceptual basket of the ACRS talks.

Within the conceptual basket, progress was also made in negotiating a Statement on Arms Control and Regional Security in the Middle East. But during ACRS plenary discussions in October 1994 in Tunis, Israel refused to accept Egypt's demand that the statement would include a specific commitment to join the 1968 Nuclear Non-Proliferation Treaty (NPT). In a subsequent meeting of the ACRS conceptual basket held in Helsinki in early 1995, Israel also rejected another Egyptian demand—that the transformation of the Middle East into a Weapons-of-Mass-Destruction-Free Zone (WMDFZ) be placed on the ACRS agenda.

The urgency Egypt attached to the nuclear issue in late 1994 was motivated by the approaching Nuclear Non-Proliferation Review and Extension Conference. The main purpose of the conference, to be held in mid-1995, was to extend the NPT indefinitely. In 1993 Egypt had refused to sign the Chemical Weapons Convention until Israel signed the NPT, and Egypt now argued that it would not support the indefinite extension of the NPT unless Israel committed itself to sign the treaty. Egypt's position was rebuffed by the Clinton administration and President Mubarak was subjected to considerable pressure—to which he eventually yielded —to have Egypt remain committed to the NPT despite its indefinite extension.

These developments produced a growing frustration within the Egyptian government. The Egyptians felt that their priorities in the ACRS process were being ignored while progress was rapid on Israel's priority, establishing an infrastructure for CSBMs in the Middle East. Consequently, in mid-1995 Cairo decided to block any further progress in the ACRS talks. During 1996–2000, not a single meeting of ACRS plenary or intersessional groups was convened.

Thus, the strategic environment favoring arms control and regional security deliberations began to deteriorate in late 1994. By that time, the sense of urgency and common purpose generated by the Gulf War had faded, and the Track-I ACRS negotiations increasingly had become hostage to the bilateral Israeli-Egyptian nuclear debate.

The Role of ACRS-Related Track-II Talks

The utility and impact of the security-related Track-II talks are very difficult to assess. The talks involve an amorphous realm—the parties' perceptions on security issues—and the extent to which these perceptions have been affected by Track-II talks is impossible to measure. In addition, the contribution of these talks has been uneven: some Track-II venues have been more productive than others.

The role of the multilateral Track-II talks changed with time. The first venues, taking place before the Track-I ACRS negotiations were launched and extending into the first period of negotiations, seem to have served a number of purposes. First, they helped to create a small intellectual community interested in enhancing regional security and stability and in supporting arms control in the Middle East. Prior to the late 1980s, there was very little interest in arms control issues in the region. Egypt's Ministry of Foreign Affairs had trained and cultivated a cadre of experts in global arms control treaties, and Israel's academic community included one or two scholars who applied arms control concepts to the Middle East. But in most of the region's states there was much less knowledge and interest in arms control issues.

The first wave of regional security and arms control Track-II meetings helped to create some of the missing expertise. The meetings served to familiarize participants with the concepts of arms control as well as with the experience gained from applying arms control agreements and CSBMs in the U.S.-Soviet and NATO-Warsaw Pact contexts. A small community gradually familiarized itself with the efforts to increase regional stability through the application of agreements and measures in Europe, such as the Conference on Security and Cooperation in Europe (CSCE) and the Conventional Forces in Europe (CFE) treaty.

In addition, the early meetings helped participants learn how to negotiate CSBM and arms control agreements. For example, the first conference held by the Mershon Center of Ohio State University in Salzburg, Austria, in July 1992, included extensive training sessions. These sessions featured Russian Ambassador Oleg Grinevsky and U.S. Ambassadors Lynn Hansen and James Woolsey, who led their countries' delegations to the Stockholm and CFE negotiations. Their instructive presentations—elaborating their experience in negotiating the CSCE framework and the CFE treaty—led to invitations to Grinevsky and Hansen to share their experience at an international conference held by the Jaffee Center for Strategic Studies in Israel in early 1992, and at a Track-II meeting held by IGCC in January 1994 in Delphi, Greece. A large number of officials and scholars from Middle East states were exposed to the Grinevsky-Hansen presentations.

A third outcome of the early Track-II talks was the personal relations fostered among participants. Many Track-II meetings were organized in a way to allow participants an opportunity to get to know one another at excursions and free time. Familiarization was also made easier by some degree of continuity in attendance, allowing participants to meet each other quite often. This proved helpful for the subsequent Track-I negotiations because some of the Track-II participants later became members of their countries' delegations to the Arms Control and Regional Security talks.

Finally, multilateral Track-II meetings allowed participants to create contacts that were later useful in pursuing bilateral relations. For example, contacts made by Dore Gold, a Senior Research Associate at Tel Aviv University's Jaffee Center for Strategic Studies and a participant in the Search for Common Ground IPCME Track-II talks, proved useful to him when he became foreign policy adviser to Prime Minister Benjamin Netanyahu. He made contacts through IPCME talks with senior officials in Amman and some of the Gulf States that allowed him easier access in these countries once he became a government official. Netanyahu's initial postelectoral contact with the PA was a direct result of Gold's contacts within the multilateral activities of the IPCME Track-II group.[3]

The multilateral Track-II talks also affected bilateral relations involved contacts between Israel and Iraq before the Gulf War. A Track-II meeting convened by the Carnegie Endowment for International Peace and chaired by Geoffrey Kemp in October 1989 provided an opportunity for an exchange of views between Israeli and Iraqi participants and the establishment of an informal channel of communication between the two sides.[4]

---

3.   Following Netanyahu's election in May 1996, the new Israeli government had no clear way to contact the PA, despite two and a half years of official contacts between Israel and the PLO after Oslo. Gold called IPCME colleague Hussein Agha in London to consult on the best way of making initial contact between the two sides. Gold requested Abu Mazin's telephone number and Agha called Abu Mazin in Gaza. The latter agreed to talk to Gold subject to the proviso that this not be misinterpreted as complicity in the new government's declared policy of downgrading contacts with Arafat. After Agha transmitted this proviso, Gold immediately established the first formal contact between the two sides.

4.   The exchange was between Shai Feldman and an Iraqi participant. The latter argued that Israel should not be concerned about Iraqi intentions because Baghdad had joined the Arab consensus regarding a peaceful settlement with Israel. He emphasized Iraq's desire to rebuild its economy after the war with Iran and stressed that Iraq had no illusions about Israel's nuclear capabilities and that Iraq had "no intentions to risk Baghdad on behalf of the Palestinian cause." Upon Feldman's suggestion, the Iraqi participant was later contacted by Laurie Mylroie, an American scholar specializing in Iraq. Her trips to Iraq and Israel in the late 1980s established a channel of communication between senior personalities and officials in the two countries. Mylroie also arranged "social meetings" in the United States between Iraqi Ambassador Nizar Hamdoun and two Israeli high ranking retired military officers: Brigadier General (Res.) Aviezer Yaari, a former commander of the Research Division of the IDF's Military Intelligence Branch, and Major General (Res.) Ori Orr, a former commander of the

Multilateral Track-II meetings proved at least as useful once the Track-I ACRS negotiations were launched. First, the meetings held parallel to ACRS became a useful venue for participants to convey their nations' threat perceptions. Clearly, it was much easier to convey such perceptions in the more informal setting provided by Track-II meetings than in the framework of official negotiations. From this perspective, informal settings that allowed for longer and less constrained discussions were particularly conducive to conveying the depth and magnitude of the concerns expressed at the formal ACRS meetings.

Second, Track-II talks provided an opportunity to gain valuable information about the other parties' threat perceptions, including the weight attached by other parties to different issues, and to convey these perceptions to Track-I negotiators. This helped members of the official delegations to better prepare themselves for subsequent meetings of the ACRS talks. For example, an Israeli participant noted that it was in a presentation given by Egyptian General Ahmad Fakhr during a Track-II meeting held in Delphi, Greece, in January 1994 that Egypt elaborated its security concept for the first time. The presentation made Israelis more aware of Egypt's sensitivity to the fact that the sources of Egypt's water originate outside its borders and to Israel's involvement in Ethiopia within this context. The issue of threat perceptions was raised in the Track-I negotiations but was not analyzed in any detail; without the Track-II talks, the Israeli side would not have understood that the threat perceptions and security doctrines of the Gulf states are very different from those of the states involved in the Arab-Israeli conflict. Neither would it have been able to understand the extent to which the Arab side regards Israel's technological superiority as a threat. Indeed, the analysis of threat perceptions conducted in the Track-II talks allowed both sides to understand why the other side adopted the positions it did in the Track-I arms control negotiations.

Another example involved a UNIDIR project focusing on national threat perceptions in the Middle East. The Israeli-Syrian dimension of this effort was probably the most important. The Syrian participant in the project, Abdulhay Sayed, submitted a lengthy paper emphasizing the manner in which Syria views Israel. The paper provided an insight into the enormous gap between the Israeli and Syrian views. Sayed expressed the basic theme that as an aggressor who appears as a victim, Israel had succeeded in deceiving the entire world. In this view, Israel could become a partner to peace only if it first underwent a "self-cleansing" process.

Central Command and, later, a chairman of the Knesset Committee on Defense and Foreign Affairs. These contacts ended with Iraq's invasion of Kuwait in August 1990.

Sayed did call for all Arabs to sit down and talk to Israel, but also stressed that this should be done in order to persuade Israel to overcome its prejudices and change its ways. As the Israeli side saw it, Sayed did not talk about interests but rather about values and rights—using a lexicon that left very little room for compromise. His views were conveyed by an Israeli participant to the top echelons of Israel's defense community, sensitizing them to the depth of the Syrian-Israeli divide.

Third, Track-II talks held parallel to ACRS meetings provided an opportunity to convey and understand other factors that affected the parties' positions on arms control issues. For example, an Arab participant explained why his country could not adopt the ratio of reserve-to-regular forces maintained by the IDF: the state of the communication and transportation systems in his country makes it impossible to mobilize reserves as fast as the Israeli Defense Forces can. Similarly, Track-II discussions allowed Israeli participants to explain why Israel could not discuss the nuclear issue in the framework of the Track-I negotiations. Without Track-II talks, this Israeli view might have been more difficult to convey to the Arab side.

Fourth, Track-II talks allowed participants to convey and understand the commitment and degree of urgency with which various positions were held in the official Track-I negotiations. For example, in the Track-II settings Egyptian participants emphasized that while Egypt demands a declared Israeli commitment to denuclearization, it understands that implementation of this commitment will span many years and will be linked to progress in the general processes of peace and reconciliation in the region. Other Track-II settings provided participants from the Gulf Cooperation Council (GCC) states an opportunity to point out that while they supported Egypt's position on nuclear disarmament in principle, they did not share the urgency Egypt attached to this issue.

Fifth, multilateral Track-II talks provided an opportunity to explore options for resolving disputes in an informal manner. For example, in a meeting hosted by Tel Aviv University's Jaffee Center for Strategic Studies in January 1993, Egyptian General Muhammad Ahmed Abdel Halim suggested that Israel should suspend operations at its nuclear reactor in Dimona. He argued that such a move would begin a process of reducing the nuclear threat in the Middle East without diminishing the deterrent value of Israel's nuclear option. The Arab states would remain aware that Israel was capable of restarting activities at Dimona should political conditions in the region deteriorate.

Sixth, Track-II talks allowed participants to expand the security-related multilateral agenda to subjects that were taboo in the formal Track-I

ACRS negotiations. One example was the blueprint presented by James Leonard (United States) and Jan Prawitz (Sweden) for transforming the Middle East into a Nuclear Weapons Free Zone (NWFZ). The blueprint, defining the conditions that might allow such a transformation, was discussed at meetings held by UNIDIR in 1996 and by UCLA in Lund, Sweden, in November 1996.

However, the Track-II talks—particularly those involving Track-I negotiators—were not entirely immune to the political sensitivities to which the official ACRS negotiations were subject. For example, in one Track-II meeting, an Arab participant delivered a particularly blunt comment on the Arab tendency to blame external factors such as Israel and "the West" for the failures that led to the rise of religious extremism in the Middle East. The participant argued that such extremism merely reflects deep frustration among Arab populations, resulting from the corruption and incompetence of Arab governments, and their failure to meet the expectations of the people. At least one Arab participant in the meeting apparently reported this comment to his government, inducing it to protest to the government of the outspoken participant. As a result, his country's minister of foreign affairs reprimanded the participant—a university scholar.

Some Track-II talks that were held parallel to ACRS negotiations also provided an opportunity to increase the degree of familiarization among Track-I negotiators who took part in these talks in an informal capacity (making them Track-I½ talks). On one occasion, IGCC made a particular effort to encourage such familiarization by inviting participants to bring their spouses to the meeting. Greater familiarization among participants proved particularly useful at times of tension in Track-I negotiations, allowing negotiators to cool off, take one another aside, and discuss ways to reduce the tension in a cordial if not friendly manner.

The paralysis of the ACRS talks since mid-1995 had two main effects on the Track-II talks. First, it created a greater perceived imperative to hold Track-I½ talks. The purpose of the talks was to maintain personal contacts among the negotiators and to create some common memory of what had been achieved before the talks had reached an impasse. Another purpose was to explore the conditions that might allow the ACRS talks to be resumed and to conduct a preliminary discussion of some issues that could not be placed on the ACRS agenda, notably the transformation of the Middle East into a Weapons-of-Mass-Destruction-Free Zone. These were the main motivations propelling the UCLA Track-II project directed by Richard Rosecrance and Steven Spiegel.

The meetings allowed participants to analyze why ACRS negotiations reached an impasse in late 1994 and to take stock of the progress made in these negotiations until that point so that the parties would not have to begin the process from "point zero" should they succeed in overcoming the impasse between them.

In some cases, however, Track-II meetings may have been counterproductive for restarting the ACRS process. For example, participants from Gulf Cooperation Council states in one Track-II meeting conveyed their discontent that their concerns regarding threats to security and stability in the Persian Gulf were not being addressed while Egypt insisted on a resolution of its nuclear debate with Israel. This expression of unhappiness—and the implied assertion that the Gulf States might not share the urgency with which Egypt regards the nuclear issue—may have further dampened the enthusiasm of Egyptian officials to a possible reconvening of the ACRS talks.

A second main effect of the paralysis of the ACRS talks was to encourage attempts to bypass the official negotiations: the issues that were blocking progress at ACRS sometimes became a central focus of the Track-II effort. This was clearly the main purpose of the project led by De Paul University in Chicago and the International Institute For Higher Studies in Criminal Sciences (ISISC) in Siracusa, Italy, directed by Cherif Bassuini. The initial goal of these discussions was to negotiate a draft agreement transforming the Middle East into a WMDFZ. While ACRS negotiators did not take part in these talks, the procedure adopted resembled Track-I negotiations in that, in contrast to all other multilateral Track-II venues, the De Paul–ISISC project participants took part in the talks as members of their countries' delegation. Each delegation was headed by an individual and the heads of the Israeli, Egyptian, and Jordanian delegations made decisions that were binding on the less senior participants.

A less sensitive but equally focused effort to address the issue of weapons of mass destruction (WMD) in the Middle East was carried out by the Search for Common Ground's IPCME project. This track was the only forum for debating WMD issues that included participants from all the major players in the region including Israel, Iran, and Iraq. The group's activities focused on regional security and on the Gulf. An offshoot of the group also examined the Chemical Weapons Convention (CWC), with Israeli, Syrian, Egyptian, Iraqi, and Iranian representatives being assisted at one stage by a senior Russian official. IPCME work on WMD issues has resulted in an agreed "common ground" text, in line with the organization's standard practice to publish texts reflecting shared views regarding key security issues.

Israeli and Arab Perspectives

For Israel, the multilateral Track-II talks—similar to the official multilateral negotiations—provided an opportunity to advance its interests in becoming integrated in the region at large. Indeed, the talks allowed Israelis to expand their contacts beyond their immediate neighbors to states with which Israel was not engaged in any formal bilateral negotiations. Thus, in Track-II frameworks, Israelis could meet colleagues from the Gulf States and discuss common interests. The informal setting allowed participants from other Arab states to convey the perceptions of Israel prevailing in their countries. For the Israeli side, the impact of Track-II talks on Track-I negotiations was clear: they engaged the North African and Gulf states in multilateral Track-I negotiations. For example, the multilateral Track-II talks clearly affected the prospects for a breakthrough in the bilateral relations between Israel and Tunisia, and Israel and Oman and were seen by Israeli officials as having helped expand the circle of relevant parties beyond Israel and Egypt to a discourse with Jordan, Tunisia, and the Gulf states.

The substance of the ACRS-related Track-II talks was also consistent with Israel's national interests. Much of the discussions in these meetings were aimed at advancing the application of CSBMs in the Middle East. Since most of these measures are cooperative in nature, any progress made in their implementation implied a higher level of integration in the region. Israelis were particularly pleased to take part in meetings where Arab participants felt free to express their differences of opinion. This was not because of any particular gratification in observing instances of Arab disunity, but rather because Israelis interpreted the willingness of Arab participants to conduct such debates in their presence as indicating that they regard Israel is a legitimate and acceptable "member of the club."

In comparison to Israel, most Arab states and their respective leaders displayed much less interest in the ACRS-related Track-II talks. For the Syrians, the Arms Control and Regional Security process in its entirety was called into question, over and above the general Syrian reticence toward Track-II type exercises. The Syrian view has been that arms control and regional security are "tail-end" issues that can only be dealt with sensibly once the bilateral territorial, political, and security issues have been resolved. Discussing ACRS issues could thus come only after an agreement on Israel's withdrawal from occupied Arab land would be reached. Otherwise the danger would be that the imbalance of power in Israel's favor would be reinforced and Israel's incentives to withdraw substantially diminished.

Basing its stance on the "land for peace" formula, Syria has consistently argued that arms control, along with economic and political normalization and the other elements of "peace," should not be granted to Israel until it keeps its side of the bargain and hands over the "land" to the Arab sides' satisfaction. These elements of "peace" should be maintained as leverage and as a measure of insurance against Israeli bad faith in the negotiations. This view has had some considerable influence in various Arab circles, despite official Arab participation in the ACRS process. Given Syria's military capabilities and its strategic regional presence, for many on the Arab side, its absence from ACRS—regardless of the rationale—seriously undermined the credibility and utility of the process.

Syria's views can be seen as a reflection of a wider Arab view that saw the genesis of the ACRS talks within the multilateral process in largely ambivalent terms. In the general Arab view, the United States conceived these talks to achieve a number of specific objectives including: First, to bring the rest of the Arab world (beyond the states bordering on Israel) into the Madrid Process. This would create a stake for other Arab parties in the process and widen the peace constituency in the region. Second, to engage the Gulf Arabs so as to facilitate the creation of open ties with Israel, irrespective of the pace of progress in the bilateral negotiations. Third, to tap Arab resources and funds—mostly from the Gulf countries—to help finance the peace process. Finally, to further isolate the region's radical states, such as Iraq, Iran, and Libya, from the rest of the Arab world by excluding them from joint economic, political, and security projects that were planned as part of the multilateral process.

The prevalent Arab perception of ACRS was that it is a U.S.-orchestrated attempt to integrate Israel into a regional security regime that could develop irrespective of the resolution of the "core" bilateral disputes, and that this would render the bilateral talks less urgent while giving priority to Israeli security requirements over those of the Arab side. In addition, the Arab side has tended to see the ACRS process as part of a wider attempt to promote Arab-Israeli "normalization" in a manner that would further erode the Arab position in the bilateral talks by depriving the Arab side of an important means of leverage against Israel. In turn, Arabs see normalization prior to a resolution of the political conflict as diminishing the Israeli incentive to offer political or territorial concessions in the bilateral negotiations. Having lost the "stick" (the military option), the Arabs would consequently lose the "carrot" (normalized relations) as well.

Equally, there was a broad Arab consensus that any attempt at regional arms control and security cannot be taken seriously in the absence of such major regional powers as Iran, Syria, and Iraq. Agreements reached without the active participation or consent of these powers would have little relevance to the real situation on the ground. It was also feared that in the absence of Iran, Syria, and Iraq the ACRS process could degenerate into new security alliances, axes, and subgroupings, leading to increased regional tensions and instability rather than the opposite. Consequently, some Arab parties participated in the ACRS process at a very low level and in an insubstantial manner to avoid antagonizing their powerful nonparticipating neighbors such as Syria, Iraq, and Iran.

Furthermore, there was a general Arab perception that the ACRS agenda was set by Israel and has only served Israeli interests. When Egypt tried to raise concerns regarding the Israeli nuclear program, its efforts were thwarted and it was blamed for a breakdown in the talks. Along with other Arab parties, Egypt kept up a constant attack on Israel's nuclear monopoly in the region and the dangers this poses to the stability and security of the area.

Rhetoric aside, Egypt maintained a cynical view of attempts to create a nuclear-free zone in the Middle East and pursued this goal more as means of leverage against Israel than as a practical achievable end. To that extent, Egypt's interest in the substance of ACRS was debatable, and should not have been taken at face value. From this perspective, the Egyptian and Syrian positions regarding ACRS were not that far apart and the differences were more stylistic than substantive. Egypt will continue to express interest in ACRS activities but will also most likely continue to view ACRS as a part of the ongoing political struggle with Israel over ascendancy in the Levant. Its objectives in the process could be summarized as follows: First, to attempt to influence Israeli decision-makers on key concerns such as the nuclear issue. Second, to attempt to elicit indirect U.S. pressure on Israel via such projects as the De Paul–ISISC exercise. Third, to create a gap between Israeli opinion makers and the Israeli government on the nuclear issue. Finally, to maintain a presence in the ACRS realm in order to avoid leaving the arena open to other regional powers such as Jordan and Turkey.

From the Arab standpoint, past attempts to build regional security systems and coordinate security issues among themselves had all failed; the current skeptical Arab attitude toward such schemes is based on historical experience. Naturally, the attempt to integrate Israel—the historic Arab foe—into regional security structures only exacerbates and complicates the problem. There was also an Arab belief that ACRS efforts had been devised to maintain the military imbalance in Israel's favor and to sustain its military superiority. The Arab side could not see why Israel would give up any of its substantive military advantages as part of future security arrangements. The development of bilateral Israeli-Turkish military cooperation further fueled Arab suspicions regarding Israel's intentions and its attempts at axis-building. From an Arab perspective, Israel could not have been serious about ACRS if it went about undermining regional security through a hostile strategic axis with Turkey.

Unlike in Israel, and despite limited efforts by Egypt, there is no serious community of Arab scholars or experts (not to mention pressure group) that could have or was ready to lobby Arab governments on behalf of ACRS-related issues. This largely explains the relative absence of Arab sponsors or mentors of the ACRS Track-II process outside Jordan and, to a lesser extent, Egypt. Nonetheless, it could be argued that one of the most important potential roles for Track-II ACRS-related talks had been to help create such a community and familiarize it with the concepts and tools of arms control and regional security. The educational impact of the ACRS Track-II process is perhaps its most salient contribution.

It is important not to misread the motives behind individual Arab states' participation in ACRS Track-I and Track-II exercises. In many cases, this participation stemmed largely from political politeness and an unwillingness to offend the (mostly) U.S. sponsorship of this track. Egypt's ACRS participation reflected its positive diplomatic profile toward the peace process as a whole. Its attempt to invest in this track can be seen as a means of furthering its own national interests, while remaining aware of its limitations. In Jordan's case, the ruling elite—and particularly former Crown Prince Hassan's office—had been genuinely committed to the ACRS process and was appreciative of its potential value. Jordan, however, is a relatively minor player; for fear of alienating the rest of the Arab world, it cannot venture too far beyond the Arab consensus. The Gulf countries, in turn, had their own particular considerations for engaging in the ACRS process. These derived largely from inter-Gulf rivalries that had little to do with the substantive issues of the ACRS process.

Participants

Israelis of different backgrounds participated in the security-related multilateral Track-II talks. Before the ACRS negotiations were launched, Israeli officials did not take part in such discussion and participants were drawn primarily from Israel's academic community instead. Senior research associates at Tel Aviv University's Jaffee Center for Strategic Studies—Shai Feldman, Ariel Levite, and Dore Gold—were particularly active in these discussions. Other Israeli scholars, including Gerald Steinberg of Bar Ilan University and Yair Evron from Tel Aviv University, had also taken part in a considerable number of such meetings. Two senior journalists also participated actively in ACRS-related Track-II talks: Zeev Schiff and, less frequently, Ehud Yaari, then Middle East correspondent of Israeli Television Channel 1.

By contrast, the Track-I½ talks that evolved after the official multilateral negotiations were launched included a number of government officials. Among them, Ariel Levite, serving as deputy for arms control to the deputy director general for external affairs at the Ministry of Defense, and Shimon Stein, then head of the disarmament division at the Ministry for Foreign Affairs, were the most frequent participants. More unique was a meeting held by IGCC in Delphi, Greece in January 1994: the entire Israeli delegation to the Track-I ACRS negotiations headed by cochairmen David Ivri and Hanan Baron took part in the discussions.

Yet even the academics involved in the more purely Track-II talks had excellent access to Israeli leaders and senior government officials. For example, Ariel Levite had served as adviser to the Ministry of Defense before he became a member of the Israeli ACRS team; Shai Feldman was close to Mordechai (Motta) Gur, who served in a number of Israeli governments, first as minister of health and then as deputy minister of defense in the Rabin Government; and Dore Gold had close relations with a number of Likud leaders, including Benyamin (Benny) Begin and Benyamin Netanyahu. Thus the three could convey the impression they gained in the Track-II talks in a way that could inform top political leaders and other decision-makers in Israel.

This was certainly the case with respect to Schiff and Yaari; both enjoyed easy access to Israeli leaders and to the country's top officials. Without violating the "off-the-record" rules that apply to Track-II talks, they found ways to share their impressions and conclusions with a wider audience. Thus the value of the exchanges that took place in Track-II talks did not remain confined to the small number of scholars, journalists, and former government and military officials taking part in the talks.

Some of the Arab participants in these talks enjoyed similar access to Arab leaders and senior officials. These included General Ahmed Fakhr and General Ahmed Abdul Halim in Egypt, Dr. Abdullah Toukan and General Muhammed Shiyyab in Jordan, and Ziad Abu Ziad representing the PA.

Mentors and Leaders

The ACRS-related Track-II talks had no mentor on the Israeli side. No senior Israeli official has ever undertaken the task of conveying the information, messages, or possibilities opened up by the multilateral Track-II talks to the country's top leaders. By contrast to the bilateral Israeli-Palestinian Track-II talks, there is no evidence that a senior Israeli official or second-echelon leader initiated a multilateral Track-II effort or sought to advance a regional security or arms control initiative through an existing Track-II venue.

Indeed, the attitude of the Israeli government and its defense establishment toward the ACRS-related Track-II talks has varied over time and has been affected by the characteristics of each venue. Until 1994 there was considerable receptivity in Israeli government circles to these talks. Deputy Minister of Foreign Affairs Yossi Beilin and then IDF Chief of Staff Ehud Barak both indicated their interest in impressions reported by Track-II participants. Senior officers in Israel's intelligence community and the IDF's planning branch expressed similar interest and encouragement. In addition, Hanan Baron, a cochairman of Israel's delegation to the ACRS talks, was extremely supportive of the Track-II efforts.

On the other hand, David Ivri, then director general of the Ministry of Defense and another cochairman of Israel's delegation to the official ACRS talks (and later Israeli ambassador in Washington) was less enthusiastic about some Track-II venues. Ivri was reportedly concerned that sensitive information might be leaked in these exchanges as well as about the possibility that the meetings would be used by Arab participants to press Israel to take steps toward nuclear disarmament. Consequently, he warned some invitees that Israel's interests might be jeopardized in such talks.

The attitude of other individuals in charge of arms control and regional security in the Ministry of Foreign Affairs and the Ministry of Defense was more favorable to Track-II talks as a channel for understanding the concerns of Israel's neighbors. They also supported Track-II efforts as serving Israel's interest in normalization and in enlarging Israeli's circle of contacts in the Arab world. Clearly, the attitude of these officials was particularly positive toward the Track-I½ talks in which they were invited to participate, notably the IGCC project.

Generally, the Israeli government's attitude toward ACRS-related Track-II venues became more reserved after 1995, when the ACRS Track-I negotiations reached a stalemate. The attitude remained quite positive toward venues that did not seem to threaten Israeli interests. This was especially true when the agenda of the talks was informally coordinated ahead of time with Israeli government officials, ensuring that the discussions did not focus exclusively on the nuclear issue and did not become a stage for propaganda against Israel's position on nuclear matters.

Conversely, there was fear that other Track-II venues might be detrimental to Israel's national interests by allowing Egypt to achieve what it failed to secure in the ACRS talks—a focus on weapons of mass destruction with particular emphasis on Israel's nuclear option. Beginning in late 1994, there was considerable suspicion in Israel that Egyptian officials were attempting to involve unofficial Israelis in a dialogue on the nuclear issue to create a constituency within Israel favoring the early application of nuclear arms control measures. There was also fear that Egypt aimed at weakening the Israeli government's resistance to discussing the nuclear issue by attempting to drive a wedge between Israeli academics and their government. Another concern was that the involvement of U.S. sponsors and participants would serve Egyptian interests by demonstrating to the United States that prominent Israelis took exception to their government's refusal to place the nuclear issue on the formal ACRS agenda.

These sensitivities reached a peak in determining the attitude of Israeli government officials toward the Track-II talks initiated by De Paul University and ISISC in late 1994. The initial effort by the sponsors of these talks to have the participants negotiate a draft NWFZ was seen by Israeli officials as meeting Egypt's priorities in the ACRS process and achieving through a Track-II process what Israel had repeatedly rejected in Track-I negotiations. As a result, Israeli government officials refused to take part in the De Paul–ISISC talks, even in an unofficial capacity. They also explained to senior Egyptians that the Israelis involved in the talks did not represent Israel's position on arms control issues. Most importantly, they pressed the U.S. Department of State and the Arms Control and Disarmament Agency to persuade the U.S. Department of Energy to cease funding the project.

Some Israeli officials saw the De Paul University–ISISC project as counterproductive to the purposes of Track-II talks because of the ill will it created within Israeli government circles that, in turn, made it more difficult to argue the general case in favor of Track-II talks. For some on the Israeli side, the De Paul–ISISC talks led to a hardening of the positions held by Israeli decision-makers and Track-I negotiators. The Israelis taking part in this venue were seen as allowing the Egyptians to dictate the arms control agenda and as having, in return, extracted from the Egyptian side no more than some "sweeteners" in the political-declaratory realm that were merely meant to assuage the Israeli government's anger. Moreover, the intensity with which some Egyptian participants initially pursued their agenda in the De Paul–ISISC talks, and the sensitivity of some Israeli participants with regard to the anxieties that these discussions created, sometimes led the discussions to deteriorate into acrimonious exchanges. Thus, at least in one venue, Track-II talks that were designed to reduce tensions sometimes had the opposite effect.

Summary

The ACRS-related Track-II talks had a unique role in the Middle East context, different than the various bilateral venues. This role was largely educational, allowing Arabs and Israelis to learn about arms control—a realm that has occupied the attention of the United States and the Soviet Union over a number of decades. As the subject matter involves attempts to employ nonmilitary means to address capabilities for military and mass destruction, it comprises one of the most complex dimensions of security policy and international affairs.

The ACRS-related Track-II venues also provided ideal settings for the exchange of information and communication regarding the parties' threat perceptions and security concerns. Indeed, as the official ACRS Track-I negotiations fell victim to the Egyptian-Israeli nuclear dispute, the various ACRS-related Track-II venues allowed the parties to continue and further develop their multilateral security conversation in informal settings.

A number of the region's states have repeatedly demonstrated the importance they attach to the ACRS process—a reflection of the extent to which they saw the subject matter of these talks as affecting their national security. Both Egypt and Israel took care to participate in every ACRS-related Track-II venue to which they were invited, even after the official Track-I ACRS negotiations were suspended de facto in mid-1995. Indeed, in one case the impasse reached in 1995 even prompted Egypt to *initiate* a Track-II venue: the Egyptian-Jordanian-Israeli De Paul–ISISC talks.

Yet the ACRS-related discussions also demonstrate the limitations of Track-II venues. While the impasse between Egypt and Israel on the nuclear issue did not prevent the continuation of "soft" Track-II venues, it prevented any ACRS-related "hard" Track-II exercise from becoming effective. Indeed, all efforts within Track-II frameworks to bridge the gap between the Israeli and Egyptian concepts of "sequencing" have failed. Israelis continued to emphasize the need to establish peace and mutual confidence through the application of CSBMs as the basis for arms control. Conversely, Egyptians continued to stress the need to approach nuclear disarmament first, given the dangerous character of these weapons. Thus, in contrast to the effect of the Oslo talks on the stalemate in the Track-I Israeli-Palestinian negotiations, the ACRS-related Track-II talks have so far failed to end the deadlock in the official Track-I ACRS negotiations.

Chapter 9

Analysis

This chapter surveys the genesis of Track-II talks and analyzes the various factors that played a role in affecting the successes and failures of such venues. It explains how Track-II discussions evolve, ascertains the various functions of such discussions, and elaborates the importance of participants, mentors, leaders, sponsors, and "third parties" in influencing the course and consequences of Track-II efforts.

Genesis

Track-II talks did not make a surprise appearance on the Middle East political landscape with the Oslo accords in 1993, nor did they become a feature of the region's diplomatic discourse overnight. Rather, the use of this tool in the Middle East evolved gradually, with very modest beginnings in the 1970s, more promising initiatives in the 1980s, and considerable impact in the first half of the 1990s.

The evolution of Track-II talks over this period cannot be explained without reference to the strategic context and the general political conditions that evolved in the Middle East over the past three decades. It could be argued that for Track-II discussions to become effective, the Arab-Israeli conflict needed to reach a measure of "ripeness" or "maturity." The maturity required was no different than that needed for increasing the odds of success of other venues such as formal Track-I negotiations as well as official but secret diplomacy. Thus, Track-II talks were unlikely to evolve immediately after the 1948 War, when the parties were still struggling with the consequences of widespread death, destruction, and displacement.

"Context" is taken here to mean the general climate that has encouraged the conduct of Track-II talks, rather than, say, the specific conditions that allowed for the Oslo breakthrough in 1993. It is also worth noting that "context" is less important for the conduct of "soft" Track-II talks that are designed to increase the parties' appreciation of one another's perceptions and concerns. Thus, when the purpose of the talks is confined to "dialoguing," no more than a general desire to acquire an understanding of the other side is required. By contrast, a much more comprehensive set of conditions must be met for "hard" Track-II talks to produce a dramatic breakthrough in conflict resolution.

Major events and developments on the ground may help "ripen" a conflict so that Track-II discussions can succeed. For example, Israel's occupation of the West Bank and Gaza during the June 1967 War allowed for the first direct contact between Israelis and Arabs not residing within the country's post-1949 borders. From the Palestinians' perspective, this development also created the most important motivation for such talks: to explore the prospects and conditions for ending Israeli occupation. Another important development that encouraged Israeli-Palestinian Track-II talks was the 1982 Lebanon War. As a consequence of the war, a growing number of Israelis reached the conclusion that the Israeli-Palestinian conflict should be brought to an end. Even more dramatic was the first Palestinian *intifada* in 1987. The uprising created an imperative for Israelis and Palestinians alike to alleviate the costs of the occupation, including the measures taken by Israel to suppress Palestinian resistance.

While wide-scale bloodshed created a negative psychological environment for Track-II talks, violence also often produced an important incentive for conducting such talks—to avoid further bloodshed. The 1973 War created such an incentive in the Arab-Israeli context at large. At a more immediate level, terrorism and violence created incentives to explore the conditions that might prevent their continuation. At the same time, terrorism and violence have had the opposite effect, as people on both sides are angered by the death of innocents. Thus, terrorism and violence may provide incentives for talks, but productive discussions are unlikely to take place in an emotionally charged atmosphere.

Developments that create great uncertainty for the parties may also encourage discussions that would otherwise have been avoided. A good example is the talks held between the Israeli settlers and representatives of the Palestinian Authority in 1995–1996. The Oslo, Cairo, and Taba accords, and the apparent determination of the Rabin government to pursue the peace process, created deep fears among Israeli settlers in the West Bank that areas where they resided would soon be subject to Palestinian control. This led some settlers to conclude that they should engage their would-be rulers with a view to exploring whether there was some ground for a *modus vivendi* with the Palestinian side.

An important effect of these dramatic developments was the conclusion reached by people on both sides that they should become more attuned to each other's perceptions and fears. During the late 1980s and 1990s, this gave rise to an important incentive to engage members of the opposing community in informal but direct dialogue. The cumulative costs of continued conflict also gradually created a deep sense of fatigue among Arabs and Israelis alike, which led to a growing desire to explore different avenues for resolving the conflict. Track-II talks gradually became a part of this larger realm.

Purposes and Functions

Track-II talks were pursued in an effort to attain a number of different objectives. We discuss eight here.

GAINING RECOGNITION

Gaining mutual recognition at the human and individual levels seems to have been a primary purpose of Israeli-Palestinian dialogue-centered ("soft") Track-II talks until the late 1980s. The best example of such an approach was the discussions organized and sponsored by Herbert Kelman at Harvard University. At the time, both sides were still highly sensitive about one another's quest for justice, dignity, and security, and they perceived recognition and acknowledgement of their respective grievances as mutually exclusive. An important objective of the Kelman exercise was to engage both sides in a dialogue about their political and ideological disputes as a kind of "political encounter therapy" in the hope that this might lead to mutual understanding of these grievances.

Track-II talks also had a more focused political objective. For the PLO, such talks were often seen as a useful avenue for reaching an important goal: gaining international recognition for the national rights of the Palestinians and for the PLO's role and standing as the sole legitimate representative of the Palestinian people. Involving a range of Israelis in a web of such discussions served the Palestinian goal of affecting Israeli public opinion and obtaining recognition by Israel and its elected government. From the outset, the ultimate political objective of the Palestinians was independent statehood and the end of occupation. Gaining recognition for the PLO was regarded as the first step toward achieving this goal.

From the Palestinian standpoint, Track-II talks that involved U.S. and European sponsors, as well as other third-party governments, also served this goal by broadening the base of such recognition. For this reason, PLO leaders often supported participation in Track-II talks almost without reservation or discrimination. Only rarely did the PLO leadership object to any particular Palestinian representation in such talks. They also assumed that the wide network of contacts created by these talks would diminish the likelihood that the PLO would be bypassed or ignored at future political and diplomatic junctures. The 1993 Oslo accords marked the triumph of the PLO's efforts to gain recognition through a Track-II process, or what started as one. A long-standing obstacle in the peace process was overcome, and a necessary precondition for any final settlement of the Palestinian-Israeli conflict was met.

Israeli leaders took a very different approach. During the 1970s and the 1980s, they did not seek recognition by the PLO or negotiations with it, but rather the opposite. Their purpose was to prevent the PLO from gaining recognition as a first step to independent Palestinian statehood. Hence, they did not encourage Track-II talks and initially regarded these talks as unfortunate developments to which they must react. But while they rarely saw a positive Israeli interest in such talks, they were willing to examine the possibility of making use of such discussions in order to explore Palestinian positions and political objectives.

The type of recognition that the two parties sought within the framework of the Track-II talks also seems to have been different. While the Palestinian leaders were mostly seeking formal recognition of their rights and of the PLO's standing, the Israeli participants in the Track-II talks often sought existential recognition—namely, Palestinian and Arab approval of the right of the Israel to exist as a Jewish state in an Arab and Islamic Middle East.

The difference between the two parties' purposes was even more pronounced in their objectives for the Arms Control and Regional Security–related Track-II talks. The Arab side generally perceived the Israeli side as eager to engage in these talks as an avenue to advancing Israel's interest in "normalizing" its standing in the region. By contrast, Israeli participants in these talks tended to perceive their Arab counterparts—particularly the Egyptians—as focused on a specific purpose, namely that of pressing Israel to abandon its nuclear option.

MAKING CONTACT

Track-II talks may help parties overcome the obstacles to constructive engagement between them. This is particularly important when exchanges are not otherwise possible due to the absence of sustained prior contact or the presence of constraints on formal contact between the parties. In Israel's case, there were long-standing political inhibitions against a direct dialogue with the PLO before 1992–1993. In 1986, these inhibitions were written into law through Knesset legislation that prohibited Israelis from direct contact with PLO members.

Track-II talks allowed for such contact by exploiting a loophole in the Israeli law: Israelis were not prohibited from participating in academic conferences that were also attended by Palestinians who were associated with the PLO. All that was required to consider such contacts as "legal" was that they could be presented as a "seminar" hosted by a third party that enjoyed some academic credentials.

Throughout the period when it was illegal for Israelis to engage members of the PLO, Track-II talks offered Israeli leaders opportunities for indirect contact with the PLO. Yitzhak Rabin, Shimon Peres, and other Israeli leaders often received verbal or written reports by Israeli participants regarding the impressions they gained from these discussions. While such contacts were clear violations of "the spirit of the law," Peres and Rabin were unconcerned about the law's rigid application. Indeed, Israeli leaders often appeared ready to turn a blind eye to "illegal" contacts where this served their purpose.

The role of Track-II talks in establishing contact among adversaries may have been more important in the Israeli-Syrian than in the Israeli-Palestinian realm. Israeli occupation of the West Bank and Gaza had made daily human contact between the two sides unexceptional, and helped to demythologize the effects of such contacts. But for Syria in particular, ideological and official constraints on contacts with Israelis were greater than those on the Palestinian side. For example, the role of Track-II talks as a means of overcoming formal obstacles to contact was a very important component of the Israeli-Syrian talks sponsored by Initiative for Peace and Cooperation in the Middle East. During 1991–1994, formal Syrian disapproval of unofficial contacts with Israelis did not extend to "academic" exercises in which other third parties were involved. The Syrian leaders' lack of objections to the participation of Syrian scholars in IPCME discussions also reflected their interest in ascertaining the limits of Israeli flexibility, particularly in view of the protracted stalemate in the formal Israeli-Syrian Track-I negotiations then being held in Washington.

From the Palestinians' standpoint, Track-II talks provided for contact with two other constituencies that were of growing significance to the PLO besides Israel: the U.S. government and—to a lesser extent—the American Jewish community. Since it made its 1975 commitments to Israel, the U.S. government could not engage the PLO directly. As a result, the PLO was constantly seeking indirect means of engaging successive U.S. administrations. Track-II talks were useful in this respect especially, but not exclusively, when sponsored by U.S. nongovernmental organizations. U.S. sponsors tended to brief U.S. government officials regarding the progress made in the talks, and the Palestinian side was keen to convey messages that would eventually reach their designated addresses in Washington.

Prior to Oslo, much of the prominence of U.S. NGOs in the Palestinian-Israeli context can be traced to the Palestinian view that the U.S. connection was vital even when working informally. Other Arab parties shared this view, as reflected in the positive Arab response to invitations to participate in the Search for Common Ground Track-II talks as well as in ACRS-related talks sponsored by other U.S. academic centers and NGOs. The desire to affect U.S. thinking was also reflected in venues sponsored by European NGOs and by European governments. In most cases, the Palestinians had a clear interest in making sure that their European hosts would brief U.S. government officials about the progress of the talks.

Track-II talks also provided the Palestinians with a venue for contacting the American Jewish community. Jewish leaders in the United States were reluctant to engage the PLO as long as Israeli law and political constraints in the United States prohibited both governments from engaging in such talks. Informal talks with U.S. Jewish leaders, such as the discussions in Sweden in 1988, allowed the PLO access to important members of the U.S. Jewish community. In addition, Track-II talks also provided opportunities for contact between the Palestinians and the Israeli right wing that could not have taken place in a formal context.

Track-II encounters helped to establish and cement personal relationships that would otherwise have been impossible. Two examples are the talks held between Palestinians and Israeli settlers and the discussions sponsored by IPCME. In the latter framework, contacts were made between Palestinian and other Arab participants and Dore Gold, then a senior research associate at Tel Aviv University's Jaffee Center for Strategic Studies. The resulting familiarity became particularly useful after the 1996 Israeli elections, when Gold became Prime Minister Netanyahu's foreign policy adviser. Such contacts had considerable impact on the Israeli-Palestinian political dynamic.

The ACRS-related multilateral Track-II talks also helped in overcoming obstacles to contact between the parties. In the absence of formal relations between Israel and most states in the Maghreb and the Persian Gulf, these talks provided opportunities for Israelis and individuals from these countries to engage in discussions of mutual interest and concern. More often than not, representatives from North Africa and the GCC states found common ground with their Israeli colleagues—a desire to address the threats to the region at large and to avoid an exclusive focus on the Arab-Israeli conflict.

By the mid-1990s, ACRS-related Track-II talks also provided venues for contacts between Israelis and Iranians, allowing for exchanges that had not taken place since the Iranian Revolution of 1979. These meetings were held on the margins of wider gatherings convened by the Stockholm International Peace Research Institute (SIPRI), the Security Group of IPCME, and later the University of California, Los Angeles. The discussions focused on arms control issues but also provided opportunities for participants to convey their respective approaches and concerns.

CONFLICT RESOLUTION

"Hard" Track-II talks were specifically intended to help negotiate a resolution of various dimensions of the Arab-Israeli conflict. While participants in the Oslo, Stockholm, and some of the IPCME talks assumed that a final resolution of most issues would need to be achieved through official Track-I negotiations, the assumption was that progress made in Track-II discussions would ease the subsequent formal negotiations. The discussions sponsored by FAFO in Oslo were initially only designed to help the Israelis and Palestinians overcome the difficulties encountered by their official representatives negotiating in Washington. Once rapid progress was made in Norway—producing a document that was far more significant than originally expected—and it became apparent that the discussions might lead to a historical breakthrough, the process was "taken over" by officials from both sides. This transformed the exercise into formal Track-I negotiations. Yet the role of the earlier Track-II phases of these talks was critical; at the time, it was only in such informal discussions that the parties' willingness to compromise could be explored.

The evolution of the Stockholm talks took an opposite course. From the outset, the discussions in Sweden were designed to help negotiate a final resolution of the Palestinian-Israeli conflict and to produce a compromise regarding the outstanding "final-status" issues at the heart of the two peoples' dispute. But the effort to produce a final status understanding was seen as separate from that of reaching a peace treaty. The participants in these talks concluded that such a treaty could be agreed upon only after the Palestinians had achieved independent statehood.

Later, however, the participants in the Stockholm talks understood that they would not be able to provide a full final status resolution and that they would have to aim for a more modest "framework agreement" that would serve as the basis for detailed Track-I negotiations. Thus, the Stockholm understandings were designed to launch the official negotiations of the final status issues from an advanced starting point. Subsequent negotiations were expected to translate the general understanding reached at the Track-II level into practical agreements that would allow Israelis and Palestinians to put their long conflict behind them.

While the evolution of the Oslo and Stockholm talks differed, their scope was similarly wide—an effort to deal with all dimensions of the conflict. This may help to explain the interest and eventual involvement of the two leaderships in these talks, and was an important cause of their success. By contrast, the earlier American Academy of Arts and Sciences effort was seen as addressing only one dimension of the problem—the security issues associated with the transfer of control of territory from Israel to the Palestinians. Consequently, these talks were less appealing to the two parties' top leaderships.

The Israeli-Syrian discussions that took place in the IPCME framework were initially also meant to achieve a limited purpose—an understanding on security arrangements should Israel withdraw from the Golan Heights. An attempt was made to summarize these arrangements in a detailed text that evolved over a number of meetings during 1992–1993.

In October 1993, however, the purpose of the talks was expanded: to reach an understanding on the principles for resolving the Syrian-Israeli dispute and for establishing peaceful relations between the two countries. An attempt was made to formulate this understanding in a one-page document that defined the general principles that might guide future Track-I Syrian-Israeli negotiations (see appendix). The Israeli-Syrian IPCME talks demonstrated that a comprehensive settlement of the Israeli-Syrian conflict, and mutually accepted arrangements in the Golan and in Lebanon, could be reached. The IPCME exercise showed that Track-II talks may assist the parties in moving toward a settlement, even if the ideas proposed are not acceptable to the two leaderships at the time, and even if the ultimate settlement does not necessarily correspond to that proposed in the Track-II framework.

In one case, an ACRS-related Track-II channel attempted to duplicate the success of the Oslo experience in conflict resolution. The talks, initiated in late 1994 under the umbrella of De Paul University in Chicago and ISISC in Siracusa, Italy, linked the Jaffee Center for Strategic Studies at Tel Aviv University, the National Center for Middle East Studies (NCMES) in Cairo, and the Department for Disarmament and Security Studies (DDSS) in Amman. Participants took part in these talks as members of delegations—thus creating a negotiation-like format. From the outset, the organizers encouraged participants to resolve their competing perspectives on a treaty that would transform the Middle East into a zone free of weapons of mass destruction (WMDFZ). Thus, the purpose of the talks was to explore whether the parties could reach an agreement that eluded their representatives in the stalled ACRS negotiations.

However, disagreements regarding priorities in enhancing regional security gradually induced the delegations to adopt more modest purposes. For the following two years, they focused primarily on negotiating a "Mission Statement"—an ACRS-related functional equivalent of a DOP. The exclusive emphasis on negotiating a WMDFZ was abandoned in favor of a more comprehensive approach to regional security that would include efforts to control conventional arms and to build regional security structures and institutions.

SENDING MESSAGES

Track-II frameworks may also provide venues for exchanging messages. The Track-II talks sponsored by Bob Ontell in San Diego in 1986–1987 (see Chapter 2) provided the first opportunity for the Palestinian side to consider the "Gaza first" option entailing an Israeli withdrawal from the Gaza Strip as a first step for creating a breakthrough in the Israeli-Palestinian conflict.

The "Gaza first" idea was raised again in late 1992, this time during the American Academy of Arts and Sciences exercise on security. In early 1993, Israeli participants prepared a paper elaborating this concept and delivered it to the Palestinian side. In March 1993, Palestinian participants in the AAAS talks discussed this option with one of the Palestinian negotiators at Oslo and examined the issue of linkage between the Gaza and the West Bank with PLO leader Abu Mazin. The emerging consensus was that any transfer of control over Gaza from Israel to the Palestinians would have to be accompanied by a transfer of control over territory— even if symbolic—in the West Bank as well. This notion was eventually incorporated into the Oslo accords.

The Palestinian side conveyed other messages to the Israelis in the AAAS talks. One such message was that the PLO was prepared to discuss Israel's security requirements on a reciprocal basis and to communicate with the Israeli government directly regarding the issues involved. This message, and the impressions gained from the resulting discussions of the issues, was transmitted to Israeli leaders and top officials through reports written and distributed by Israeli participants in the talks.

In July 1995, the Palestinians conveyed a different message in their talks with Israeli settlers. At that time, the Palestinian Authority decided to send an official representative to the talks, signalling that the PA was "here to stay" and that it was ready to engage the settlers in discussions of their problems. More significantly, it signalled to the settlers, as well as indirectly to the Israeli government, that the PA recognized the reality of the settlers' presence, and that it understood the value of the contacts between the two sides as a possible confidence-building measure.

Israelis used the same channels to deliver messages to the Palestinians. In early discussions regarding the "Gaza first" option, Israelis signalled to the PLO that a successful beginning in Gaza would create an atmosphere conducive to further Israeli concessions in the West Bank. It was pointed out that such a success would demonstrate that the prospective Palestinian authority was capable of preventing violence in the territory under its control. Similarly, in the talks between Israeli settlers and the PA, each side emphasized its human concerns in an effort to de-demonize itself in the eyes of the other.

In the IPCME Syrian talks, the Syrian participants conveyed the notion that they were serious about their willingness to negotiate a settlement with Israel. Israeli participants in these discussions conveyed to the other side the importance they attached to securing Israel's water resources, and, consequently, to the Sea of Galilee. The Israeli participants also used this channel to make clear that they were prepared to accept some degree of reciprocity in implementing postwithdrawal security arrangements.

GAINING INFORMATION

Track-II talks can help the parties gain information about one another. In the Palestinian-Israeli context, each side has used Track-II discussions as a venue for gathering information about and understanding the inner workings of the other side's political system. Personal contacts established in these talks facilitated such exchanges, given the political and psychological obstacles to gaining such knowledge through formal negotiations. One reason why the PLO leadership rarely objected to informal contacts with Israelis was its interest in utilizing every possible source for additional information and new ideas.

For the parties involved, gathering information and gaining an appreciation of the other parties' perceptions and concerns provided an important motive for engagement in the ACRS-related Track-II talks. For example, Israeli participants in these talks were curious to find out how their Arab counterparts perceived Israel's nuclear option and the manner in which different developments affected Israel's deterrent profile. They were also interested to learn how their Arab neighbors viewed their own security imperatives—partly in an effort to ascertain the extent to which Arab governments continue to regard Israel as an adversary.

In an effort to assess their neighbors' capabilities and intentions, Israeli participants in ACRS-related Track-II venues were interested to learn how participants from Middle Eastern states viewed other states and their respective leaders. For example, they were interested in Jordanian insights into the Iraqi leadership and in Egyptian insights into Iran's intentions and its involvement in encouraging terrorism and instability in the region. Similarly, Arab participants in these talks attempted to ascertain Israel's threat perceptions in order to have a better judgment of what might trigger a decision to use force.

There may be an inherent trade-off between using Track-II talks for information gathering on the one hand, and using them for conflict resolution on the other. Making good use of information requires that it be disseminated within the governmental and institutional structures. But the larger the number of officials aware of this information, the greater the likelihood that either the information or its source may be leaked. This, in turn, could lead one or more of the parties to abort the discussions, thus undermining any possibility that the talks could become a venue for effective conflict resolution.

Track-II talks have been particularly useful for gaining information about the other side's intentions. The Syrian side appears to have used the IPCME channel to test Israel's seriousness and commitment to reaching an agreement. The Syrians were also interested in exploring Israel's "red lines," particularly in matters related to the security arrangements required as a condition for its withdrawal from the Golan Heights. Similarly, the Palestinian side used the AAAS talks to explore Israel's position regarding the future of the Jewish settlements in the West Bank and Gaza and its security requirements after a possible withdrawal from these areas.

Leaders can utilize one Track-II channel to corroborate information or understandings gained from other Track-II channels. For example, they may use one Track-II channel to test the intentions of the other side as reflected in another channel. Although such cross-checking does not appear to have been widely exercised in the Middle East, Prime Minister Rabin may have used information gained in the AAAS talks (as transmitted through Deputy Defense Minister Mordechai Gur) to corroborate the messages received in the Oslo framework. Similarly, the PLO leadership may have used information gained in the AAAS talks to corroborate the impressions given by Israeli participants in Oslo regarding Israel's willingness to transfer responsibility for internal security to the PLO following Israel's withdrawal.

TESTING IDEAS

Track-II talks have allowed the parties a deniable venue for testing creative ideas and have been used to float such ideas and elicit reactions without incurring significant political costs. In the Middle East, however, it was mostly the Israeli side that made use of this particular facet of Track-II talks during the late 1980s and early 1990s. This is because Israeli participants in these talks generally benefited from a social and political system that demonstrated greater tolerance for independent thinking. Even more importantly in the Israeli-Palestinian context, Israeli participants were virtually free of the safety concerns faced by the Palestinians taking part in these talks.

The Israeli-Syrian talks conducted under the sponsorship of IPCME are a case in point. The Syrian participants in these talks generally refrained from generating ideas and commented instead on ideas presented by the Israeli side. The Syrians never volunteered texts but limited themselves to examining and reacting to texts suggested by others. Indeed, even the degree of their commitment to ideas that seemed to comprise an "agreed text" remained vague and uncertain. At one stage, it was hoped that an IPCME paper would be acceptable to the Syrian participants, and that through this the Syrian government would signal its indirect approval. But after the meeting in Istanbul in May 1993, it became quite clear that the paper would be "filed" and that the Syrian participants were hesitant to put their signature to an agreed document that would be signed by all participants.

INFLUENCING THIRD PARTIES

As the weaker party in the conflict, the PLO saw Track-II talks as a useful means of influencing third parties—primarily the United States. Palestinian participants often saw themselves as communicating simultaneously with two audiences: their Israeli counterparts across the table and U.S. government officials in Washington. Since they acknowledged U.S. influence in the Middle East and were convinced that Washington's approach to the Arab-Israeli conflict was biased in Israel's favor, Palestinian participants utilized Track-II talks to try to persuade their interlocutors that the PLO's positions were both moderate and justified. They also regarded these talks as an opportunity to correct what they believed to be U.S. misperceptions about the conflict.

By contrast, Israel, which enjoyed more effective channels for influencing opinions in the United States, did not try to affect Washington's approach through Track-II talks. At the same time, Israel did not object to the third-party role of the United States in Track-II venues. By and large, Israel preferred that the United States play such a role rather than the Europeans, due to the prevalent Israeli view that the latter tended to lend "automatic" support to the Arab cause.

While Israelis did not need Track-II venues to communicate with the

United States, they were often interested in keeping U.S. officials informed of developments taking place in Track-II venues. This was especially true for "hard" Track-II talks, due to an understanding that Washington's position would be crucial to any effort to implement whatever agreements might be advanced as a consequence of Track-II activities. The Israelis generally assumed that the United States would compensate Israel for whatever concessions it would need to make in an agreement with its Arab neighbors by offering military aid, economic assistance, and strategic assurances. This was particularly relevant with regard to an Israeli agreement with Syria. More broadly, the Israeli side also tended to assume that U.S. support would be needed to gain international recognition and legitimacy—primarily in the United Nations—for any agreement reached with its Arab neighbors. Therefore, there was no attempt to dissuade the sponsors of Track-II talks from briefing U.S. officials regarding the progress made in these discussions.

ADVANCING TACTICAL INTERESTS AND PERSONAL PROBLEM SOLVING
Track-II talks were also used to advance tactical interests. For example, the Palestinians taking part in the Stockholm talks were interested in affecting the Israeli electoral process. They hoped that the outcome of the talks would provide Prime Minister Rabin with a framework that would help him in the struggle over the Labor Party's platform with respect to Israeli-Palestinian final status issues, as well as in the subsequent Israeli general elections. Israeli participants in the talks also hoped that their positive results might serve the Israeli mentor of these talks—Minister of Planning Yossi Beilin—in his quest for a leading position in the Labor Party by making it clear that he should be credited for his part in creating the breakthrough.

Another example concerns the Palestinian attempt to engage Likud leaders or individuals close to Likud. Sometimes the Palestinians regarded forums that did not include Likud members or individuals close to Likud as incomplete. While PLO leader Yasser Arafat had enormous respect for some Labor leaders, by the late 1980s the PLO leadership concluded that it should not limit its contacts with Israelis to those associated with the Israeli peace camp or the Labor party.

This ultimately led to the talks held between the Palestinian Authority and Israeli settlers, in which some attempt at problem solving also took place. Before the elections to the Palestinian Legislative Council in January 1996, the Palestinian Authority feared that Israeli settlers might resort to activities, including violence, that would disrupt the elections or increase the popularity of more extreme candidates. Consequently, PA participants in the talks requested that the settler leadership make every effort to prevent such disruptive action; the request seems to have been generally heeded.

In the ACRS-related talks, Egypt attempted to affect the Israeli public debate on arms control issues and to encourage greater willingness among the country's intellectual elite to question the utility of parts of Israel's strategic deterrence. The Egyptian side seemed to be attempting to drive a wedge on these issues between Israeli defense intellectuals and their government. Thus, on more than one occasion, Egyptian leaders made reference to ongoing Track-II talks as indicating that some Israelis were willing to adopt a "more flexible" position on these issues than their government.

Contacts made through Track-II talks also helped solve problems of individuals. For example, one Israeli participant in these talks helped a Palestinian colleague to obtain entry and exit permits. Having discovered that a rival in the PA intelligence services was preventing the Palestinian participant from entering Gaza, the Israeli participant helped devise a way that might enable him to enter and remain in the city.

The Players

Participants

Not all participants in the Middle East Track-II talks have been private individuals acting in an independent capacity. Indeed, the most often cited example of Track-II talks—the Oslo talks—was never a purely Track-II exercise: the Palestinian participants in these talks were high-ranking PLO officials. From the outset, the Oslo talks constituted a Track-I½ framework involving a mix of officials and non-official individuals.

Similarly, a number of ACRS-related talks—notably the talks sponsored by the University of California's Institute for Global Cooperation and Conflict and by the University of California at Los Angeles (UCLA)—included high-ranking Israeli and Arab officials "acting in an independent capacity." This was particularly the case for the "military-to-military" talks held by IGCC beginning in 1997. A large number of active-duty senior military officers from Israel and a number of Arab states took part in these talks, focusing on issues related to regional security and arms control. Hence, these discussions could also be characterized as Track-I½ frameworks.

While some of the officials taking part in Middle East Track-II talks did so at the behest of their superiors, private individuals participating in these discussions seemed to have had a different profile. By and large, these individuals were motivated by a sincere concern for the fate of the region and were committed to advancing the cause of peace in the Middle East. Some were deeply concerned by what they perceived as the negative direction of developments in the region. They were convinced that they should try to change the course of these developments. In addition, a measure of curiosity may have been involved, including a desire to become familiar with and to better understand former adversaries.

Participation in conflict-resolution "hard" Track-II frameworks may also have reflected a desire to leave a mark on history. In addition, participants may have been motivated by the simple concern that there was a task to be performed and by the conviction that others would not be able to execute the mission as effectively. A more modest wish was to become involved in the policy process outside rigid bureaucratic governmental or semigovernmental structures.

Another motivation for individuals to take part in Track-II talks was political ambition. For example, a number of Israelis with aspirations for leadership hoped that their involvement in efforts to end the Arab-Israeli conflict would affect their image positively. For these individuals, Track-II meetings constituted a source of ideas that they could bring back to their political circles. In addition, the meetings allowed leaders to test their own proposals and obtain direct feedback from Arab participants about notions they had developed for solving the conflict.

Yet in the late 1980s and early 1990s, Israeli and Arab participants in Track-II talks often differed considerably in the relative weight they attached to these talks. In some cases, Israeli participants seem to have been moved by a deep psychological need to enter into a dialogue with their Palestinian counterparts. This points to an interesting paradox: while Palestinian leaders were usually more interested in Israeli-Palestinian talks than their Israeli counterparts, Israeli participants were often more eager to engage in these talks than their Palestinian colleagues, despite the Israeli view—widely held at the time—that it was not possible to engage PLO-related Palestinians except on the subject of independent statehood. Consequently, while the Palestinians approached these talks as one among many efforts launched to advance their interests, the Israelis taking part in these talks seemed much more eager to secure positive results.

Participants' willingness to take risks also affected the course of Track-II talks and their outcomes. For example, the potential impact of the AAAS talks may have been undermined by the refusal of Israeli participants in these talks to travel to Tunis to meet with the PLO's top leaders, possibly missing an opportunity to make the AAAS channel a more central venue of Israeli-Palestinian engagement.

For Palestinians during the 1980s, participation also required personal courage, as they were implicitly if not explicitly threatened by militant groups that had assassinated a number of Palestinian individuals for having conducted a dialogue with Israelis, notably Issan Sartawi and Said Hammami. Indeed, it was only after 1988, when the Palestinian National Council accepted the "two-state solution," that the physical risk to Palestinian participants in Track-II talks began to recede.

The status of Palestinian and Israeli participants in Track-II talks was very different. The Palestinian participants in many Track-II activities saw themselves more often than not as unofficial representatives of their "government." With some exceptions, however, most Israeli participants appeared conscious of representing only themselves, albeit with connections to the Israeli political establishment. Indeed, while many of the Israelis involved in these discussions were truly independent—before 1991 some were even estranged from their country's establishment—their Palestinian counterparts rarely acted without some form of sanction by the PLO leadership. Yet prior permission to participate in these discussions was not always necessary. More often than not, Palestinian participants in these talks would inform the PLO leadership of their participation after the talks had taken place.

The Israelis taking part in talks with Palestinians assumed that the latter sought permission from PLO leaders in Tunis to participate in the talks and that they kept Tunis informed regarding the progress made in these discussions. In one sense this was to the Palestinians' benefit—the Israelis often assumed that their Palestinian counterparts were more representative and authoritative than they were.

Palestinian and Israeli participants in Track-II talks also demonstrated different spectrums of opinion. Israeli participants—particularly in the IPCME framework and the PA-settlers talks—occasionally included individuals close to Likud and other right-wing movements, even though it was not always easy to persuade Israelis who were associated with Likud to take part in such discussions. By contrast, Palestinian participants in Track-II talks almost never included members or followers of Hamas or other opposition groups that were critical of the PLO. While this may have been the result of some reluctance to bring in anti-PLO factions, it also reflected the reluctance of the Palestinian opposition to engage in the Track-II process.

The conceptual flexibility demonstrated by Israelis and Arabs in these talks also differed. Israeli participants generally displayed greater willingness to propose options and scenarios than their Arab counterparts, while Palestinian and Syrian participants often found it difficult to suggest options that were at odds with the official line. Given Israel's control on the ground and the general imbalance of power in its favor, Israelis could afford to develop and discuss different scenarios for withdrawal and disengagement. The consensus on the Israeli side was also weaker, with no clear red lines regarding the ultimate fate of the territories conquered in 1967; Israeli options regarding this issue ranged from full withdrawal to full annexation. By contrast, the Arab consensus allowed little scope for exploring anything but a full Israeli withdrawal to the lines of June 5, 1967. Consequently, Israeli scenarios and maps often set the pace and agenda for Track-II discussions, with the Palestinian-Arab side responding to ideas generated by the Israelis.

To a lesser degree, the ACRS-related Track-II talks also showed the different degrees of "independence" enjoyed by Israeli and Arab participants. In most cases, Arab participants in these talks were strongly tied to their respective governments. Even when participants were members of private research centers, these institutions and their members exercised more limited independence than their counterparts in Israel and the other "Western" advanced states. The Israeli-Egyptian-Jordanian talks, sponsored by De Paul University and ISISC in Siracusa, provided the most extreme example of this contrast. While the Arab participants were encouraged to take part in these discussions by their respective governments, Israelis participated in the talks despite the deep misgivings that senior Israeli government officials held about these discussions—at least until early 1998.

Ultimately, the effectiveness of Track-II participants depends very much on their access to the country's highest authorities. The structure of decision-making in all Middle East states is such that the effect of Track-II talks is minimal unless lessons, messages, and ideas that are generated in these meetings reach the very top policy echelons and are regarded by the latter as of real value.

MENTORS

Yossi Beilin, who served in 1992–1995 as deputy minister of foreign affairs and in 1995–1996 as minister of planning, serves as a good example of a mentor on the Israeli side. Abu Mazin, Secretary General of the PLO executive committee and a high-ranking PLO official, played a similar role on the Palestinian side. The two mentors guided the participants in the Oslo talks—at least until these talks were transformed into Track-I formal negotiations—as well as the subsequent discussions held in Stockholm. They were able to perform this role because they met all the prerequisites for playing an effective part in the talks and because they shared a tacit understanding regarding the purposes and significance of the exercises in which they were involved.

The AAAS and PA-settler talks clearly lacked mentors willing to take political risks in the fashion demonstrated by Beilin in Oslo and Stockholm: taking action first and obtaining authorization later. The Israeli-Syrian discussions sponsored by IPCME also illustrate the consequences of the absence of a mentor. While the talks may have had tacit acceptance from the Syrian leadership, they lacked a conduit through which Israel's top leaders could be presented with the progress made and persuaded of the opportunities provided by the discussions. As it was, none of the Israeli officials familiar with the IPCME track carried the political weight necessary to persuade Rabin to pay serious attention to the talks. Moreover, some government officials involved in the Israeli-Syrian Track-I negotiations were interested in preventing the Track-II talks from competing with the formal negotiations that they were conducting. For example, Ambassador Walid Mua'lim, who led the Syrian delegation in the Washington talks, reportedly asked his government to assure him that negotiations were not being conducted through more than one channel. Mua'lim's Israeli counterpart, Ambassador Itamar Rabinovich, seems to have been equally dubious about the talks.

An effective Track-II mentor on the Arab side was Jordan's former Crown Prince Hassan, who played an important role in the ACRS-related talks. Since the late 1980s, Hassan had encouraged senior Jordanians to engage Israelis in informal talks on bilateral and regional security issues. He demonstrated genuine interest and intellectual curiosity in the impressions they gained from these talks. Hassan's view seems to have been that as a weak country, sandwiched between significant military powers like Israel, Iraq, and Syria, it was incumbent upon Jordan to use all available venues for learning everything possible about the surrounding states, particularly Israel. Hassan's involvement in the Track-II process could be described as the product of genuine commitment to the notion of arms control. The knowledge and understanding gained through these contacts also helped Jordan conduct its formal negotiations with Israel in 1993–1994, and in the subsequent talks that focused on the implementation of the agreements reached.

Another Arab mentor for the ACRS-related Track-II talks was Nabil Fahmy, adviser to Egypt's minister of foreign affairs (and later ambassador to the United States). Fahmy did not encourage Track-II talks with the same enthusiasm as Yossi Beilin, Abu Mazin, and Prince Hassan. As a government official, his position was junior to that of the three leaders and his objectives were different. While Beilin, Abu Mazin, and Prince Hassan were interested in pursuing Track-II talks primarily as an avenue for conflict resolution (and gathering information and understanding), Fahmy saw the process first and foremost as a venue for advancing Egypt's interest in Israeli nuclear disarmament. Nonetheless, Fahmy played an important role in guiding Egypt's participation in the Track-II process. Participation in significant ACRS-related Track-II talks was cleared with him, positions were coordinated with him in advance, and information and assessments gained in these meetings—as well as conclusions reached afterwards—were injected into Egypt's policy process through his office.

By contrast, Israeli participants in ACRS-related Track-II talks lacked a mentor. Some Israeli participants in these talks conveyed their impressions and the information they had gathered to some leaders and government officials. A number of officials—notably then IDF Chief of Staff Lieutenant General Ehud Barak and Deputy Minister of Defense Mordechai (Motta) Gur—expressed genuine interest in these talks. But none were willing or capable of giving the time and energy required to provide sustained guidance to Israeli participants in these talks.

LEADERS

For "hard" Track-II talks to succeed, leaders must be receptive to the information and assessments gained in the talks and to the options and possibilities floated in them. In the 1990s, Middle Eastern leaders varied in the extent to which they were willing to attach any weight to Track-II venues. Israeli Prime Minister Rabin, who presided over the most dramatic breakthrough achieved in what began as a Track-II process at Oslo, was disinclined to use this tool. Rabin was often obsessed with the fear of losing control. By all accounts he was negatively predisposed toward the idea that individuals who were not accountable to the prime minister could conduct important talks on Israel's behalf.

Rabin's skepticism was particularly pronounced with regard to talks conducted by academics; he was very much an anti-intellectual. He was also obsessed with secrecy and felt that independent individuals involved in such talks would seek publicity and personal credit, and that, consequently, they might leak the fact that the talks had been taking place, if not their content. For this reason, when made aware of the talks conducted with the PLO in Norway, Rabin's immediate reaction was to request that a government official join and then lead the talks. This may also explain why Rabin apparently discounted the reports he received from Israeli participants in the IPCME talks.

While Beilin and the Israeli participants in the Stockholm talks maintain that they refrained from informing Rabin of the existence of the track, it is likely that he was informed by Israeli intelligence sources that the talks were taking place. Indeed, it is probable that he tacitly colluded in the continuation of the discussions pending some substantive progress.

Rabin's concerns about Track-II venues did not extend to the more benign "soft" discussions. In the mid-1970s—during his first term as prime minister—he was curious to hear from Israeli participants about the impressions they had formed from their encounters in dialogue-oriented talks with Palestinians. In the early 1990s, he was similarly interested in the reports he received from Israeli participants in the AAAS talks. However, Rabin never initiated a query or asked participants in these talks to explore an issue or convey a message. His approach to the ACRS-related talks was even more passive—there is no evidence that he ever reacted to any of the many reports provided by Israeli participants during course of these discussions.

The Syrian leadership had a number of reservations about the Track-II process. First, they regarded informal talks with Israelis as a form of normalization. In their view, normalization was an important card that the Arabs could play in order to extract Israeli concessions. More important, the Syrian leadership was as obsessive as Rabin about keeping control over the process and about conducting diplomacy with utmost secrecy. Hence, it did not regard a channel conducted by academics as a serious venue for negotiations. Moreover, it did not regard the talks held between Israelis and Syrians in the IPCME framework as intended for deal-making. Rather, it viewed these discussions as providing an opportunity to probe Israel's willingness to make the concessions necessary for a political settlement.

Once it had been leaked to the press that the IPCME talks had taken place—and that Syrian and Israeli participants in these talks might have reached agreement on the formulation of a joint document—the Syrian side quickly retracted its tacit approval for the talks. Syrian participants in the IPCME effort were instructed to "lie low," blocking their participation in other Track-II venues as well. As far as can be ascertained, they refrained from taking part in any Track-II channel during 1994–2000.

The approach of the PLO leadership and Chairman Arafat to the Track-II process was very different than that of Syria's leaders. Since the early 1970s, PLO diplomacy was primarily geared at gaining international legitimacy and recognition. Gaining recognition from the United States received top priority. This was particularly evident when Track-II talks were sponsored by U.S. NGOs and when the exercise included a significant number of U.S. participants. Such talks provided an important venue for gaining sympathy for the PLO's positions, thus enhancing its legitimacy. Arafat conducted the PLO's affairs during that period from a position of weakness, and felt that he could not ignore any avenue—including Track-II discussions—for advancing the PLO's cause.

For all these reasons, Arafat regarded the talks conducted at Oslo as an opportunity that should not be missed. Yet, while receptive to the information and assessment gained through the Track-II participants, and while gradually convinced that the Oslo talks held good prospects for advancing Palestinian interests, Arafat had little patience for the details of the talks conducted. He generally depended on Abu Mazin—the Palestinian mentor of these talks—to alert him to important developments in the discussions.

In Jordan's case, King Hussein seems to have delegated the task of following Arab-Israeli Track-II discussions to his brother, the Crown Prince Hassan, who became the mentor of his country's participation in these talks. Given the close family and working relationship between the king and the crown prince (until just prior to the king's death in early 1999), the positions of the king and his brother on Jordanian participation in Track-II discussions were virtually indistinguishable.

While there is not enough evidence to evaluate the attitude of Egypt's President Hosni Mubarak toward the Track-II process, there are some indications that Foreign Minister Amr Mussa supported the efforts to explore whether Egypt's national interests could be advanced through this framework. In particular, Mussa approved of efforts to use ACRS-related Track-II and talks that included officials acting in an unofficial capacity in order to convey to Israelis—as well as to third parties, primarily the United States—Egypt's approach to arms control, particularly with regard to nuclear weapons. He authorized the participation of Foreign Ministry officials in a large number of such discussions, hoping that they would make the case that Israel should sign the Nuclear Non-Proliferation Treaty (NPT) and agree to negotiate the establishment of a Nuclear-Weapons-Free Zone (NWFZ) or a Weapons-of-Mass-Destruction-Free Zone (WMDFZ) in the Middle East, and that it should, at the very least, allow these issues to be placed on the ACRS agenda. Mussa also appointed his top adviser, Nabil Fahmy, to coordinate Egypt's participation in ACRS-related Track-II venues as of 1992, thus making Fahmy the informal mentor of Egyptian participation in these talks.

In 1994–1995, at the height of the Israeli-Egyptian nuclear debate associated with the efforts to extend indefinitely the NPT, Mussa personally approved the participation of Egyptians in the De Paul–ISISC talks. The extent to which President Mubarak was also receptive to these talks remains unclear.

In Egypt, the participation of retired diplomats and senior military officers in Track-II meetings held in Israel requires the approval of the presidency; the position of Egypt's leaders on this issue clearly changed during the 1990s. In 1992, approval to participate was denied, but in early 1993 a similar involvement was authorized. Since 1994, security experts were allowed to take part in meetings held in Israel in the framework of the De Paul–ISISC project and in conferences sponsored by the Jaffee Center.

Sponsors and Third Parties

Sponsors have had a decisive impact on the success and failure of Middle East Track-II talks. The creativity demonstrated by sponsors, their willingness to invest in making continuous talks possible, the degree of sensitivity demonstrated when orchestrating the talks, and the degree of intrusion they exercised all have clearly affected the talks.

Parties in conflict who have been divided by a long history of violence are generally incapable of managing Track-II meetings on their own. Third-party sponsorship is usually required to initiate and sustain such talks. In the political environment of the early 1990s, it was highly unlikely that Israelis and Palestinians could have engaged in sustained talks without the umbrella of a third-party sponsor. It was even less likely that Israelis and Syrians could hold such meetings outside a framework created by a "neutral" sponsor.

Middle East Track-II talks have been sponsored by governmental as well as by nongovernmental organizations. The Stockholm talks were the best example of the former—arranged, financed, and secured by the government of Sweden. More common, however, were Track-II talks sponsored by NGOs such as the Search for Common Ground, the American Academy of Arts and Sciences, and the International Friends Service Committee. Some of the NGOs sponsoring such talks were academic research centers: the Carnegie Endowment for International Peace in Washington, D.C., the Institute on Global Conflict and Cooperation (IGCC) in San Diego, and the Center for International Relations of the University of California in Los Angeles (UCLA).

In some cases, the distinction between governmental and nongovernmental sponsors of Track-II talks was unclear. The Oslo talks were a good example of this phenomenon. While FAFO provided the formal umbrella, for all practical purposes the venue was orchestrated by Norway's Ministry of Foreign Affairs. Indeed, very soon after the talks began, even the facade of FAFO sponsorship was abandoned as Foreign Minister Holst played an increasingly central role in bringing the talks to a successful conclusion.

Likewise, the Olof Palme International Center provided the umbrella for the Stockholm talks with the support and backing of successive Swedish governments that saw these talks both as a means of facilitating a resolution to the conflict and as means of maintaining a Swedish role in the peace process. To a lesser extent, the U.S. Department of Energy (DOE) and the Arms Control and Disarmament Agency (ACDA) also played a key role in funding and guiding the IGCC and UCLA ACRS-related Track-II venues.

Generally, government-sponsored Track-II talks enjoyed better funding than NGO-sponsored discussions. While NGO sponsors were in constant pursuit of the funds necessary to hold additional meetings—usually one at a time—government sponsorship allowed for continuity. This was particularly important for "hard" Track-II talks, where efforts to resolve the parties' conflict required continuous negotiations. For example, as sponsor of the Stockholm talks, the Swedish government sponsored twenty-one Israeli-Palestinian meetings, providing logistical support and robust security at the meeting sites. No NGO could equal such an intense and sustained effort. Indeed, for NGOs funding is very often the critical factor in deciding not only whether a project can be launched but also whether it can be sustained and brought to fruition. By contrast, a government decision to support a project normally ensures a better prospect for its sustainability.

Sponsors of Track-II talks have differed in the degree of intrusion they exercised in the talks. In some such venues, notably the talks convened by the AAAS and IPCME, the sponsors exercised minimal intrusion, allowing participants to set the agenda and the pace of the talks. During the Stockholm talks, the Swedish government exercised similar restraint. Indeed, the Swedish approach was to allow the talks as much leeway as possible without any overt intervention and with no attempt at arbitration unless specifically asked—which never happened. At some stage in the talks, the Palestinians considered the possibility of Swedish aid in providing technical assistance such as aerial photographs of the West Bank. Ultimately, however, this was not deemed necessary or practical. Nonetheless, the Swedish sponsors were always aware of the possible need to assist in transforming any understanding reached into political reality. They were both ready and willing to exercise their influence with the PLO and Israel to achieve that end if necessary.

By contrast, the Norwegian hosts of the Oslo talks played a relatively intrusive role. The Norwegians intervened on more than one occasion, in Oslo as well as at the highest levels in Jerusalem and Tunis, to prevent the talks' collapse. Surprisingly, most sponsors of ACRS-related "soft" talks were also quite intrusive, particularly in setting a rather rigid agenda and schedule. Indeed, some of these sponsors erred by imposing a schedule that included too many sessions and did not leave enough time for informal interactions among participants. More sensitive sponsors of ACRS-related talks consulted the parties as they set up the meetings' schedules and agenda.

NGO sponsors of Track-II talks obtained both government and private funding for such activities. Private funding was raised from individuals as well as foundations. Large U.S. foundations were involved in supporting ACRS-related Middle East Track-II as well as AAAS activities: Carnegie, Ford, MacArthur, and Rockefeller. However, smaller foundations also supported such meetings, notably W. Alton Jones and Ploughshares. By contrast, the financial assistance provided by European foundations for such activities was minimal.

Governments providing financial support for Track-II activities have also exercised different degrees of intrusion in the talks. For example, the U.S. Arms Control and Disarmament Agency (ACDA, which was dissolved in 1999 and its role assumed by the U.S. Department of State) involved itself in the process of setting the agenda and choosing the participants in Track-II discussions hosted by IGCC and by UCLA. By contrast, European governments supporting such activities, notably the Dutch government supporting IPCME discussions and the Swedish government supporting IPCME and UCLA-sponsored talks, refrained from micromanaging the talks.

Third-party sponsorship has been motivated by a number of factors. In some cases, state and governmental sponsorship can be traced to *raison d'etat* and the desire to protect and expand state interests in the region. Security and stability in the Middle East have long been prime objectives of the U.S. and European governments, and there is general recognition that Track-II exercises may advance these goals. Attempts to preempt or manage potential crises in the Middle East are another motivation. This can be linked to a perception that the area is of considerable strategic and geopolitical importance for the West, and that Europe in particular may pay a high price if the Arab-Israeli conflict is not resolved.

Competition probably also played a role in convincing the U.S. government to support Track-II activities, particularly after Oslo. Given the magnitude of the overall U.S. involvement in the Middle East peace process, Washington was unlikely to yield to Europeans the sole credit for pursuing a venue that seemed to yield, at least in one case, dramatic results. Despite such competition, government sponsors or financial supporters of Track-II talks have sometimes kept other governments informed of the progress made. For example, the Norwegian sponsors of the Oslo talks provided U.S. government officials with at least partial reports of these discussions. Similarly, the Dutch government— which supported the IPCME talks on the proliferation of weapons of mass destruction in the Middle East—informed Syrian government officials of the progress made in these talks.

Personal factors have also influenced the sponsorship of Track-II talks. In Europe and the United States, the historical background to the conflict and the continued legacy of World War II and the circumstances surrounding the creation of Israel also have had an important impact on both the governmental and personal levels. Equally, religious beliefs and other compassionate considerations account for the activism and dedication shown by many of the sponsor-participants. For many, advancing "Peace in the Holy Land" has had a strong and multidimensional appeal. For example, a sense of contribution to the prospects of peace was at the root of the initiatives undertaken by a wide variety of NGOs, including Search for Common Ground and the AAAS project. NGO activities in the Middle East have also benefited from the readiness of governments and other grant-giving individuals and institutions to finance such projects, providing an additional motive to work in this area.

In rare cases, local NGOs have sponsored Track-II talks. One example is the series of discussions held in 1995–1996 between the Israeli settlers and the Palestinian Authority. These talks evolved from an April 1994 tour to the Middle East by participants in the AAAS talks. Yet all subsequent meetings between these protagonists were held under the auspices of the Middle East Office of the American Jewish Committee, located in Jerusalem. In June 1995, Joseph Alpher, director of this office, arranged for the first of these meetings to be cosponsored by the Foundation for International Security and to be funded by a private source.

Another example of a local NGO sponsor of a Track-II venue is IPCRI —a joint Israeli-Palestinian research group based in Jerusalem. Supported by U.S. and European NGOs and foundations, it has sponsored and encouraged Palestinian-Israeli dialogue over a broad range of issues. IPCRI's modest success, however, highlights the difficulties facing Track-II talks between conflicting parties without assistance from a "third party." It may be argued that IPCRI is not removed enough to qualify for such a role. Israelis tend to regard it as biased in favor of the Palestinians while the latter regard it as an Israeli-dominated joint venture.

The Political Environment

As noted earlier, Track-II talks have been affected significantly by changes in the strategic environment and the region's political climate. A number of major developments since the mid-1980s have left a distinct imprint on the nature and prospects of such talks.

THE 1987 INTIFADA

Beginning in late 1987, the first Palestinian *intifada* affected Israeli-Palestinian Track-II talks in a number of ways. The initial reaction to the outbreak of the uprising was surprise and shock among Israelis and Palestinians alike. This immediately elicited a strong desire to assess whether or not the violence doomed Track-II efforts to failure. This was felt clearly by participants in the Ontell and Kelman projects. In most cases the tendency was to persevere with the talks.

However, the 1987 *intifada* also affected Track-II talks logistically. Palestinian participants residing in the West Bank and Gaza found it more difficult to enter and exit the territories for the purpose of attending meetings abroad. Paradoxically, this sometimes contributed to group cohesion among Israeli and Palestinian participants as they consulted about ways in which the Israelis could intervene with their authorities to obtain travel permits for their Palestinian counterparts.

The first *intifada* also affected the delicate internal balance among the Palestinian participants who resided in the occupied territories and those who lived abroad—in Tunis or Europe. Participants from the West Bank and Gaza appeared to have more to contribute than had previously been the case, since they came from the epicenter of the most important developments. Finally, the first *intifada* affected the substance of discussions as Palestinian participants attempted to persuade their Israeli counterparts to support their cause. This generated even more animated discussions of the motives and aspirations affecting both sides to the conflict.

THE 1990 INVASION OF KUWAIT

Iraq's invasion of Kuwait in August 1990 and Yasser Arafat's ambivalent position during that crisis had a similarly dramatic effect. Israeli participants in Track-II talks were deeply disturbed by what they perceived as a Palestinian decision to ally with the worst of Israel's enemies. Arafat's public posture also induced a change in the balance between the Israeli and Palestinian participants in Track-II talks, weakening the position of the Palestinians, at least temporarily.

Iraq's invasion of Kuwait also aborted contacts made in multilateral Track-II frameworks. For example, a pre-ACRS Track-II effort launched in the late 1980s by the Carnegie Endowment for International Peace had produced an informal Iraqi-Israeli dialogue. This was ended by the Gulf crisis and war.

TERRORISM AND VIOLENCE

In the 1990s, acts of violence included knifings of Israeli citizens by Palestinians in the early 1990s; the 1994 massacre of Palestinians in Hebron by an Israeli settler; various Hamas suicide bombings against Israeli citizens since 1994; the Qana bombing of Lebanese civilians in 1996; and the violence resulting from the opening of the Hasmonean "tunnel" near the Western Wall in Jerusalem in September 1996.

The immediate effect of such acts was to divert Track-II participants' attention from the basic issues at dispute and to compel them to invest more of their time and energy in discussing the implications of specific events. In almost every Track-II meeting that took place during or immediately after major acts of terrorism or violence at that time, substantive talks had to be preceded by "a venting phase," allowing participants to express their anger at the consequences and causes of such violence. Such acts presented participants with specific dilemmas, including whether they should address the implications of these events directly—for example, by issuing a joint statement or by communicating jointly an appeal to both sides to prevent further bloodshed.

Not surprisingly, reactions to acts of violence later in the period were quite often more positive and constructive, including a renewed determination to continue the peacemaking efforts. A good example was at an IPCME meeting that followed the 1994 massacre in Hebron. Most Arab participants gave clear expression to their deep anger but they were restrained by a senior PLO security official who urged participants to continue their work, stressing that the unfortunate development should merely reinforce their determination to make every effort to seek a resolution of the conflict.

Just as Arafat's reluctance to condemn Saddam Hussein during the 1990–1991 Gulf Crisis weakened the Palestinian position in Track-II talks, the Hebron massacre had a similar effect on the Israeli participants. For these participants, the initial feeling was that Israel had lost the moral high ground, as Israelis could now be shown to be engaged in what could only be described as "fundamentalist terrorism." Later Hamas bombings, however, tended to soften this feeling. This type of violence also led Track-II sponsors and participants to ask whether a dialogue between religious leaders on both sides—even those known to have extreme views—should be encouraged. Consequently, IPCME invited a Palestinian journalist close to Hamas to take part in a Track-II meeting in Vienna.

Another set of developments that affected the course of Track-II talks at that time was Israel's propensity to impose a "closure" of the West Bank and Gaza. These partial or complete closures—extending from days to several months—imposed enormous hardships on the Palestinians residing in these areas, affecting their access to workplaces, commerce, and medical treatment. The recurring acts of violence and "closure" also affected the substance of Track-II discussions, forcing participants to confront a dilemma that has accompanied the peace process since the late 1980s: The apparent contradiction between the desire to separate the two peoples and the requirements of mutual security, economic well-being, and peaceful coexistence.

THE 1995 ASSASSINATION OF RABIN

The strategic and political environment can affect not only the course of Track-II talks but also their consequences. The most extreme example was the effect of the assassination of Israeli Prime Minister Rabin in November 1995 on the outcome of the Stockholm talks. Rabin was to have been briefed about these talks only days after he was assassinated. Had he not been assassinated, and had the briefing taken place, it is likely that Rabin would have taken exception to some of the understandings reached in the Stockholm talks. But it is also possible that despite such reservations, Rabin would have regarded the "package" of understandings reached through the Swedish venue as providing sufficient basis for subsequent Track-I negotiations. Moreover, it is likely that Rabin enjoyed greater flexibility to pursue such a package than his successor, Shimon Peres. Thus, Rabin's assassination—and the transformation in the political environment it caused—may have had a decisive impact on the ultimate consequences of the Stockholm talks.

THE 1996 ISRAELI ELECTIONS

During the 1990s, Arab-Israeli Track-II talks were affected by political events in Israel such as the 1996 election of Benyamin Netanyahu as Israel's prime minister. The general setback to the peace process resulting from this development was exemplified by Netanyahu's initial refusal to meet with Yasser Arafat and his decision to open a new exit from the Hasmonean tunnel, near the Western Wall in Jerusalem in September 1996. The opening fueled Islamic fears that Israel intended to excavate under the Haram ash-Asharif/Temple Mount. The violence that erupted following this decision became a focus of discussion in Track-II talks, as Arab participants expressed their anger and frustration and, even more significantly, their desire to understand what motivated Israel's new leader. Discussions of Netanyahu's ambitions and character thus became a near obsession of participants in a number of Track-II meetings for some time after 1996.

A second consequence of the 1996 Israeli elections was the termination of the Track-II talks held previously between Israeli settlers and representatives of the Palestinian Authority. This resulted from the diminished motivation of the settlers to take part in such discussions once they became hopeful that the Oslo process could be reversed. They now believed that the premise underlying their engagement in the talks—namely, that they were likely to find themselves residing in Palestinian-controlled areas—would be invalidated.

The substance of Israeli-Palestinian Track-II talks was also affected by the various unilateral actions taken by the Netanyahu government, such as the early 1997 decision to authorize a housing project at Har Homa/Jebel Abu Ghneim in East Jerusalem. Interpreted by Palestinian participants as attempts to pre-judge the outcome of the final status negotiations, such actions created a perceived Palestinian imperative to focus the talks on issues that were to have been left to later negotiations.

Potential Pitfalls

Alongside their many advantages, there are also a number of pitfalls to the use of Track-II talks as a venue for communication and conflict resolution between disputing parties.

OPPORTUNITIES FOR MISPERCEPTIONS

While one of the purposes of Track-II talks is to convey perceptions and concerns, participants in such venues are not immune to misperceptions.

Indeed, Track-II participants and other observers may well misperceive the meaning of a Track-II venue. For example, the IPCME talks that in October 1994 resulted in a one-page understanding between Israeli and Syrian participants could be seen as constituting an Israeli-Syrian Track-II venue. But in reality, these talks were conducted in the framework of IPCME's Security Group, which included other nationalities such as Jordanians and Egyptians. The Syrian government was unlikely to have authorized participation in serious negotiations in such an environment.

For a considerable time, discussions of Israeli-Syrian issues were conducted in this venue without the participation of individuals residing in Syria. Two participants who had resided in London for some years—a Syrian and a Lebanese—represented Syrian views in these discussions. It is unlikely that the Syrian government would have trusted either participant to act on its behalf.

The two academics from Syria who eventually joined the talks saw their role primarily as probing Israeli positions and intentions and not as representing Syrian positions. With this objective in mind, their approach was one of "political reconnaissance," which may have been misconstrued as showing greater flexibility than their government had. In addition, while the paper under discussion in the talks focused on security measures, neither of the two Syrians involved in the talks was an expert in security affairs. In retrospect, these considerations raise some doubt regarding the extent to which the Syrian participants could have been considered as representing their country in these talks. Yet the Israeli participants in these talks clearly perceived their counterparts as representing the Syrian government's views.

Another possible misperception within Track-II venues relates to the importance and standing of specific participants. For example, participants in the AAAS talks seem to have overestimated the influence of particular individuals in one another's team. The Israeli participants seem to have believed that Nizar Ammar, a PLO security official, had more influence with Chairman Arafat than he did. Similarly, the Palestinian participants in these talks believed that Israeli colleagues, such as Shlomo Gazit, had greater influence and access to Prime Minister Rabin than was actually the case.

Under some circumstances, misperceptions can develop as a result of straightforward confusion. For example, prior to Oslo the PLO was confused by the multiplicity of venues and the contradictory messages that were often received through different tracks. Consequently, at one point the PLO decided that the Oslo talks would become the sole venue of authoritative Israeli-Palestinian discussions. Other venues—such as the talks conducted by Israeli Knesset member Ephraim Sneh and Palestinian leader Nabil Shaath—were either downgraded or abandoned. Similarly, in late 1994 the Stockholm talks became the main venue for Israeli-Palestinian discussions of final status issues. In both cases, the need to prevent confusion was the main reason for reducing the multiplicity of venues.

In other cases, misperceptions can arise from misleading messages delivered within Track-II discussions. For example, in the discussions conducted by an Israeli and Iraqi participant in the framework of the Track-II talks hosted by the Carnegie Endowment in October 1989, the principle Iraqi message was that Baghdad had abandoned its militant position in the Arab-Israeli conflict and that it was prepared to endorse any settlement of the conflict that would be acceptable to "the Arab consensus." It was further explained that Iraq knew that Israel was equipped with a deliverable nuclear capability and that it was not willing to risk Baghdad on the Palestinians' behalf. Clearly, this message of "moderation" did not entirely accord with Iraqi President Saddam Hussein's subsequent behavior, such as targeting Israeli cities during the 1991 Gulf War and attempting to forge a violent link with the Arab-Israeli conflict.

TENSIONS BETWEEN TRACK-II AND TRACK-I

The success of the Oslo talks exacerbated the danger that government officials involved in Track-I negotiations would feel threatened by Track-II venues. Government officials on both sides became concerned that they might be strategically surprised and upstaged by another Track-II breakthrough. After Oslo, Track-I negotiators made efforts to reduce the "danger" that they would be similarly upstaged again. For example, the head of Syria's delegation to the Washington negotiations asked for assurances that the talks he was conducting constituted the only venue of Syrian-Israeli negotiations. Similarly, some claim that Israeli negotiators were somewhat uncomfortable with the understanding reached between the Syrian and Israeli participants involved in the IPCME talks.

This points to a more general dimension of the potential tension between the two tracks. Track-I officials are often convinced that Track-II participants in "hard" Track-II venues aimed at conflict resolution lack the professional expertise for negotiating and drafting international treaties. They further argue that as a result of such shortcomings, Track-II participants are not aware of the various possible interpretations and implications of the wording used to summarize the understandings reached. The Israeli team to the Oslo talks, for example, experienced considerable tension between its Track-II participants, Hirschfeld and Pundik, and their Track-I superior, legal adviser Joel Singer.

Among Israelis, the Oslo agreement created even greater tension between those who took part in these talks and those who were executing the parallel Track-I negotiations in Washington. The latter felt that they were deceived by their superiors and had wasted many months of their lives in a futile exercise, while the "real" action—consuming the attention of Israel's top political leaders—was taking place in Norway. Moreover, some of Israel's Track-I negotiators felt that they were unduly deprived of achieving a similar breakthrough in Washington by their government's refusal to engage PLO officials in direct negotiations—a restriction from which the Oslo talks were exempted. Israel's Track-I negotiators later said that had the talks they were conducting been similarly exempt from this restriction, an equally dramatic breakthrough could have been achieved in Washington.

The Arms Control and Regional Security–related Track-II talks were also affected by the hypersensitivity that the Oslo success created. This was reflected in the approach of some Israeli government officials to the De Paul–ISISC talks. These officials strongly suspected that the sponsors of this venue wished to achieve in the ACRS context what Oslo achieved in Israeli-Palestinian relations: an understanding among Arab and Israeli academics on the modalities for transforming the Middle East into a weapons-of-mass-destruction-free zone (WMDFZ). This suspicion was reinforced by the fact that the participants in these talks were organized as delegations and efforts were directed, at least initially, at negotiating a treaty-type WMDFZ agreement. This was interpreted as a Track-II effort to emulate, and possibly substitute for, Track-I negotiations. It was also feared that Arab governments—primarily Egypt—would present such an understanding as evidence that the refusal of the Israeli government to discuss a similar agreement in the framework of the ACRS talks was unreasonable. There was concern that this development, in turn, would invite international pressure on the Israeli government to moderate its stance on this issue.

These concerns were exacerbated by two additional perceptions of Israeli officials: first, that Israeli participants in the De Paul–ISISC talks were willing to accept an agenda dominated by Egypt's concerns with nuclear weapons, and second, that the U.S. government may have been backing the efforts to use the De Paul–ISISC talks to produce a more flexible Israeli position regarding key issues on the arms control agenda. This perception was based on the knowledge that the U.S. Department of Energy was funding the De Paul–ISISC meetings and that the Cooperative Monitoring Center (CMC) at the Sandia National Laboratories—an organization funded entirely by DoE—was involved in providing educational support on verification technologies to the venue participants. It thus seemed that an effort was underway to place an official stamp on what at first glance might have appeared an innocent Track-II venue.

While the formal position of Israeli government officials was that the Israeli participants in the De Paul–ISISC talks enjoyed academic freedom and that, consequently, the Israeli government did not oppose the project, the very same officials took steps to register their deep displeasure about the venue. They asked the U.S. government to refrain from any steps that might be interpreted as backing these talks. Thus, instead of contributing to conflict resolution, the De Paul–ISISC talks initially created considerable tension—at least within Israel—between Track-I officials and Track-II participants.

UNINTENDED CONSEQUENCES

Track-II participants may not always be aware of what they are doing or of how their presence or presentation affects the other side. Not every Track-II participant will necessarily have a premeditated or clearly defined objective in the talks or a strict line that he will wish to pursue. Unlike formal talks the scope for off-the-cuff improvisation is quite wide and can even be seen as one of the positive attributes of Track-II informality. Such discussions thus carry some measure of "trial and error," with all the risks and advantages that this may entail.

Particularly when the contact is new or untested, there is a danger that the opposing side may read too much or too little into what is being said. This may be correctable over a sustained period, but may also be damaging if uncorrected. The AAAS experience indicates that there may be a certain asymmetry in perceptions about the utility and status of the venue; in this case the net result was seen as positive—a reinforcement of the Israeli leadership's readiness to deal with the PLO.

Track-II talks and their consequences are no exception to the general proposition that international politics is the realm of unintended consequences. The Oslo talks were initiated to support the Track-I negotiations in Washington; they later became a substitute for these negotiations. The talks focused on providing a framework for resolving the conflict between Israel and the Palestinians; they resulted in mutual recognition between the Israeli government and the PLO. Likewise, the Stockholm talks were intended to demonstrate that Israeli-Palestinian final status issues were solvable; one unforeseen consequence was that they eventually became the basis of an effort to forge a new Labor-Likud consensus within Israel itself.

Similarly, the talks conducted in 1995–1996 between Palestinians and Israeli settlers were intended to explore whether there might be some basis for future coexistence between the settlers and the Palestinian Authority. But once the fact that the talks had taken place was revealed, their effect was to "leglitimize" the PA in the eyes of the Israeli right, thus making it easier for Prime Minister Netanyahu to enter into a dialogue with Chairman Arafat.

The Israeli-Syrian discussions conducted in the IPCME framework provide another example of Track-II talks' leading to unintended consequences. Despite the absence of any intention by Syria or Israel to utilize these talks as a deal-making framework, the one-page "understanding" reached in the talks had the potential for leading to a significant substantive breakthrough.

Track-II talks often build on other Track-II discussions. For example, a conversation between an Israeli and a Palestinian that took place during the first meeting on regional security held by the Friends International Service Committee led to the security talks sponsored by the AAAS. The AAAS talks laid the basis for the PLO-settler dialogue. Similarly, the Stockholm talks were launched by an Arab participant who encountered a Swedish government official at a social function that took place at the edges of a meeting held by IPCME.

Yet, in other cases Track-II discussions may have made the pursuit of other such talks more difficult. For example, it is quite possible that the Oslo accords made Syria more sensitive to such discussions. This may explain its decision to ban further participation in Track-II talks following the October 1993 leaking of the Israeli-Syrian talks. Syria did not react in this way to press reports of Israeli-Syrian talks published before the Oslo accords.

The effects of positive developments on Track-II venues were also not always positive. For example, it may well be that the reluctance of Prime Minister Rabin to explore the possibilities opened by the Israeli-Syrian document negotiated in the IPCME framework was affected by the Oslo breakthrough. Simply, Rabin may have feared that Israeli public opinion would not tolerate the risks associated with perceived Israeli concessions to the Palestinians and the Syrians simultaneously.

Chapter 10

Lessons from the Middle East

The Middle East's experience with different forms of Track-II diplomacy has been unusually rich and extensive over the past three decades. Whatever the roots of Track-II talks in the specific needs and requirements of U.S.-Soviet crisis management during the Cold War, this tool clearly found fertile ground for development in the Middle East in general, and in the Palestinian-Israeli context in particular during the late 1980s and early 1990s.

The specifics of the Middle East case hardly preclude the possible extension of Track-II techniques, and lessons learned in this arena, to other arenas and conflicts.[1] In the Middle East, as possibly elsewhere, Track-II talks should be seen as most effective and useful in internal or interstate conflicts where, at a certain stage, the parties involved are unwilling or unable to bridge their differences using the traditional tools of official Track-I diplomacy and direct formal negotiations. In almost all cases, Track-II talks have provided—or at least were intended to provide—a bridge to Track-I negotiations.

In fact, the Middle East experience points to the complex and multifaceted nature of Track-II talks and the confusion that can often surround them. Since there is no single route for Track-II talks to follow, and because Track-II talks are often the result of ad hoc personal initiatives and fortuitous contacts, rather than any extensive planning, the attempt to devise universally valid formulas for their initiation or success may be

---

1. See, for instance, the paper on the role of Track-II diplomacy in resolving the internal conflict in Tajikistan, given by Harold Saunders at a conference held by the Carnegie Corporation, New York, November 1997.

misleading or counterproductive. What was useful and successful in the context of the Arab-Israeli conflict may not necessarily have the same effect in another context. Conversely, what was of limited utility in the Middle East may have a more positive effect elsewhere.

Nonetheless, it is equally misleading to suggest that nothing can be usefully derived from the Middle East experience and potentially applied to good effect in other conflicts and regions. Overcoming formal obstacles, establishing contacts, promoting dialogue, exchanging messages, corroborating other negotiating inputs, testing out ideas, managing crises, resolving problems, and reaching negotiating "closure" have all been part of the broad menu of Track-II talks in the Middle East. Other conflicting parties who seek to achieve one or more of these objectives may find insight in the experience of Middle East Track-II talks. The following sections suggest some general rules and lessons that may be usefully derived from the Middle East experience through the mid-1990s.

On Sponsorship

Sponsors that can provide the necessary financial support, logistics, and facilitating experience may make the difference between the success or failure of Track-II talks. A government sponsor can also provide invaluable protection when a physical threat to the participants is possible. Most sponsors can provide a physical location and a sense of distance, both real and psychological.

A sponsor should make a special effort to provide an opportunity for maximum interaction between the participants. Socializing is an integral part of the process and should be actively encouraged (but not forced) by the sponsors. Free time should be allocated for such socialization beyond the time allocated for active engagement in the talks. Equally important, the sponsors should be aware of the stress and strain often engendered by the discussions and should allow time for complete rest and nonengagement where possible.

One major advantage of having an external sponsor is that the third party may insulate the participants from the pressure of daily developments. However, such insulation cannot be complete, and short-term developments on the ground often impinge on Track-II encounters even when the issues under debate are of much longer-term import. Third-party political neutrality and the physical distance provided by foreign locations play a vital insulating role. This seems to have been a characteristic of all the venues studied here, and comprised a vital ingredient of their viability.

Although it may be difficult to prescribe a general rule regarding the degree of intrusiveness that should be exercised by a third-party sponsor, the participating parties need to agree on the sponsor's role and this should be conveyed to the sponsors themselves. A facilitating role may be common to all exercises, but active mediation by the sponsors may not always be welcome.

Prospective third-party sponsors may need to exercise some sensitivity about the degree of intrusiveness that is tolerable to the negotiating parties. The Middle East experience suggests that by and large, a light touch is more productive than an assertive approach. Successful facilitation requires flexibility, initiative, and a creative outlook on the sponsor's part. Although a clear definition of roles may be important in establishing confidence between the sponsor and the participants, these roles may change or develop as the exercise proceeds even without any formal acknowledgement. In some instances, however, the distinctions between sponsorship, facilitation, and active intervention can be blurred and a positive outcome may be secured regardless, depending on the nature of the track and the group dynamic it generates.

Despite seeming heavy-handed or unduly assertive to the participants, sponsors may need to step in to give Track-II talks a final push, particularly when valuable opportunities may be otherwise lost. In the end, sponsors naturally seek to maximize their own advantages. Governments may seek to enhance their international image and establish their role (as did Norway); institutions may have other objectives, ranging from pursuing their own implicit political agendas to strengthening their grant-raising capabilities. At some stages the sponsors and participants may differ over how and when to go public over a particular track or whether, how, and with whom to advertise its achievements. A noticeable feature of Middle East Track-II sponsorship is that many of the sponsors have maintained a commitment and extended their activities over time (e.g., Kelman, AAAS, IPCME, Norway, and Sweden). A Track-II "success" may thus impose a commitment to follow up in order to maintain a sponsor's profile over the long term. This may not always be self-evident at the outset of an exercise.

On Procedure

THE IMPORTANCE OF INFORMALITY

Track-II activities should be as free as possible from the formal constraints that are characteristic of official diplomacy. This does not mean that there should be no agreed procedural framework for the talks, only that rules of conduct seem to work best if set by consensus among the participants themselves. Agreed rules of conduct are best settled at the outset of the talks, but they should remain open to revision, if necessary, as the exercise continues.

Part of the value of Track-II talks is that they normally allow for a much wider and more comprehensive exchange of views than do formal negotiations. Formal delegations usually have a strict hierarchy with a head of the delegation who sets the tone and pace for the party he represents. Delegates rarely speak without prior clearance from their superiors and usually express themselves only in their narrow field of competence. For example, in the 1991–1993 formal Madrid-Washington negotiations, the Israeli, Jordanian, and Syrian heads of delegations were often the only ones to speak. Other delegates sat through months of negotiations without making a single intervention. In comparison, Track-II talks are generally free-ranging and unencumbered by the hierarchic diplomatic structures and constricting conceits of formal negotiations.

Serious conceptual engagement and formality can often act against one another: the further apart conceptually, the easier it is to be civil. Formality and apparent "civility" can thus disguise deep disagreement and act as a substitute for the proper and thorough airing of differences. Barring blatant personal attacks, Track-II exchanges should remain as open and uninhibited as possible.

While this does not mean that Track-II participants should be overtly rude or uncivil to each other, they should be ready to disagree strongly and vociferously with their counterparts (and on occasion perhaps even with members of their own camp). Thus, when appropriate, they should not shy away from expressions of politically charged emotions.

AVOIDING CONTENTIOUS ISSUES AT THE OUTSET

At the commencement of Track-II talks, it may be better not to address the more contentious issues frontally and without careful preparation. In "soft" Track-II exercises, the initial phase may consist of participants' recounting their personal histories in order to help humanize the two sides and promote empathy within the circle of participants.

In "hard" Track-II talks, some consideration may be given to examining the contours of the potential relationship between the two sides after an agreement would be reached. It may thus be useful to look at some long-term post-settlement issues and establish some common horizons or aspirations for dealing with them. A common vision of this nature can serve as a confidence-building mechanism and as a means of facilitating the management of disagreements over the more immediate and potentially contentious issues.

ALLOWING IDEOLOGICAL EXCHANGES

Although it is understood that no meaningful political action can be entirely nonideological, usually Track-II talks are not an appropriate forum for ideological debate or an arena for scoring points against the other side. Ideological differences can rarely be resolved by argument, and the focus of Track-II discussions should be on positive exchanges, dialogue, problem-solving, and conflict resolution. However, in "soft" Track-II talks where there are profound existential differences—such as in the Palestinian-Israeli case—it may be important to allow time for an overtly ideological debate. Such a debate may help to "clear the air" and facilitate a more focused approach later.

In such a context, ideological exchanges need not be forced and may depend on the nature of the talks as well as the inclinations of the participants. But where such debates occur naturally, they should not be discouraged, since they are often a necessary preliminary to further progress. At the same time, parties need not feel that they are bound to reach a joint understanding of their respective histories or agree on a single narrative in describing the past. Agreement on the past can be helpful, but it is not a prerequisite for progress in resolving current or future problems.

DEVISING RULES OF ENGAGEMENT

Unlike in most Track-I diplomacy, Track-II participants often need to set up their own track-specific rules of engagement. Based on the general principles above, Track-II participants may need to be clear from the outset about some basic procedural rules, and may need to give consideration to the following:[2]

UNDERSTANDING REGARDING THE PURPOSE OF THE EXERCISE. The purpose of the exercise should be well defined and mutually agreed, but should also be sufficiently flexible to allow for any changes along the way—as happened in both the Oslo and Stockholm talks. A clear program of action may be more important for "hard" Track-II talks that are oriented toward problem solving or deal making than for "soft" talks that have a broader purpose, such as the PLO-settler talks. Other "soft" Track-II talks, such as those aimed at promoting dialogue and mutual understanding (such as the Kelman project), could possibly commence with a less precise understanding on their intent and purpose, and then work toward a more clearly defined purpose (e.g., a signed document) as the exercise develops.

---

2. See the "Stockholm Rules" in Appendix 3.

AGREEMENT ON TIMETABLE, FREQUENCY, AND PLACE OF MEETING. This may be necessary for the cost-effective management of "hard" Track-II talks, particularly when acting against a particular political backdrop—such as the possibility of Israeli elections that emerged during the Stockholm talks. "Soft" Track-II exercises may require a less rigid timetable. In both cases, time management may also depend on the role and outlook of the third-party sponsors, which may want to reach a particular goal within a particular time frame and at a predetermined cost.

UNDERSTANDING THE ROLE OF THE THIRD PARTY OR SPONSOR. Where relevant, an understanding reached among participants regarding the role of the sponsor may or may not be shared with the third-party sponsor, depending on the nature of its role and function. The effect of such an understanding may even be to exclude the third party from certain decisions or actions, but may also leave room for third-party activism if necessary. However, an active third party may develop its own intrusive agenda even if this was not its initial purpose—as became evident with Norway in the latter stages of the Oslo talks.

A MECHANISM FOR ARBITRATION. Such a mechanism is not necessary in "soft" Track-II exercises but may be essential for "hard" Track-II talks. In the latter case, it is most likely to involve the third-party sponsors. It may also include the adoption of agreed internal mechanisms that are mutually satisfactory. The understanding reached among participants on this matter should also define when arbitration is relevant (e.g., at the point of total breakdown) and to what degree its findings would be binding.

AWARENESS OF A POTENTIAL CONFLICT OF INTEREST OVER INTELLECTUAL OWNERSHIP OF ANY COLLECTIVE WORK. Clearly, the ownership of the Oslo "Declaration of Principles" was ultimately irrelevant insofar as it was formally signed by Israel and the PLO, and achieved the status of an international agreement. But where there is no formal agreement on the status of a document or understanding, its intellectual ownership may be open to question. Not all joint documents are the product of equal work or labor, and some parties may feel that they deserve more credit for such work than others. Group work that is drafted or facilitated by third parties may equally obfuscate the contribution of participants from either side. For example, the IPCME Syrian-Israeli drafts put together by IPCME staff were based on the participants' deliberations. Sponsors may also want to take credit for their substantive input, which may not always correspond to the views of the parties themselves.

AN UNDERSTANDING ON CONDITIONS OF CONFIDENTIALITY AND RELEASE OF INFORMATION. The parties need to agree on whether and when to divulge the activities of the Track-II talks and what portions of it should remain subject to total or partial confidentiality. For example, the AAAS "soft" exercise was public but its "hard" component was kept confidential by agreement. Confidentiality can help to protect participants and ensure their physical safety. In all circumstances there must be some measure of mutual good faith in the ability of all sides to maintain an agreed silence in any Track-II talks, at least as long as the discussions continue. Generally, in the Middle East Track-II talks described in this book, confidentiality regarding issues of substance was preserved while the tracks remained active, and almost nothing of what was said in such talks was divulged at the time. Generally, even when participants' names have been identified, no particular statements have been ascribed to them.

CONDITIONS FOR ANY NEW ADDITIONS TO THE GROUP.   Once a Track-II exercise has been established, the core founding group tends to develop its own modus operandi and idiosyncratic group dynamics. New additions to this core can be disruptive and may interrupt the flow of the exercise. In some cases, the third-party sponsor may have to be consulted before any new additions are made. Political leaders on either side may mandate such additions in order to examine the channel and test its credibility, as, for example, when Israeli Prime Minister Rabin sent legal expert Joel Singer to Oslo in June 1993.

AGREEING ON CHANGES IN DIRECTION.   New developments may impose a change in the talks' agreed agenda or objective. Similarly, new ideas may be proposed that redirect the exercise away from one agreed purpose or modus operandi to another. This may be dealt with either by agreement within the group or by appeal to arbitration. Given the political nature of Track-II talks, it may be necessary to allow for such changes of direction so as to remain relevant and in tune with developments "on the ground."

CAUCUSING.   Some Track-II parties may feel the need to share some of their work with an outside group in order to test ideas and gain additional inputs into the discussions (the Israeli side at Stockholm did this, for example). While potentially useful, this may also increase the dangers of premature leakage. Much depends on the nature of the exercise and whether the various parties feel the need for political caucusing. A measure of mutual agreement on the nature and extent of such caucusing may help to avoid disruptions or misunderstandings.

On Participation

SELECTING PARTICIPANTS

Methods of selection and the qualifications for participation in Track-II talks may differ according to the nature of the exercise. In the Middle East, participants have often been self-selected. In the Oslo and Stockholm talks, the core participants chose themselves by mutual agreement, and were then supported by their political mentors and leaders. Any changes in the composition of the teams were largely a function of the relationship between the negotiating teams and their political leaderships. On the Israeli side, Uri Savir and Joel Singer were sent to Oslo to override the Track-II Hirschfeld-Pundik team. On the Palestinian side, Hassan Asfour was added to the original Stockholm team at the behest of Abu Mazin to present an "informed" official input.

In other cases the third-party sponsors have chosen participants. In the case of the AAAS and PLO-settler talks, the initial participants were invited by the sponsors to join the talks. In the case of the AAAS, agreement from the political echelons on the PLO side was also necessary to move beyond a "soft" format and provide official representation at the talks. In many cases, participants have chosen other participants who have appeared to them as most useful and constructive for the exercise. Participants thus tend to nominate or bring in professional colleagues with whom they share a common outlook and who may also have prior Track-II experience. In some cases, participation has been contingent on agreement from the source financing the talks (when the funders are not the sponsors themselves). This appears to be mostly relevant to academic or NGO-type sponsorship, since government sponsors usually provide financial support for Track-II projects themselves. A determined academic or NGO sponsor may find other sources of financial backing. For example, when IPCME faced legal barriers to funding a U.S.-Iranian dialogue in 1997–1998, Sweden stepped in to take on a sponsorship role.

AGREEING ON NUMBERS

Most experience suggests that Track-II talks seem to work best with a relatively small circle of core participants. Small groups tend to develop their own modus operandi and group interest. Such an interest may naturally intensify as the group comes closer to success.

Yet considerations related to personal interactions should be regarded differently, depending on whether bilateral or multilateral talks, and "soft" or "hard" Track-II talks, are involved. Bilateral "hard" Track-II talks may require that the number of participants be limited in order to maintain group cohesiveness, maximize efficiency, and preserve confidentiality. However, multilateral or "soft" Track-II discussions involve a larger circle of participants and a less demanding schedule.

A larger group may dissipate the energy and focus of the discussion and increase the tendency or temptation to posture. The size of the group and the frequency and location of their meetings may also depend on the sponsor and the resources allocated for the project. Multilateral talks, which usually involve a larger group of participants, can be made more manageable by dividing them into smaller subgroups, based on either technical expertise or regional concerns. A "core" group can be maintained with specialized subgroups included when necessary or desirable. For example, Search for Common Ground had a balanced "core" group set the overall approach, and core representatives took part in more dedicated or specialized subgroups.

Occasionally, however, participants may resist such a fragmentation on the grounds that all issues are interconnected and that such divisions are imposed artificially on a unified subject matter. In part, this may reflect the participants' desire not to miss out on any interesting discussions in the subgroups that they are not attending. Maintaining a large plenary, however, is almost invariably unwieldy and unproductive to serious engagement.

GENERATING A GROUP DYNAMIC

Track-II talks tend to generate their own group dynamics. The process of engagement often creates its own momentum, and a common incentive to succeed may transcend the national division between participants. Whereas Track-I negotiations may also generate a common will to succeed, official talks usually face greater political and systemic barriers to mutual concessions and place stricter constraints on the ability of the group to develop its own "team spirit." In "soft" Track-II talks, the urge to succeed may be less relevant, although intergroup and interpersonal interactions in these talks are equally significant as a means of creating viable and productive exchanges.

Indeed, one important side effect of the group dynamic in almost all Track-II exercises, regardless of their goal, is the establishment of a network of strong personal relations that can carry over beyond the exercise. Although this effect may vary widely, depending on the personal and political outlooks of the participants, Track-II talks can act as a valuable means of self-education and personal political development. In this sense, Track-II participants can "evolve" and can emerge from the exercise with modified and occasionally more moderate views on the issues at hand. In many ways the informal nature of Track-II talks allows for more rapid education and change than does the less flexible environment of Track-I negotiations. The educational aspect of Track-II talks may even help to promote the career prospects of participants who may be seen as having gained a certain expert status within their own academic, professional, or governmental communities.

Group dynamics may act as a barrier to late additions, particularly if their mindset is substantially different than that of the original core group. New members may have to be taken through issues that have already been thrashed out, and they may not fully grasp why and how certain understandings were reached. Veteran members may be tempted to suppress any reopening of issues that have been agreed and resolved, but some allowance may be needed for redundancies of this nature. On the other hand, new blood can enrich the debate and help prevent the exercise from falling into predictable patterns or outcomes. Of course, new additions are most effective when they are on the same political wavelength as the core group and accept its basic rules and objectives. With judicious management by the veterans, a new group dynamic can quickly take hold.

PARTICIPANTS' QUALIFICATIONS

Regardless of their means of selection or exact number, Track-II participants must have certain qualities and characteristics. These can make a vital difference in facilitating or compromising the success of the exercise. Clearly, however, not every Track-II participant can or need have all the characteristics discussed below.

AVAILABILITY.   A key element is the degree of availability and commitment any Track-II candidate can or is willing to provide to the exercise at hand. For core groups to function most effectively, it is desirable to minimize abrupt changes in personnel or discontinuity in participation. Even participants who may be brought in on an occasional "specialized" basis need to have a measure of commitment to the talks to maintain their integrity and flow. Serious Track-II engagement requires considerable time and effort, and may be especially demanding in "hard" talks as they approach closure. Without a real commitment of time and effort, "hard" Track-II talks are unlikely to produce results.

A WILLINGNESS TO TAKE RISKS, A READINESS TO MAKE DEALS.   Risk-taking is a prime quality of effective Track-II practitioners. "Hard" Track-II talks that aim at reaching a deal cannot succeed without the willingness of participants on both sides to take political and sometimes personal risks. Insofar as "hard" Track-II talks require challenging or bypassing official positions or articulating creative ideas that do not correspond with the established "common wisdom" within each camp, Track-II participants must be willing to "enlarge the envelope" and seek a deal that may run the risk of personal or political exposure. Governmental third-party sponsors of Track-II talks may provide good physical protection to participants while they are meeting but they cannot extend a permanent "safety umbrella" to areas outside their jurisdiction.

A PROBLEM-SOLVING APPROACH.   Although problem solving as such may not be the main focus of a particular Track-II exercise, a problem-solving *approach* will facilitate the discussions and help to overcome political or psychological impasses. A problem-solving approach is essential for "hard" Track-II talks. It implies a nonideological perspective and a readiness to acknowledge that practical solutions on the ground are not always fully compatible with longstanding ideological or political aspirations.

EXPERTISE. Where operational issues are under discussion (for example, matters relating to security arrangements or trade and economic issues), specific technical expertise may be necessary. Generally, however, the Middle East experience suggests that it may be better to have knowledgeable generalists rather than specialists who may slow down the process through overemphasis on matters of detail. In this respect, legal advice, though useful, may not always be a *sine qua non* for broad or conceptual agreements and may even deflect the talks from their original course. This is not to suggest that documents and understandings should not be reviewed for their legal import, but that Track-II sponsors and participants should be wary of getting bogged down in legal debates or legalistic differences.

A SHARED LANGUAGE AND OUTLOOK. Fluency in a common language is highly desirable for the success of a Track-II exercise. A common language (e.g., English) may help prevent misunderstandings but does not necessarily eliminate all problems of textual interpretation. Persistent misunderstandings over the Oslo agreement have been partly a matter of differing interpretations and partly a matter of textual ambiguities, both deliberate and unintended. Conversely, a common language helps to establish some mutual cultural and psychological frame of reference even where deep political differences exist.

WIDENING THE POOL OF PARTICIPANTS

In the Middle East, Track-II participants have tended to be drawn from the same limited pool. Many Track-II participants took part in several of the different exercises described in this book. This may have added to the efficacy of Track-II talks across the board, but may equally have helped to create a relatively closed, self-sustaining circuit of practitioners, with limited potential for extension and renewal. Veteran participation may be useful but may also offer diminishing returns. As with any relatively closed circle, a group may develop an inability to progress beyond certain boundaries that have been fixed by the inability of the individuals involved to develop new and creative ideas or break away from longstanding political or psychological presuppositions. Individuals who may appear fresh and interesting at first can also lose their appeal and credibility through overexposure. On the other hand, Track-II novices may waste time and opportunities through sheer inexperience. Some balance between veterans and novices may be necessary, depending on the object of the exercise.

"MODERATES" OR "HARDLINERS"?

Track-II talks can pose a conundrum; understandings are ostensibly best achieved between moderates of both camps who are most likely to have a similar outlook and a common political language. Yet in Track-II talks (as in Track-I negotiations), agreements are likely to be more lasting and durable if they obtain the consent of more "hardline" or "extreme" elements. Equally, in the absence of "hardliners," moderates may feel the need to argue on their behalf in order to appease, preempt, or bypass their likely opposition.

Sometimes moderates are oversensitive to the hardliners' views and sensibilities, and are paradoxically less willing to make the necessary compromises than the hardliners themselves. In the Stockholm talks for example, the Israeli participants (who represented the moderate end of the Israeli political spectrum) were unwilling to go far on the Jerusalem issue out of concern that they would not be able to carry hardline opinion with them. Hardliners such as former Israeli Prime Minister Ehud Barak were subsequently willing to go considerably further than the Stockholm moderates.

Thus, the inclusion of "hardline" representatives may actually facilitate the talks and promote their ultimate chances of success by making them more truly representative and by allowing both "moderates" and "hardliners" to speak for themselves, without mediation or second-guessing. Track-II discussions can also potentially pull those with extremist views toward a "common ground." The upshot is that "hardline" participation should not be excluded and that "hardliners" who have the necessary pragmatic qualities may make a valuable contribution. Nonetheless, while political homogenization may be artificial and counterproductive, some irreducible common understanding between participants may be necessary—a commitment to a resolution of the conflict by diplomacy and negotiations rather than violence or the use of force.

The issue of the scope of political views and representation in Track-II talks can be highly complex and may not be amenable to any predetermined formula. First, "moderate" and "hardline" are in themselves difficult to define and can be utterly misleading as a true measure of dedication to dialogue, deal-making, or problem solving. Second, such positions naturally tend to vary depending on the nature of the exercise and the subject at hand. The role of "hardliners" may differ according to whether the Track-II venue is "hard" or "soft." In "soft" Track-II talks that focus on dialogue or existential issues, "hardliners" tend to give the debate extra emotional and political depth. Equally, a moderate position in one Track-II or on one issue can be translated into a "hardline" position in another forum on another issue. Third, given the nature of the Track-II process, positions can evolve as the exercise progresses. "Hardline" in this context is thus potentially changeable and not necessarily immutable. Indeed, it could be argued that helping to transform "hardline" attitudes is one of the prime functions of all Track-II venues. Finally, in small, tightly knit Track-II groups, personal attitudes and antagonisms can be as powerful a negative influence as combative "hardline" views. A "hardliner" who is prepared to subscribe to the group ethos and common purpose of the exercise without personal acrimony can be more effective in enhancing the Track-II exercise than an ostensible "moderate" who cannot or will not fit in. In some cases it may even be necessary to accommodate "nonplayers" regardless of their political outlook if their intellectual contribution or representative status is difficult to obtain elsewhere.

Ultimately, sponsors and participants alike may need to show considerable flexibility. While socialization and building personal relations among the participants can be an important by-product of Track-II exercises, ensuring true and credible representation of the political spectrum may be as important as ensuring that all participants have workable personal relations. Until the mid-1990s, one of the great difficulties facing Track-II organizers in the Middle East was that of finding suitable and representative participants from the Israeli right. This changed somewhat after the 1996 elections as the Likud-led government became more engaged in the official process of negotiations. But there are still comparatively few Israeli Track-II players who can be identified—or who identify themselves—clearly with the right. There are also very few, if any, Track-II players on the Arab side who clearly and unequivocally represent a viewpoint hostile to the peace process (such as that represented by the Palestinian Islamic group Hamas). The Palestinian side has been either unable or unwilling to bring such representatives to Track-II forums, and those representing the Palestinian opposition have not always been keen to participate in Track-II type forums.

Clearly, a Track-II exercise dominated by extremist views on both sides is unlikely to be very productive. But the Middle East experience suggests that those who agree to participate in Track-II talks are almost by definition interested in making the best of the exercise. This also points to the self-selected nature of Track-II participants: those who are bent on deliberate obstruction and those who have no real faith in the exercise tend to stay away from the process irrespective of their political coloring.

PARTICIPANTS' RELATIONSHIP TO MENTORS AND LEADERS

The relationship between Track-II participants and their national leaderships (including their political mentors) is perhaps the most crucial and decisive element in determining the outcome of any Track-II exercise—bilateral, multilateral, "hard" or "soft." Clearly, when Track-II talks are focused on deal-making or when the participants are seeking to provide precise answers to particular problems, progress is contingent on the nature and viability of the participant-leader relationship. We identify five important factors:

ACCESS AND MUTUAL TRUST. Access to the leadership and a sense of mutual trust can be vital to the success of a Track-II exercise. This is particularly important in "hard" exercises where a deal is sought. In return for accepting a certain degree of risk by entrusting such a deal to unofficial delegates, it may be in the leadership's interest to maintain a measure of credible deniability if the talks fail or are prematurely aborted. Track-II participants in "hard" exercises should be of a certain stature, but they should not be so senior as to give the impression that they are conducting covert or quasi-camouflaged Track-I talks. High-level participation might make talks as sensitive as Track-I negotiations and could thus be self-defeating. The leadership's exposure to risk thus needs to be diminished by a buffer of deniability provided by less than high-level participants.

WILLINGNESS TO ACT WITHOUT SANCTION. Track-II participants should also be ready to take the initiative. This may require a readiness to propose ideas and notions the political leadership has not cleared in advance and that may even be rejected by it, at least initially. In some cases, Track-II participants may need to challenge their own side's "common wisdom" or presuppositions in order to generate enough momentum to bring the talks to fruition. The Middle East experience suggests that, on occasion, Track-II participants should be ready to "lead" the leadership if necessary.

By their nature, political leaderships rarely have the time or luxury to engage in conceptualization or detailed thinking through of problematic issues. In many cases, it may be necessary for Track-II participants to "do" first and consult with their leadership later. In this case, however, the participants carry the burden of the risk that they will fail to deliver.

KNOWLEDGE OF "RED LINES." Keeping in touch and in tune with the domestic political mood and its potential shifts is another vital ingredient of effective Track-II participation. This is primarily a matter of instinct and experience. Track-II participants need to have a solid understanding of their own constituency and a sharp sense for what may or may not be acceptable to the political echelons and the general public. They should be aware of the political and psychological "red lines" affecting their leadership and its broader domestic constituency. They must be sensitive to the potential tension between the need for creative thinking on the one hand, and the need to avoid violating the implicit or explicit political mandate granted to Track-II participants on the other. A readiness to take risks should not be equated with a presumption of being able to transgress what is politically acceptable and deliver "solutions" that are fundamentally unworkable.

UNDERSTANDING THE OTHER SIDE'S LIMITS. Track-II participants should also be sensitive to the other side's political and psychological "red lines." While striving to protect their own interests, participants should understand and take into account their counterparts' domestic constraints. Each side should be aware that while it may be possible to outsmart or out-maneuver the other, the outcome might not be acceptable to the other side's domestic camp. The informal nature of Track-II exercises may tempt one side to believe that it can extract more from the other than would be possible in formal negotiations. But this may be self-defeating. Ultimately, formulations that emerge from Track-II exercises must be acceptable to both sides if they are to be of any practical political value.

MAINTAINING A DISTANCE. In some circumstances it may be desirable for Track-II participants to maintain a certain physical and psychological distance from their leaderships. Excessive intimacy or exposure to a political leadership can erode the participants' credibility. Paradoxically, leaderships sometimes appear to give more weight to views and ideas that are not perceived to emanate from their immediate political circles. Clearly, much depends on the participants' initial standing with the leadership as well as on the leadership's perception of its team's standing with the other side. Where there is the requisite degree of mutual respect, the leadership may be more receptive to new ideas from relative "outsiders" who are not viewed as having an institutional or bureaucratic agenda or as belonging to any internal group or faction within the bureaucracy.

On Method and Substance

FINDING A SOLUTION

There is an important gap between realizing that a solution can be found and actually formulating an optimal solution. Track-II exercises can provide a forum for resolving negotiating problems, but participants need to be aware that solutions often appear more elusive the closer one comes to them. On the whole, Track-II exercises should be wary of seeking to provide comprehensive answers, and are generally best suited to deal in concepts, principles, and frameworks for solutions. In this manner, Track-II talks can act as grand breakthrough mechanisms, leaving the minutiae and micro-details to the formal negotiators.

In Track-II activities, problem solving is not the same as reaching agreement: the latter suggests some official acceptance, while the former does not. By suggesting possible solutions, Track-II discussions can provide *a range of options* for formal agreement without binding the formal negotiator or decision-maker to any one outcome. For instance, the IPCME Syrian-Israeli track provided a major service simply by demonstrating that it is possible to devise security arrangements on the Golan that are agreeable to both sides at least in principle. Indeed, merely by confirming that a solution is possible, Track-II talks can facilitate the peacemaking process, even if the solution ultimately agreed in formal negotiations is different than that reached in earlier Track-II talks.

DEALING WITH CRISES

Generally, Track-II participants should refrain from attempting to deal with daily crisis management unless this is expressly part of their brief. Due to their access to decision-makers, the temptation to get involved in "real" ongoing issues or disputes may be strong. Pressure may also come from decision-makers who may wish to use Track-II venues for dealing with immediate and urgent issues. When Track-II activities are aimed at long-range problems, however, involvement in the daily grind can erode the track's credibility and divert it from its more substantive purpose. In both the Oslo and Stockholm talks participants made a determined—and mostly successful—effort to avoid dealing with issues outside their agreed brief.

In some circumstances, however, a successful attempt at resolving immediate or current crises in a Track-II forum may create a sense of mutual trust and greater credibility in pursuing the exercise. Where relevant, successful crisis management may impress the sponsors, mentors, or both, of the track's ability to deliver, thus enhancing confidence in the prospects of its success in dealing with its primary brief. By and large, however, attempting crisis management is risky and the cost of failure may be high, outweighing the advantages.

WORKING ON A TEXT

Texts are clearly less relevant to "soft" than "hard" Track-II exercises. In the latter, deal-making may require fixing any agreement in a mutually acceptable text. It may be theoretically possible—if perhaps not always advisable—to rely on oral understandings alone. "Soft" Track-IIs may produce texts, but these tend to be closer to a basic record of the encounter rather than an agreed program of action. In the case of the PLO-settlers talks, both sides explicitly agreed—for political reasons—not to have any common texts, despite an attempt by the sponsor and organizer to suggest a framework "code of conduct." Thus, although some understanding was reached orally, this was not put down in writing. A number of different factors may be important in deciding whether or not an agreed text is appropriate to a particular Track-II venue.

POLITICAL "RIPENESS." By and large, the value of agreed substantive texts should be gauged according to the prevailing political conditions. If the conditions are not "ripe" for such documented agreements or understandings, their effect may be limited or counterproductive. While "ripeness" itself may be hard to measure, there should be some consensus among the participants as to whether aiming for a particular text is politically viable. On the other hand, agreed texts can also be used to "enlarge the envelope" and help to hasten the "ripening" process itself (e.g., at Oslo and Stockholm). Ultimately, decisions on "ripeness" may depend to a large extent on the political instincts of the participants, sponsors, and mentors. The greater the concordance between and within these three groups, the more likely it is that an agreed text will have political utility.

THE VALUE OF THE WRITTEN WORD. Written agreements have a power of their own. A text helps to "fix" both sides into positions that may be difficult to retract later. For this reason, Track-II exercises can be seen as problematic by political leaderships that are hesitant to commit themselves to any particular line or outcome, even after taking into account the extra protection of deniability that Track-II venues provide. But without a written text, Track-II exercises may also lose the moment. In some cases a text can be prepared and kept in abeyance pending agreement on when the moment is ripe to reveal it.

WHO PREPARES TEXTS? For most purposes, substantive texts are best prepared by the participants themselves. One side may derive a certain advantage by preparing the first draft, given that the structure and language of a text may be strongly influenced by the side that designs it. On the other hand, yielding the initiative to the other side may help to draw the opponent out before there is any need to divulge one's own positions. In some instances, a third-party draft may be invaluable, especially if neither side seems ready or able to "commit" itself, as with the IPCME staff position papers in the Syrian-Israeli Track-II talks. In "soft" Track-II exercises, the third-party sponsor may be more active in preparing the agenda or in summing up the debate. This was true of the Kelman exercise, the AAAS talks, and Project "Charlie." The text that emerges can then be modified according to the wishes and objectives of the participants. A third-party paper can be adopted as a joint paper, or can remain merely a record of each side's views and concerns.

MARKETING IDEAS

In certain circumstances, Track-II participants may play a vital role through their access to opinion-makers and the media. In "soft" dialogue-oriented Track-II exercises, such access may help to accelerate the circulation of new ideas and concepts within each side's society. Where participants themselves are opinion-makers (e.g., senior journalists or publishers), access to the media may be an important factor in transmitting the knowledge and insight gained in the talks to a wider audience. Indeed, a case could be made to suggest that political opposition to the Oslo accords could have been mitigated by better media presentation to the Israeli and Palestinian publics. In multilateral Track-II discussions such as the ACRS-related talks, participants may need to be very enterprising in marketing their impressions and in ensuring that they can reach the relevant policy elite. Equally, participants in "hard" Track-II talks may be better placed to explain or defend any agreement if they are able to make good use of contacts and access to the media.

On Secrecy

THE NEED FOR SECRECY

Given that Track-II talks may entail some painful concessions by both sides, premature leakage of their content can often spell their doom. In most cases, every attempt should be made to preserve confidentiality and prevent leaks that can seriously undermine the prospects of success. At the same time, allowance should be made for some percolation of ideas and concepts developed in Track-II frameworks in order to mollify, minimize, neutralize, or coopt potential centers of opposition (whether political, bureaucratic, or personal) and win over as much support for the Track-II exercise as possible.

Generally, secrecy may be more of an issue in "hard" Track-II talks than in "soft" discussions. Actual or potential deal-making exercises may be disrupted or destroyed by a leak. But secrecy may also be a prime requirement of "soft" talks where the very fact that two sides are meeting may embarrass one or both of the parties or their leadership (as with the PLO-settler talks). In other cases, the forum itself or the list of participants may not be a secret, but the content of the debate or discussion must be kept confidential (as with the AAAS, Search for Common Ground, and the ACRS-related exercises).

Secrecy serves six goals. First, it allows deniability. This may be vital for political leaderships that wish to test ideas without indicating a prior commitment to them. Track-II venues provide an insulating blanket that protects the leadership while allowing it to experiment with ideas that it may otherwise find very difficult if not impossible to approach. Second, secrecy allows for the airing of ideas that can be considered seriously within a small group and that may otherwise be killed as a result of media pressures or public debate. Third, secrecy may allow participants, mentors, or sponsors an important degree of political maneuverability with the political leadership on either side. For example, secrecy at Oslo allowed Beilin to maneuver between Peres and Rabin and increased the chances of obtaining their consent. Fourth, secrecy allows mentors and political leaders a degree of control over the talks and helps to ensure that directives are being followed. Fifth, secrecy very often adds to the political credibility of the exercise in the eyes of the political leadership. (Part of the attraction of the Oslo process for both Rabin and Arafat was that it met both leaders' propensity to deal in confidential and controlled channels.) Sixth, secrecy limits the number of those who need to know, or of those whose intervention in the process may be politically disruptive or complicating for the decision-maker.

THE DANGERS OF EXCLUSION

The Middle East experience indicates that ideas emanating from Track-II talks run the risk of rejection, not necessarily as a result of principled objection to their content, but rather because a significant body of opinion- or decision-makers feels slighted or surprised at being denied knowledge of the talks or their results. Much of the internal opposition to the Oslo accords on both sides seems to have been the result of this factor. Furthermore, there seems to be a natural tendency among those who have been excluded from a Track-II exercise to suggest that they could have achieved better results had they been privy to the talks or involved in their deliberations. Such attitudes may create serious problems for a Track-II deal if senior decision-makers learn of the track only after the fact. At the same time, the need for consultation and inclusion must be balanced against the requirements of strict confidentiality and mutual trust within the track itself—and this may be difficult to do.

THE RISKS OF ABUSE

Partly as a result of their confidentiality, the results of the Track-II efforts may be open to abuse, particularly where the understandings achieved have no clear formal status (as with the Stockholm talks). Through sheer political opportunism, one side may deliberately misrepresent informal understandings. A particular sponsor, mentor, or leader may seek to distort or misrepresent the outcome of a Track-II exercise either to defend against accusations of a "sell out" or to claim political or electoral credit for a breakthrough.

Deliberate misrepresentation may also be a way to increase the political leverage against the other side in parallel or subsequent Track-I talks. If one party concedes a position informally in a Track-II context, the opposing party may assume that this position can be further eroded in parallel or subsequent Track-I negotiations. Informal talks may be seen to reveal "bottom lines" that are then used by the other side as the starting point for demanding further concessions when Track-II talks are converted to Track-I negotiations.

Track-II venues thus require a modicum of mutual trust and common commitment to avoid abuse. It is important to bear in mind, however, that there can be genuine misunderstanding, as well as abuse. Agreements can be interpreted differently by different sides, and perceptions of what may have been agreed may also differ over time, or as a result of changes in political circumstances. Common texts are clearly a better guarantor of mutual understanding but are naturally not immune to dispute. Nor may it always be within either side's ability to maintain control over the substance of Track-II understandings, let alone the possibility of manipulation, misrepresentation, or simple misconstruction of what has been informally agreed. After 1996, for example, the Palestinian leadership was deeply perturbed by the dissemination and misrepresentation by various Israeli sources of the Stockholm understandings under the guise of the so-called "Abu Mazin–Beilin" agreement. Track-II understandings or agreements may thus develop a life of their own that may not correspond with the intentions or desires of one or both sides. This may be one of the greatest areas of concern regarding Track-II talks.

On Leakage

Leakage from Track-II talks may occur for a number of reasons. These can include a deliberate attempt to sabotage the talks by parties within either camp who wish to prevent their continuation. Track-I negotiators may leak information on Track-II talks—even if sponsored by their leadership—to prevent any possible "bypass" solutions. Even elements within one side's leadership may leak information in order to discredit other elements within the same side. For instance, there is some evidence to suggest that leadership elements on the Palestinian side used inaccurate leaks to the press about the Stockholm talks (the "Abu Mazin–Beilin agreement") to mount politically motivated attacks on Abu Mazin himself. Leaks can thus become an extension of internecine political and personality conflicts.

LEAKAGE AS A MEANS OF MANAGEMENT

It may be misleading to suggest that leaderships have only one unchangeable attitude to leaks of Track-II talks. Much depends on the nature of the talks and their perceived purpose and utility. In some cases, leaders may initiate a leak for any or a combination of the following purposes: to protect themselves against any accusations of a secret "sell-out"; to "demystify" the channel by a partial disclosure of its content; and, to indirectly share the information and challenges presented by the talks with the opposition, thus circuitously co-opting the opposition. Equally, leaders may leak information about a Track-II exercise simply because they do not take it very seriously. In addition, a party may leak information about a Track-II channel to embarrass or discredit the other party to the channel. For example, the PLO's August 1993 leakage of IPCME's work on a Syrian-Israeli framework for security arrangements on the Golan was largely designed to embarrass Damascus and forestall criticism of the PLO's own secret channel at Oslo.

Leaks about Track-II discussions can also be used to protect other Track-II or informal talks. During early to mid-1993, the PLO leadership deliberately leaked reports of talks being held between Nabil Shaath and Israeli Knesset members Ephraim Sneh and Yossi Sarid. The purpose of the leaks was to draw attention to these discussions—which the PLO considered expendable—and away from the Oslo talks.

THE EFFECTS OF LEAKAGE

Regardless of the intentions of the parties themselves, the experience of Track-II efforts in the Middle East suggests that there is a strong possibility of premature leakage. Indeed, Track-II exercises seem highly leak-prone and information about all the talks examined in this volume were leaked in one way or another while still ostensibly operative. While the leaks may have seriously jeopardized some talks, they seem to have had less effect on other tracks. An early leak of the first AAAS-IPCRI meeting in London 1992 in the British press passed without any significant wider notice (but led to the separation of IPCRI from the project).[3] Press reports

---

3. Leaks can also have the effect of increasing mistrust between different participants or organizations involved in a project. In this case, Israeli participants were still

of the Oslo meetings in 1993 were dismissed and seem to have had no real effect on the prospects of the channel's continued progress. In part, this may have been the result of the perceived importance of the participants and venue. For most observers of the Middle East scene, reports of "secret talks" in Norway in spring 1993 involving Abu Ala' and some then obscure Israeli academics did not seem to portend a major political breakthrough.

Similarly, the first full-scale leakage of IPCME's Syrian-Israeli track in the Arab press elicited virtually no response, whereas a subsequent leak in the Israeli press effectively ended the whole exercise. After Israeli reports about the Israeli-Syrian IPCME talks in December 1993, the Syrian government banned any further participation of Syrians in Track-II discussions. This reflected Syria's loss of any faith it might have had in "free-lance diplomacy." It also demonstrated Syria's aversion to being "tainted" by any Oslo-like deal, particularly in light of its strong criticism of the means and substance of the Oslo accords (which it had called "a secret deal struck behind the back of the Palestinian people").

The Syrian-Israeli example shows the importance of context. Whereas the first leak happened prior to the PLO-Israeli Oslo breakthrough, the second occurred after it, and thus seemingly enhanced the significance of the talks, particularly as the last pre-leak IPCME meeting had taken place—coincidentally—in Oslo as well. Leaks regarding the talks between Israeli settlers and the Palestinian Authority also terminated the talks—the Israeli participants were exposed to strong political and psychological pressures within the settlers' community—but their future was equally affected by the elections of the Likud-led Netanyahu government. In the case of the Stockholm talks, the leaks came after the project had already been derailed by the assassination of Rabin, and may thus have had less effect on its immediate prospects of success. On the other hand, the leaks may have made it more difficult for the parties to resume discussions on the same basis at a future date.

On Formal and Informal Talks

There are significant similarities in the scope and substance of formal Track-I and informal Track-II talks. In both cases, the object of the exercise may vary from long-range problem solving to urgent crisis management and from a superficial exchange of positions to deep substantive agreement. In both cases as well, it is important that participants (or delegation

---

subject to the official ban on contacts with the PLO and their mistrust of IPCRI was aggravated by the leak—without any evidence that IPCRI was in fact responsible.

heads) enjoy easy access to their leaders and be able to speak confidently on these leaders' behalf, especially for "hard" Track-II talks. As in Track-I diplomacy, "hard" Track-II players should know the limits of their brief and should know how to remain within their explicit or implicit mandate. Given the informal nature of Track-II discussions, Track-II players need to be doubly aware of the risks of exceeding their mandate or misleading the other side as to the limits of what may be possible. But there may also be marked differences between the two modes; we discuss four.

THE PARTICIPATION OF NON-OFFICIALS

Given their nature, Track-II talks are best conducted, at least in their initial stages, by non-officials. This preserves an important measure of freedom of action for Track-II participants, and at the same time allows for credible official deniability by the respective leaderships. Sometimes a mixed model may emerge, in which both officials and non-officials become Track-II participants, with each adopting some of the characteristics of the other. In the initial phases of the Oslo talks, the Palestinian side was nominally "official" while the Israeli side was nominally "academic." In reality, however, these distinctions were blurred; both sides were engaged in the attempt to strike a political deal with official sanction. In this instance, the unofficial nature of the first phase of the Oslo talks was largely—but not entirely—a function of Israeli nonrecognition of the PLO. In other instances, where the two sides do face obstacles to direct contact, the participation of officials may only be necessary when Track-II talks are on the verge of becoming Track-I negotiations, and there is an agreed need to clinch a formal agreement.

One of the important consequences of the informal nature of Track-II talks is that participants are likely to be less inhibited about shedding formal positions than they would be in Track-I negotiations. This means that the gap between Track-II parties is usually narrower than in Track-I conditions, or that this gap is easier and quicker to bridge than in Track-I negotiations. This may not hold over all issues and circumstances. But it is worth noting that issues resolved in Oslo over six months (and that were effectively renegotiated after the intervention of Singer and Savir) had been totally stalemated in Washington for over two years. That the PLO had deliberately prevented any progress in the formal negotiations in Washington merely confirms the potential utility of a Track-II "bypass."

THE IMPERATIVE TO AGREE

While it may be difficult to generalize, in most Track-II exercises the two sides have a shared interest in reaching an agreed common ground. Track-II talks are thus less likely to be the venue for spoiling or delaying tactics or attempts to actively disrupt or prevent the achievement of an agreed goal. By contrast, Track-I talks may be aimed at frustrating the other side or denying it a particular goal, and may have as their primary objective the maximization of gain, rather than the attainment of a common ground. Clearly, this does not mean that Track-I negotiations are not appropriate for those who seek to reach formal agreement or a common understanding, only that Track-I talks may allow for a negative purpose as well as the more positive one. The chances of any Track-II exercise proceeding very far based on a strategy of denial or frustration are limited, and there seems to be little incentive for a party to embark on Track-II talks if its object is obstruction.

THE DANGER OF "SLIPPERY SLOPES"
While Track-II talks can help to bring conflicting states and non-state actors closer to resolving their disputes or, at a minimum, to conduct a dialogue regarding their different perceptions and concerns, such talks are not without serious risk. The imperative to agree and the group dynamic of Track-II talks can create a "slippery slope," pushing the participants in directions that may diverge from the parties' official stances. A good example can be found in the Oslo talks. In embracing the declaration of principles negotiated in Oslo, Israel may be seen to have "slipped" into granting recognition to the PLO. Having concluded the DOP, Israeli Prime Minister Rabin could not refuse a U.S. request that the agreement be signed in Washington, where Rabin finally found himself on stage—and practically at the same level—with PLO Chairman Arafat, under the auspices of U.S. President Bill Clinton. This established the PLO's new position as a coequal partner and may have reinforced Arafat's claim to independent statehood.

In this sense, the informality of Track-II venues can be contrasted with the formality of Track-I talks. Formality in the latter can act as a means of control and as a hedge against "slippage." An experienced party to a Track-II venue may thus exploit the tendency toward "slippage" in the relatively congenial and uncontrolled atmosphere of these talks and turn this to its advantage. In turn, "slippage" in Track-II talks or its purposeful exploitation (or misinterpretation) by one party may affect its positions in parallel Track-I negotiations.

TRACK-II AS RECONNAISSANCE
Any talks or negotiations may involve some measure of testing out the other side and seeking a response to suggested solutions or ideas for possible breakthroughs and mechanisms. One of the most important virtues

of Track-II venues is that this can be done without any real cost to the parties' leadership. In Track-II talks, reconnaissance can work at different levels.

First, it can be used to see whether the other side is serious about ongoing or potential Track-I negotiations, as in the Oslo, Stockholm, and ACRS-related talks. Track-II frameworks can become venues for checking out the intentions of the other side regarding negotiations per se. Second, given the element of deniability, Track-II channels can be used for sending "trial balloons" and experimental solutions that may be difficult to approach in Track-I negotiations without incurring a high political or psychological price. Third, Track-II talks can be an effective vehicle through which the leadership—again at little or no cost—can bypass its own bureaucracies and establishments. Through such frameworks, the leadership can check the reliability of its own establishment's political or intelligence assessments or see how far a certain political line can be pursued without serious interference or impediment from the establishment.

Finding the Right Environment

Not all problems that have not been resolved in a Track-I context will yield to Track-II treatment. The same factors that impede progress in Track-I negotiations can also impede progress in Track-II venues. For example, Israeli-Lebanese Track-II activities before the Israeli withdrawal from Lebanon in May 2000 faced many of the same problems seen in the formal Lebanese-Israeli negotiations, most of which stemmed from the broader issue of Lebanon's limited freedom of action and its inability to act independently of Syria on major policy issues. Although Track-II provides a possible "bypass" around Track-I obstacles, it cannot build a bridge between two parties that do not have the will or the means to act according to their independently defined national interest.

For some practitioners, Track-II talks have a vital role to play precisely when Track-I negotiations break down. Some believe that Track-II talks are particularly important when Track-I negotiations are stuck because it is then that Track-II allows continued communication and contacts among Track-I participants. Indeed, if under such circumstances Track-II talks did not take place, what had been achieved in Track-I negotiations prior to the breakdown would soon be forgotten. This view further argues that in times of high tension, it is preferable to hold Track-II talks. The mutual familiarity achieved in Track-II is seen as important because it means that if Track-I negotiations are resumed, the negotiators will not have to familiarize themselves with each other from scratch. This view, however, seems to be based on the assumption that the same teams would participate in both Track-I and Track-II functions, and that there would be a political operational continuum between the two, which is rarely the case.

On the other hand, post-Oslo experiences in the Middle East suggest that prospects for Track-II talks have been at their brightest and potentially most fruitful when the PLO and Israeli leaderships have developed a real working partnership, such as that between Arafat and Rabin in 1994–1995. This does not deny the Track-II function as a breakthrough mechanism, but it does suggest that Track-II talks may be redundant or ineffective if there is total breakdown at the Track-I level or if there is a complete loss of confidence between the two sides, such as between the PA and the Netanyahu government after February–March 1997. For Track-II venues to work, the political leaderships on both sides must be willing to give it a chance, and this, in turn, may depend on each sides' perception of the good faith and intent of the other.

When a breakdown occurs in Track-I negotiations, the effectiveness of Track-II channels can also depend on their purpose: in such circumstances any Track-II approach may have to be more cautious and less ambitious than it would be otherwise. In real life, complete and irrevocable political breakdowns are rare even between the most vehement of enemies, and there is almost always some mutual interest in maintaining contact for one reason or another. In such conditions, Track-II venues may still be useful if only to limit the possibilities of unintended escalation or to avoid mutual misunderstandings and misreading of intentions. (The PLO-settler contacts fit into this category to some extent.)

However, where Track-I and Track-II efforts are conducted in parallel, Track-I activities may impinge on the freedom of Track-II talks. For example, it may be more difficult to deal with problems creatively in Track-II talks if either or both political leaderships perceive this as undermining their formal Track-I positions. In the Middle East, the Syrian side has often been unwilling to pursue Track-II opportunities largely for this reason. Given its concern about a possible "loss of control" in Track-II talks, Syria has been wary of pursuing any sustained Track-II effort lest this erode its formal positions or give the Israeli side the impression that the Syrian side is merely posturing in the formal discussions and is actually open to a more flexible resolution. Leaderships' attitudes to Track-II talks can thus vary from the consistent interest and occasional enthusiasm of the PLO, to the suspicion and hesitancy leading to outright hostility of Syria.

Moving from Track-II to Track-I

By their nature, Track-II forums attract an academic or quasi-academic audience usually reinforced by retired or semi-retired officials and experts (Oslo was an exception in that the Palestinian side included officials from the start). Most Track-II participants are not professional negotiators. Except in circumstances where a Track-II venue has a direct input into Track-I talks, the value of "solutions" reached in the former may lie less in their potential or immediate impact on decision-makers, and more in their general effect on the realm of opinion-making institutions, party political circles, or the media. In this context, the value of understandings reached in Track-II venues can be seen as important not because they will necessarily resemble what is ultimately agreed upon at the Track-I level, but rather because Track-II understandings can point the way out of a political logjam. In other words, work done at the Track-II level can indicate that solutions *are possible* given the will and the opportunity to work them out. The very fact that problems widely perceived to be intractable—such as Palestinian-Israeli final status issues, or security arrangements on the Golan—are demonstrated to have a potentially mutually agreed resolution can have a powerful political impact.

If and when Track-II talks are transformed into Track-I negotiations, or when Track-II participants are "elevated" to Track-I talks, the crossover from the Track-II experience may facilitate the resolution of Track-I logjams. But there is also the danger that Track-II methods, precepts, and participants may be lost in the Track-I political and bureaucratic morass, and that participants may lose their presumed comparative advantage. The Middle East experience thus suggests that Track-II expertise may be lost, stifled, marginalized, or opposed by professional and career diplomats operating in a Track-I setting.

Measuring Success and Failure

Generally, "hard" Track-II exercises appear to work best when problems are of a bilateral nature. The Oslo talks—the most apparently successful "hard" Track-II exercise in the Middle East—were bilateral and a product of secrecy, dedicated deal-making, and "ripeness." Regional and multilateral issues appear less amenable to "hard" Track-II resolutions, primarily due to the difficulty of problem solving when there are too many conflicting national agendas. It is also more difficult to keep a serious multilateral or regional Track-II effort confidential and secure, or to ensure workable logistics.

CRITERIA OF SUCCESS

In one sense, Track-II venues become a success when the deliberations, and the understandings and agreements reached in their framework, are adopted at the Track-I level. But this may be too simplistic and linear a criterion for measuring success. For one thing, the measure of success in "hard" Track-II talks is intrinsically different from that of "soft" tracks. In the former, agreed texts or other substantive evidence are obvious measures of progress toward a common goal. In the latter, the measures of success may be less quantifiable or visible; the results of dialogue, empathy, and political networking may also take a longer and more complex route to fruition.

Track-II success can be measured by the extent to which the exercise fulfilled its stated purpose. But in many instances, success (or failure) may not be evident to the participants, the sponsors, or others at the time. In some cases, Track-II work may disappear in one form, only to reappear in another. For example, the Stockholm talks became transformed into the "Abu Mazin–Beilin" agreement, which first formed the basis for a joint Labor-Likud document in 1996, and ultimately the Clinton bridging proposals of December 2000. Track-II participants may also have a natural tendency to overestimate the importance of their work at the time. This tendency applies to some extent to the AAAS and the PLO-settlers talks, whose real significance appears to have been arguable at best. Conversely, some Track-II exercises may seem more important retrospectively while their significance was much less clear around the time they were conducted. Equally, a project that apparently failed to reach its immediate goals—such as the Stockholm channel—can continue to resonate politically long after its termination. In this sense, positive outcomes (i.e., "success") can be more of an unintended consequence of the exercise rather than the formal attainment of its stated goal.

Who judges Track-II venues as a "success" or "failure," and at what stage is this judgment made? From a sponsor's perspective, "success" may be attained once its role is recognized. A Track-II exercise may be a success from the point of view of the sponsor's own interests if it generates a political profile or role (as for Norway) or more grants for subsequent exercises and projects (for NGOs).

Bearing in mind the difficulty of establishing clear criteria, five criteria for establishing the success or failure of Track-II talks seem reasonable:

First, in some cases, the mere readiness of two differing sides to sit together can be seen as a measure of success. This is clearly a necessary but not a sufficient condition for any other progress.

Second, success may be seen as the outcome of agreement on some common frame of reference. Short of a substantive resolution of all or most basic differences, this could include any or all of the following:

- long-term joint conceptualization about future common goals or aspirations;
- finding potential operational solutions to common problems;
- defining the principles required for an agreement;
- defining areas of agreement or disagreement between the two sides;
- reaching a joint statement of intent;
- reaching a common agenda;
- reaching a procedural agreement; and
- agreement on confidence-building measures.

Third, success can mean the attainment of substantive agreements or understandings. In a formal sense, Track-II talks ultimately succeed most perfectly when their findings are adopted at the Track-I level.

Fourth, Track-II talks can succeed by establishing informal contacts and political networking between opposing sides. Track-II exercises can create their own ripple effect that could not have been anticipated and that may have an important positive effect on conflict resolution.

Finally, success can come through the seepage of new and positive ideas into the political psyches of the respective constituencies as a result of public disclosure of Track-II talks, including discussions, intellectual exchanges, the development of new terminology and language, etc.

To Whose Advantage?

Track-II talks can distort the balance of power between the two parties in favor of the weaker party. This is because the ebb and flow of argument in "hard" Track-II talks tends to depend less on the objective balance than on the abilities, experience, and dedication of the participants themselves. In some ways, Track-II forums can help to level the political and psychological playing field by presupposing a nominal equality between the two sides. At the same time, the group dynamic acts in favor of an outcome where both sides have an equal stake in success. The stronger party, interested in reaching an agreement but finding it difficult to achieve in the "real" world, also gains from a perceived correction of the imbalance, without which an agreement may not be possible.

Citizen Diplomacy

The Middle East experience between the late 1980s and mid-1990s suggests that Track-II talks can offer considerable scope for citizen or private diplomacy. In most of the examples reviewed, Track-II venues were set up at the initiative of private individuals acting outside—if not without—their government's consent. Track-II talks thus appear to arise and be effective when determined participants see a real need. Much depends on the calibre and dedication of these initiators and on their relationships with their leaderships. Citizen diplomacy cannot flourish without a special relationship built on mutual trust between participants, mentors, and leaders.

Equally important are the nature and quality of the sponsor and the role of the third party. The Middle East experience indicates that without an effective and sustained sponsor, Track-II efforts may have a limited life span or limited prospect of success. In this context, the viability of citizen diplomacy appears contingent on the availability, dedication, and objectives of an outside sponsor.

Citizen-diplomats may also have to bear the consequences of acting outside or beyond the formal consent and protection of their governments. As ostensibly free agents, citizen-diplomats may thus be politically vulnerable to pressure or intimidation from opponents within their camp as well as from the other side. They may also be in danger.

However, no matter what effort and sense of enterprise have been brought to bear by private citizens, not all Track-II venues bear fruit as intended. Of the various "hard" Middle East case studies reviewed here, only Oslo can be seen as a "success" in terms of its own initial objectives, and its broader political success remains debatable. Clearly, some of the "soft" Track-II frameworks initiated with more modest purposes in mind met their objectives. Backed by suitable sponsors, Track-II talks can achieve a wide range of objectives: from the consolidation of an ongoing peace processes, to the creation and generation of new peace networks; and from the stimulation of public debate on basics issues, to the creation of new and dramatic political realities.

Appendix 1:
Oslo Talks

The Principles of an Israeli-Palestinian Negotiating Plan[1]

Israeli-Palestinian negotiations will concentrate on achieving agreement in regard to three documents: A DoP (Declaration of Principles), a CWP (Cooperation and Working Programme) and Guidelines for a Marshall Plan.

1. DRAFT FOR DOP (DECLARATION OF PRINCIPLES):

1. The aim of Israeli-Palestinian negotiations is to obtain agreement regarding arrangements for establishing a Palestinian Interim Self-Governing Authority (Body), the elected Palestinian Interim Council, for a period leading to a permanent settlement based on Resolutions 242 and 33.
   [It is understood that the interim arrangements are an integral part of the whole process leading to the implementation of 242 and 338.]
2. In order that the Palestinian people in the West Bank and Gaza may govern themselves according to democratic principles, direct, free and general political elections (under international supervision) (in which all Palestinians from the West Bank and Gaza, as on the fourth of June 1967, would participate) would be held three to six months after the signing of the DoP.

---

1. Draft presented by the Israeli side, Oslo, 11.02.1993

3. The elections for the establishment of the Palestinian Interim Council will constitute a significant interim, preparatory step towards the realization of the legitimate rights of the Palestinian people their just requirements.

4. Immediately after the signing of this DoP a transfer of authority from the Israeli military government and the Israeli Civil Administration to the Palestinians and such committees that will be appointed by the Palestinian delegation will start. The transfer of authority to the Palestinian committees will be of temporary and preparatory nature and will include Palestinian control over taxation, tourism, education, health and social welfare, as well as other agreed upon spheres.

5. In order to guarantee optimal economic development and growth, immediately with signing of this DoP, a Palestinian Land Committee and a Palestinian Water Administration Committee will be established. The Palestinian Land Committee and the Palestinian Water Administration Committee will be given immediate powers as mutually agreed upon. A coordinated land and water resources development plan will be negotiated between the Palestinian Land Committee and the Palestinian Water Administration Committee on the one, and Government of Israel on the other hand.

6. In order to guarantee optimal security arrangements for the Palestinian inhabitants of the West Bank and Gaza, the Palestinian Interim Council will establish a strong police force, responsible for internal security and public order.
Preparatory steps, necessary for the establishment of the Palestinian police force, will be taken immediately (after the signing of the DoP), in liaison with the Israeli and Jordanian police forces regarding the West Bank, and in liaison with the Israeli and Egyptian police forces, regarding Gaza.

7. In order to enable the Interim Self-Government Authority, the Palestinian Interim Council, to promote economic growth, several institutions will be established at the time of its inauguration: a Palestinian Land Authority, a Palestinian Water Administration Authority, a Palestinian Electricity Authority, a Gaza Port Authority, a Palestinian Development Bank and a Palestinian export Promotion Board.
In order to determine the powers, rights and obligations of these institutions, the Palestinian committees will negotiate with the Government of Israel the necessary relevant agreements.

8. The Palestinian Interim Council will be empowered to legislate for all the authorities that are mutually agreed upon. Both parties will reassess jointly all laws and military orders presently in force.

9. In order to allow the Interim Self-Governing Authority, The Palestinian Interim Council, to operate in harmony with the Government of Israel, agreements on cooperation and liaison will be negotiated in order to provide for security and mutual understanding between the concerned parties.
   An Israeli-Palestinian Liaison Committee will be established and will deal with all issues of dispute and common interest.

10. Further liaison and cooperation arrangements will be negotiated and agreed upon between the Government of Israel and the Palestinians on one hand and the Governments of Jordan and Egypt on the other hand.

11. Even in case the necessary agreements will not be finalized in time, the elections to the Palestinian Interim Council and its inauguration, shall be held on the agreed upon date (i.e. six months after the signing of the DoP). In this case, the elected Palestinian Interim Council will continue negotiations with the Government of Israel. Accordingly, the delegation of powers and the transfer of authority, regarding those specific issues that will not have been agreed upon before the date of elections, will be postponed until mutual agreement will have been achieved.

12. Immediately after signing the DoP the transitional period of five years will begin. As soon as possible, but not later than the beginning of the third year, negotiations will take place to determine the final status of the West Bank, Jerusalem and Gaza, and its relationship with its neighbours.

13. After the signing of the DoP, Israeli-Palestinian negotiations on the redeployment of Israeli military forces in the West Bank and Gaza will start. A first redeployment of forces will be carried out on the eve of elections for the Palestinian Interim Council. Further redeployments will be gradually implemented in line with the introduction of other agreed upon security measures. At the end of the second year of the interim period, Israeli military forces will withdraw completely from Gaza, in the spirit of partial implementation of 242 and 339.

14. After the Israeli withdrawal from Gaza a trusteeship will be established, as agreed upon between the Government of Israel and the Palestinians.

Appendix 2:
AAAS Talks

Withdrawal from Gaza "By Agreement"[2]

FIRST: FACTORS AFFECTING THE ISRAELI SIDE (FROM ISRAELI PERSPECTIVE)

1. Sovereignty: Acknowledging the relinquishment of annexation (Gaza) but no acknowledgement of Palestinian sovereignty
2. Security: prevention of terrorist activities based in Gaza aimed at Israel
3. Political and security stability
4. Economic stability
5. Refugees and displaced persons: A permanent solution to the problem (condition) of the refugees, the displaced persons of 1967 and a resolution of the situation of the Gazans living outside Gaza.
6. Settlements: What effect a resolution of the settlers issue in Gaza may have as a precedent regarding the future of settlers in the rest of the occupied territories
7. The future of economic relations (Israeli-Gazan) in particular the movement of Gazan workers
8. The effect of a withdrawal from Gaza on the Israeli domestic scene

---

2. Words between brackets denote suggested alternative formulations. Draft internal memo prepared at PLO Directorate for International Relations, Tunis, March 1993, based on AAAS Track-II discussions December 1992–March 1993.

9. The effect of a withdrawal from Gaza on the escalation of violence (*intifada*) in the rest of the occupied territories
10. The question of 'linkage' between the withdrawal from Gaza and the future of negotiations over Jerusalem and the West Bank
11. The party that will take over (including possible third parties) and the nature of the structure of the Palestinian authority.

SECOND: FACTORS AFFECTING PALESTINIAN SIDE:

1. The Principle of 'linkage': No agreement on "Gaza first" can be a substitute for an agreement on the interim phase in the rest of the occupied territories.
2. Full Israeli military (and security) and settlement withdrawal [from Gaza]
3. The mechanism for a transfer of authority and for defining the role of third parties
4. The nature of Palestinian governing authority and its powers
5. Palestinian security preparedness
6. Economic stability and external support; the external economic environment (relations with Israel–Egypt–the West Bank)
7. The effects and repercussions of an agreement on Gaza on the Palestinian internal scene
   a. Relations between Gaza and the West Bank
   b. Relations between the Palestinian factions (including Fateh-Hamas)
   c. Effect on the Palestinian political scene in the Diaspora
8. The effect of the agreement on the Arab-Israeli negotiating situation
   a. The Syrian-Israeli track
   b. The Jordanian-Israeli track
9. The effect of any agreement on refugees-displaced people on the issue of "refugees-displaced people" in general
10. Effect of agreement on Palestinian-Arab relations, in particular: Jordan-Syria-Egypt

Appendix 3:
Stockholm Talks

Final Agreed Working
Papers 1 – 4[3]

Document One

PROCEDURAL AGREEMENTS

1. The work of the two teams will proceed on the basis of an 'open agenda.'
2. The role of the 'third party:'
   a. In case of difficulties the two teams will consult with our Swedish host regarding:
      i.   Data and/or the assessment of data
      ii. Achieving a breakthrough from an impasse situation
   b. A dialogue with other third parties, including the US, will be carried out in the future by agreement.
3. Henceforth, both teams undertake not to take part in any future negotiations on final status issues. Other current and future negotiations will be channelled and subsumed into this project.
4. Participation by relevant political actors and experts will be invited by agreement. The intention of both teams is to ensure the active engagement of their respective political leaderships in this endeavour.
5. All understandings obtained are to be committed to paper in one standard draft.

---

3.   Agreed First session, Stockholm, 04.09.1994.

6. Both sides will have the right to ask for separate consultations among their own team, at any point of time.
7. The two teams agree to provide our hosts with a detailed verbal briefing at the end of each session and a written report every quarter.

    Note: The two teams have agreed to meet monthly until the end of 1994 to identify and discuss the issues, problems and subjects related to a final status agreement.

Document Two

GUIDING PRINCIPLES FOR REACHING AN ISRAELI-PALESTINIAN AGREEMENT ON FINAL STATUS ISSUES.

An Agreement should:

1. Be durable
2. Be stable
3. Not pose a security threat to any party
4. Enhance both Israeli and Palestinian security
5. Promote bilateral and regional stability
6. Not threaten the religious, cultural and political identities of the parties
7. Be politically viable for the respective communities
8. Take into account Arab concerns and sensitivities
9. Promote the free association of peoples
10. Provide for and promote the freedom of movement of people, goods and capital
11. Provide for the non-violent resolution of future disputes and conflicts
12. Adhere to the principle of equitability
13. Promote a comprehensive peace

Document Three

ISSUES TO BE DEALT WITH IN AN ISRAELI-PALESTINIAN FINAL STATUS AGREEMENT

The Israeli-Palestinian final status agreement will address the following issues in the context of a permanent peace:

1. The final and irrevocable delineation of secure and recognized borders
2. The creation and implementation of agreed security arrangements
3. The political nature of the emerging Palestinian entity/state
4. The creation of normal and stable inter-state relations
5. Relations with neighbouring countries
6. The future of settlements
7. Arrangements regarding the future of Jerusalem
8. The settlement of the refugee problem
9. Property rights in Israel and the Palestinian territories
10. Freedom for cooperation in areas of mutual interest
11. Mechanisms for disputes resolution
12. The use of water resources
13. The international role including guarantees to the parties involved
14. Verification and inspection mechanism
15. The status of former agreements
16. Modes for the implementation of the final status agreement
17. Preliminary measures for the implementation of a peace treaty.

Document Four

STEPS TOWARDS A FUTURE MIDDLE EAST

First Stage: Peace between states

Second Stage: Sustaining non-violent means of resolving disputes

Third Stage: Entering into voluntary civil association between the peoples of the region through economic and cultural interaction

Fourth Stage: Guarantee stabilization within communities

Fifth Stage: Create representative government-enhancing democratic forms of conduct

Sixth Stage: Moving towards a cooperative Middle East with the appropriate superstructure

Appendix 4:
Project "Charlie"[4]

"Charter for Good Neighbourly Relations"
(not agreed)

Dec. 1 1995

The PLO and the Settlers of Judea, Samaria (West Bank) and Gaza:
A Charter of Principles for Good Neighbourly Relations

PREFACE

The Oslo agreements have made us political neighbours. On the basis of
the present political reality, all the settlements in Judea, Samaria (West
Bank) and Gaza will remain the neighbors of the Palestinian Authority,
led by the PLO, at least until a final status agreement is reached.

Accordingly, it is fitting that we sit and discuss the possibilities for dialogue in the spirit of good neighbours; attempt to solve problems with
civility; and exchange views with regard to the long-range political options—even as we acknowledge the broad divide between our views.

PRINCIPLES

At this juncture, we agree upon the following points:

1. With the application of autonomy in Judea and Samaria (West
Bank), both parties pledge to deal with one another with civility, to

---

4.   Proposed by Joseph Alpher, December 1, 1995.

prevent and condemn any instance of violence, and to maintain normal and tranquil life in the region.

2. The parties confirm that the Oslo I and II agreements, along with the laws prevailing in Israel and in the Palestinian Authority, constitute the shared basis for living together, until such time as a new agreement supersedes any of these.

3. With regard to local disagreements, e.g. concerning land rights or environmental issues, the settlers and the PLO seek to address them themselves, at the local level, and will turn to the authorities only in the event of failure.

4. At the ideological-political level, the two parties will seek to continue and expand their dialogue, with the goal of defining additional common denominators.

5. The parties also seek to cultivate dialogue at the local level between the residents of settlements and the residents of nearby villages and towns.

Appendix 5:
IPCME Talks

Proposed Principles for an Israeli Withdrawal from the Golan.[5]

1. Israel reaffirms Syrian sovereignty over the Golan; Syria pledges its commitment to full peace.
   a. Israel commits itself to full withdrawal from the Golan during a mutually acceptable period of time. This time period will be determined by both parties in order to activate any and all of the provisions of this settlement. Consistent with the provisions of the agreement, and in accordance with Syrian sovereignty, special arrangements shall be negotiated to determine the future of Israeli settlers in the Golan.
   b. Syria's commitment to peace includes the following: establishment of full diplomatic and consular relations, the development of economic and cultural relations, the end of the economic boycott, and the free movement of people and goods.
2. Israeli withdrawal and Syria's steps to normalize relations will be at parallel stages and phased in accordance with a schedule to be negotiated by the parties. These phased steps will be simultaneous and interdependent and will be accompanied by the introduction of mutual security measures on a schedule to be agreed upon by the parties. Mutual security measures will extend beyond the timetable for withdrawal.

---

5. Drafted Oslo, October 1993.

3. Consistent with the provisions of this agreement both parties recognize each other's concern over water resources and commit themselves to negotiate in good faith their use during and after the period of phased withdrawal.

About the Authors

Hussein Agha is a Senior Associate Member of St. Antony's College at Oxford University.

Shai Feldman is Head of the Jaffee Center for Strategic Studies at Tel Aviv University.

Ahmad Khalidi is a Senior Associate Member of St. Antony's College at Oxford University.

Zeev Schiff is Defense Editor of Ha'aretz.

Index

BCSIA Studies in International Security

Published by The MIT Press

Sean M. Lynn-Jones and Steven E. Miller, series editors
Karen Motley, executive editor
Belfer Center for Science and International Affairs (BCSIA)
John F. Kennedy School of Government, Harvard University

Agha, Hussein, Shai Feldman, Ahmad Khalidi, and Zeev Schiff, Track-II Diplomacy: Lessons from the Middle East (2003)

Allison, Graham T., Owen R. Coté, Jr., Richard A. Falkenrath, and Steven E. Miller, *Avoiding Nuclear Anarchy: Containing the Threat of Loose Russian Nuclear Weapons and Fissile Material* (1996)

Allison, Graham T., and Kalypso Nicolaïdis, eds., *The Greek Paradox: Promise vs. Performance* (1996)

Arbatov, Alexei, Abram Chayes, Antonia Handler Chayes, and Lara Olson, eds., *Managing Conflict in the Former Soviet Union: Russian and American Perspectives* (1997)

Bennett, Andrew, *Condemned to Repetition? The Rise, Fall, and Reprise of Soviet-Russian Military Interventionism, 1973–1996* (1999)

Blackwill, Robert D., and Michael Stürmer, eds., *Allies Divided: Transatlantic Policies for the Greater Middle East* (1997)

Blackwill, Robert D., and Paul Dibb, eds., *America's Asian Alliances* (2000)

Brom, Shlomo, and Yiftah Shapir, eds., *The Middle East Military Balance 1999–2000* (1999)

Brom, Shlomo, and Yiftah Shapir, eds., *The Middle East Military Balance 2001–2002* (2002)

Brown, Michael E., ed., *The International Dimensions of Internal Conflict* (1996)

Brown, Michael E., and Šumit Ganguly, eds., *Government Policies and Ethnic Relations in Asia and the Pacific* (1997)

Carter, Ashton B., and John P. White, eds., *Keeping the Edge: Managing Defense for the Future* (2001)

Elman, Colin, and Miriam Fendius Elman, eds., *Bridges and Boundaries: Historians, Political Scientists, and the Study of International Relations* (2000)

Elman, Miriam Fendius, ed., *Paths to Peace: Is Democracy the Answer?* (1997)

Falkenrath, Richard A., *Shaping Europe's Military Order: The Origins and Consequences of the CFE Treaty* (1994)

Falkenrath, Richard A., Robert D. Newman, and Bradley A. Thayer, *America's Achilles' Heel: Nuclear, Biological, and Chemical Terrorism and Covert Attack* (1998)

Feaver, Peter D., and Richard H. Kohn, eds., *Soldiers and Civilians: The Civil-Military Gap and American National Security* (2001)

Feldman, Shai, *Nuclear Weapons and Arms Control in the Middle East* (1996)

Feldman, Shai, and Yiftah Shapir, eds., *The Middle East Military Balance 2000–2001* (2001)

Forsberg, Randall, ed., *The Arms Production Dilemma: Contraction and Restraint in the World Combat Aircraft Industry* (1994)

Hagerty, Devin T., *The Consequences of Nuclear Proliferation: Lessons from South Asia* (1998)

Heymann, Philip B., *Terrorism and America: A Commonsense Strategy for a Democratic Society* (1998)

Kokoshin, Andrei A., *Soviet Strategic Thought, 1917–91* (1998)

Lederberg, Joshua, *Biological Weapons: Limiting the Threat* (1999)

Shaffer, Brenda, *Borders and Brethren: Iran and the Challenge of Azerbaijani Identity* (2002)

Shields, John M., and William C. Potter, eds., *Dismantling the Cold War: U.S. and NIS Perspectives on the Nunn-Lugar Cooperative Threat Reduction Program* (1997)

Tucker, Jonathan B., ed., *Toxic Terror: Assessing Terrorist Use of Chemical and Biological Weapons* (2000)

Utgoff, Victor A., ed., *The Coming Crisis: Nuclear Proliferation, U.S. Interests, and World Order* (2000)

Williams, Cindy, ed., *Holding the Line: U.S. Defense Alternatives for the Early 21st Century* (2001)

The Robert and Renée Belfer Center for Science and International Affairs

Graham T. Allison, Director
John F. Kennedy School of Government
Harvard University
79 JFK Street, Cambridge, MA 02138
Tel: (617) 495-1400; Fax: (617) 495-8963
http://www.ksg.harvard.edu/bcsia bcsia_ksg@harvard.edu

The Belfer Center for Science and International Affairs (BCSIA) is the hub of research, teaching and training in international security affairs, environmental and resource issues, science and technology policy, human rights, and conflict studies at Harvard's John F. Kennedy School of Government. The Center's mission is to provide leadership in advancing policy-relevant knowledge about the most important challenges of international security and other critical issues where science, technology and international affairs intersect.

BCSIA's leadership begins with the recognition of science and technology as driving forces transforming international affairs. The Center integrates insights of social scientists, natural scientists, technologists, and practitioners with experience in government, diplomacy, the military, and business to address these challenges. The Center pursues its mission in four complementary research programs:

- The **International Security Program** (ISP) addresses the most pressing threats to U.S. national interests and international security.

- The **Environment and Natural Resources Program** (ENRP) is the locus of Harvard's interdisciplinary research on resource and environmental problems and policy responses.

- The **Science, Technology and Public Policy Program** (STPP) analyzes ways in which science and technology policy influence international security, resources, environment, and development, and such cross-cutting issues as technological innovation and information infrastructure.

- The **WPF Program on Intrastate Conflict, Conflict Prevention and Conflict Resolution** analyzes the causes of ethnic, religious, and other conflicts, and seeks to identify practical ways to prevent and limit such conflicts.

The heart of the Center is its resident research community of more than 140 scholars: Harvard faculty, analysts, practitioners, and each year a new, interdisciplinary group of research fellows. BCSIA sponsors frequent seminars, workshops and conferences, maintains a substantial specialized library, and publishes books, monographs and discussion papers.

The Center's International Security Program, directed by Steven E. Miller, publishes the BCSIA Studies in International Security, and sponsors and edits the quarterly journal *International Security*.

The Center is supported by an endowment established with funds from Robert and Renée Belfer, the Ford Foundation and Harvard University, by foundation grants, by individual gifts, and by occasional government contracts.